FORMS OF SPEECH IN
VICTORIAN FICTION

FORMS OF SPEECH IN
VICTORIAN FICTION

Raymond Chapman

LONDON AND NEW YORK

Longman Group UK Limited,
Longman House, Burnt Mill,
Harlow, Essex CM20 2JE, England
and Associated Companies throughout the world.

*Published in the United States of America
by Longman Publishing, New York*

© Longman Group UK Limited 1994

First published 1994

ISBN 0 -582-087465 CSD
ISBN 0 -582-087457 PPR

British Library Cataloguing-in-Publication Data

A catalogue record for this book is
available from the British Library

Library of Congress Cataloging-in-Publication Data

Chapman, Raymond.
    Forms of speech in Victorian fiction / Raymond Chapman.
        p.   cm.
    Includes bibliographical references and index.
    ISBN 0-582-08746-5. -- ISBN 0-582-08745-7 (pbk.)
    1. English fiction--19th century--History and criticism.
    2. Speech in literature. 3. English language--Spoken English.
    4. Conversation in literature. 5. Dialogue. I. Title.
    PR878.S64C43   1994   93-5699
    823'.80926--dc20   CIP

set in 10/12 Goudy
Produced by Longman Singapore Publishers (Pte) Ltd.
Printed in Singapore

Contents

FOR PATRICIA

who tolerates my frequent departures
into the nineteenth century

CHAPTER 1
Introduction: Speech in fiction

'What is the use of a book without pictures or conversations?' reflected Alice before her descent into Wonderland. Illustrated novels are no longer in fashion, but even the most experimental developments in fiction still contain dialogue, for speech is a necessary element in any literary text which purports to represent human life: people who come together invariably talk. The mimetic function of dialogue is less important than its power to reveal character and to develop the complex relationships which help to distinguish the novel proper from simple prose narrative. Dialogue serves also to develop the plot as things which are said cause the story to go forward. It may give narrative information in the guise of speech to break up the continuous flow of objective story-telling. The author's skill is tested by keeping the idiolect of the speaking character consistent when the purpose is mainly informational.

Yet in so fundamental an aspect of the novel, there is cheating and collusion. Even in the most realist fiction, dialogue has an artificial quality; trying to read a novel which accurately reproduced real conversations would soon be wearisome. The novelist selects and economises, excluding the many features which are accepted in reality but would become intolerable if they were reproduced on the printed page. Speech is full of hesitations, repetitions, anacolutha and non-semantic noises. 'Nobody speaks at all like the characters in any novel, play or film. Life would be intolerable if they did; and novels, plays or films would be intolerable if the characters spoke as people do in life' (Abercrombie 1965, 4).

Speech is not only tidied up for the printed page; it is given a uniformity which it does not possess as a spoken reality. Variations in accent, social or regional, and in personal voice quality, are tacitly ignored unless the text requires that they be made specific. Standard spelling neutralises speech and puts the onus on the author to show any special features. Novelists have for long grasped this nettle and

1

developed a written code which can approximate to dialect or show contrasts of class and education among their characters. Deviant spelling and punctuation convey non-standard speech. The omitted aspirate and some deliberate misspellings for the vocalic elements in words can support the objective assertion of the text that the speaker is a cockney.

Departure from the expected norm is more important than the accuracy of transcription – an accuracy which can never be attained within the normal resources of the alphabet. The ear-code of speech has to be rendered into the eye-code of writing, and the two codes do not match. English offers an alphabet of twenty-six letters to accommodate a spoken language which contains over forty phonemes, or semantically significant sounds, in Received Pronunciation and more in various dialects. There can be no perfect visual recreation of the auditory experience without the use of a phonetic alphabet inaccessible to most readers and writers. The best that can be done is to develop a visual convention that will suggest the deviations and idiosyncrasies of speech, ranging from the quotation marks which tell the reader that narrative has changed to dialogue, to the deviant spelling that conveys cockney, or Scots or other special forms. Punctuation denotes the intonation of the question or exclamation, the hesitations and incomplete sentences which give verisimilitude if they are not overdone. The resources of typography can offer italics or capitalisation for emphasis or loud speech. Convention accepts 'ha, ha' for laughter, 'brr' for the involuntary reaction to cold.

The prosodic features of speech, stress and intonation can only imperfectly be suggested by the resources normally available. Written dialogue may be naturalistic and idiomatic in its choice of words and syntax, well marked by punctuation, but it can never give a full impression of what we hear in life. Nor can the phonational qualities be shown by any established convention. The individual qualities of voice are many, in terms of natural pitch, smoothness or harshness, and so on. Qualities may be affected by physical changes, as the slurred speech of intoxication or the huskiness of a cold; or situationally by whispering or shouting. In all these things the novelist must use the equivalent of stage-directions, indicating by verbal commentary how the character is to be 'heard' by the reader.

We acquiesce in the deception, as part of the broader collusion of reading a novel at all. We enter a world in which all experience is verbalised and no longer directly available to the other senses. We accept that dialogue is not intended to give the sensation of listening to a real conversation but is part of the author's imaginative world which we have agreed to enter. The characters are performers, each with a role to play in the total structure. Their speech is not only purged of the redundancies and hesitations of real conversation; it is better planned and more purposeful. The speech even of uneducated characters is better structured, richer in vocabulary, than absolute realism would demand. The 'turns' by which a conversation is managed are usually longer than in life, more informational and suggesting a continuity of thought which most of us lack. 'No real-life bore utters speech as purposeful and informational as Miss Bates in *Emma*, and no gin-sodden old woman ever held forth in the disciplined rhetoric of Dickens's Mrs Gamp' (Page 1973, 10). At the same time, the novelist must contrive to make us suspend our disbelief and read as though we were of the company. The reader comes to the text in a dual role, as addressee and eavesdropper. He or she is the ultimate observer, to whom the whole book is addressed and for whose benefit the dialogue is written. Yet the reader is outside the story, the silent eavesdropper who overhears what other people are saying, with no part in their affairs.

Nevertheless, readers tend to demand credibility even while they connive at artificiality. Dialogue is expected to be 'true to life' and not to sound like a contrivance to further the plot between quotation marks. Expectation is inevitably based upon experience, and it may not be easy to accommodate to the conventions of an earlier period. In judging whether dialogue is natural and convincing, a certain amount of subjectivity is exercised even by the most acute critic. There are passages in Victorian fiction which convince us, which 'ring true' as if people might actually, allowing for the tidying convention of fiction, have spoken them. We feel that our role as eavesdropper is being fulfilled.

Here is an example of written dialogue which seems convincing. In Chapter 6 of Trollope's *Barchester Towers* (1857), the forceful Archdeacon Grantly is talking with his gentle father-in-law about the new Bishop's chaplain:

'He is the most thoroughly bestial creature that ever I set my eyes upon,' said the archdeacon.

'Who – the bishop?' asked the other, innocently.

'Bishop! no – I'm not talking about the bishop. How on earth such

a creature got ordained! – they'll ordain anybody now, I know; but he's
been in the church these ten years; and they used to be a little careful
ten years ago.'

'Oh! you mean Mr Slope.'

'Did you ever see any animal less like a gentleman?' asked Dr
Grantly.

'I can't say I felt myself much disposed to like him.'

'Like him!' again shouted the archdeacon, and the assenting ravens
again cawed an echo; 'of course you don't like him: It's not a question
of liking. But what are we to do with him?'

The quick exchange of views, the different tones and lengths of
utterance, carry conviction, aided by the occasional but not too
frequent commenting words like 'innocently' and 'shouted', and given
dimension by the presence of the ravens. At the same time, we need
to adapt our minds to the heat which the Victorians could feel about
ecclesiastical appointments, and to their elusive concept of the
'gentleman'. In a different social milieu, there is conviction in the first
chapter of George Moore's *Esther Waters* (1894). William, a cook's
son and potential footman, sees books in the bundle of the new
housemaid:

> Sarah Tucker – that's the upper housemaid – will be after you to lend
> them to her. She's a wonderful reader. She has read every story that has
> come out in *Bow Bells* for the last three years, and you can't puzzle her,
> try as you will. She knows all the names, can tell you which lord it was
> that saved the girl from the carriage when the 'osses were tearing like
> mad towards a precipice a 'undred feet deep, and all about the baronet
> for whose sake the girl went out to drown herself in the moonlight. I
> 'aven't read the books mesel', but Sarah and me are great pals.

On the other hand, it is hard to believe that even an early-
Victorian undergraduate spoke to a friend in the way that Newman
gives to Charles Reding in his *Loss and Gain* (1848):

> 'I am just going for a turn into the meadow,' said Charles; 'this is to me
> the best time of the year: *nunc formosissimus annus*; everything is
> beautiful; the laburnums are out, and the may. There is a greater variety
> of trees here than in any other place I know hereabouts; and the planes
> are so touching just now, with their multitudinous green hands
> half-opened; and there are two or three such fine dark willows
> stretching over the Cherwell; I think some dryad inhabits them: and as

you wind along, just over your right shoulder is the Long Walk, with the Oxford buildings seen between the elms.'

This surely is Newman's own nostalgia for the Oxford he had left for ever after his secession, rather than students' talk. However, the beauties of nature seem to bring out the worst in fictional dialogue. Here is a passage from Chapter 2 in the fifth section of Thomas Hardy's *A Laodicean* (1881):

> Abner Power was quite sentimental that day. 'In such places as these', he said as he rode alongside Mrs Goodman, 'nature's powers in the multiplication of one type strike me as much as the grandeur of the mass.'
> Mrs Goodman agreed with him, and Paula said, 'The foliage forms the roof of an interminable green crypt, the pillars being the trunks, and the vault the inter-lacing boughs'.

When we say that such passages do not ring true as renderings of speech, what exactly is meant? Do they seem contrived and out of place in relation to the characters who are supposed to speak them, or are they remote from what can be discerned about actual speech at the time when they were written? Can we judge the credibility of Victorian dialogue in its own time? The attempt is not entirely futile, though judgements need to be cautious. Victorian speech was often more formal, and more allusive, than we are accustomed to hear today. The opinions of contemporary critics and commentators need to be taken into account, but there remains much that is uncertain about the readerly approach to the dialogue in Victorian novels. Reading aloud was popular, both in family circles and among groups of the less privileged who would jointly buy the new serial part of a novel and get one of their more educated members to read to them. Was any attempt made to reproduce the distinctive qualities of different speakers? Mimetic effects may not have been confined to the cultured and talented; it will be recalled that Sloppy in *Our Mutual Friend* (1865) was able to 'do the police in different voices' when he read from the newspaper. Dickens also relates how Wopsle, reading a newspaper account of 'a highly popular murder', 'identified himself with every witness at the Inquest . . . The coroner, in Mr Wopsle's hands, became Timon of Athens; the beadle, Coriolanus' (*Great Expectations* 1861).

The points that are chiefly addressed in this book concern the effect of dialogue in creating and developing character and for placing speakers in their social standing, their beliefs and their relationships to one another within the novels. Examples are treated for their semantic content, their lexis and their syntax. Examination of attempts to show prosodic and phonational features would have extended the study beyond its planned limits.

There is of course a more fundamental critical issue. This study of nineteenth-century novels accepts the relationship between the known world and the fictional presentation of it which was assumed by the novelists and their readers. Fiction was generally expected to be 'true to life' and could be unfavourably reviewed if it strained credulity too far. It was acceptable to discuss fictional characters as if their presentation in the novels were part of real biographies. This approach was encouraged by the way in which novelists described their characters' emotions and motivations as well as words and actions, and by the frequent practice of a closing chapter which tells briefly the future lives of the principal actors. It was a fashion which paved the way for the excesses of character-criticism and questions like 'How many children had Lady Macbeth?' which later marred the often brilliant Shakespearean criticism of A.C. Bradley. It is possible to read Victorian novels simply as products of a social and economic system; it is possible to treat their characters as a piece of language, generated by the whole text. For the present analysis, it is necessary to accept, with eyes open to other approaches, some of the original collusion between author and reader.

This is the principal aim, but there is another which constantly accompanies it. Besides the reality of characters speaking within their texts, there is the question of how closely their speech related to what was heard in daily conversation. The necessary adjustments of untidy colloquial speech to the demands of the printed page have already been mentioned. Apart from this, did Victorian characters speak like their counterparts in Victorian society? Here the investigation is limited by the fact that fiction is our major source of information about speech, as it had been for the whole of literate history. However, there are other sources: social observers, diarists, newspaper reports, books of etiquette with advice about conversation. These can sometimes provide a control for the accuracy of fictional dialogue; and, as will be seen, what seem to be wild extravagances in the novel are sometimes not far from reality. It is possible to analyse the effect of dialogue in its own world of fiction and thereby learn more about the art as it was conceived and accepted. If something, however tentatively, can be done to relate it to the reality around it, the validity of the novel as a social record is also confirmed.

Secondary sources contemporary with the novels are briefly identified in the text with reference to detail in the bibliography. A perspective of some of the principal observers may be useful. Henry Mayhew (1812–87) found time within a varied literary career to make the social survey which he published as *London Labour and the London Poor* between 1851 and 1864; it is not always possible to distinguish his own reports from those of his collaborators. J. Greenwood, who has left little personal record to posterity, was one of those middle-class Victorians who were impelled by a mixture of curiosity and social conscience to wander around the unfashionable and deprived parts of London; he wrote a number of books on his observations and a novel, *Dick Temple*. J.E. Ritchie, who edited the *Ilustrated News of the World* from 1860 to 1863, pursued and recorded similar activities. A.J. Munby (1828–1910) was a civil servant and minor poet who was fascinated by the lives of women engaged in menial work and took every opportunity of talking with them. He secretly married a servant and kept his journal for many years. Little is known of the American D.J. Kirwan except that he was the London correspondent of the New York *World*. In 1870 he published his memoir of aspects of London life in the previous decade. Others who are quoted as factual observers, such as Edward Bulwer-Lytton, are sufficiently well known as imaginative writers to need no further introduction. Others again, the authors of manuals on etiquette and social conventions, have left no record of themselves beyond their names.

Yet even this evidence may be subject to qualification. Surviving speech records have been subjected to the constraints of using the written code for the spoken. In this period, when non-literary sources become more frequent, they are likely to be affected by the same conventions, accepted by contemporary readers, as governed literary texts. Social constraints not directly related to the problem may yet add to it. Reports of trials are found to be less idiomatic and convincing in the nineteenth century than in the eighteenth. 'Barmaids and crossing-sweepers begin to *observe* and *perceive* instead of just seeing, or their *attention is directed* to suspicious characters who in their turn have a way of inquiring which is Mr. So-and-so's *residence*' (Sutherland 1953, viii). Nor can we be sure about matters which were universally accepted and thus received no comment. Was the general pace of speech slower in the last century than it is now? Was intonation less marked when some of its function was served by other register features? Probably we shall never know; the few recordings of Victorian voices – Queen Victoria, Tennyson, Florence Nightingale – are the stylised tones of old age which tantalise us with their remote and artificial quality.

There are at least two things of which we can be certain. One was the popularity of the novel, which increased as the century lengthened. Novels were widely read and discussed, at least by those who had money to buy or borrow them[1] and leisure to read them. If those factors excluded a large section of the population, they included a growing number who were shaping the distinctive ethos of the period, and therefore of the years that were to come. Anthony Trollope wrote in 1879:

> The number of those who read novels have become millions in England during the last twenty-five years, with our artisans, behind our counters, in third-class railway carriages, in our kitchens and stables, novels are now read unceasingly.
>
> (*Nineteenth Century* January 1879)

In the same year, a reviewer of Meredith observed, 'The two principal agencies whereby literature puts itself in relation with human life in general, and the life of the age in especial, are the newspaper and the novel' (*British Quarterly Review* April 1879).

The other matter that lies beyond controversy is that the novel as a genre contains many different voices. It depends partly on conversations between two or more people of different personal types and social class, placed in a number of different physical settings. It possesses the multiplicity of language varieties conveniently called *heteroglossia* (Bakhtin 1981).

Any treatment of the Victorian novel confronts the reader with a formidable expanse of published books. The corpus offers wide coverage of many aspects of contemporary life and a great range of human types. It also poses problems of selection. I have tried to combine breadth and depth by close attention to a number of novels and more extensive references where points of particular interest are found. The major authors have naturally received most attention, but some of those usually placed lower in the hierarchy of evaluative criticism have been valuable sources.

The Victorian age was a long one and was not homogeneous throughout. Dates of novels may sometimes be important in considering them as evidence for spoken usage. When there seems to be a marked difference between the speech of generations I have drawn attention to it. However, the nineteenth century, an era of immense change in so many ways, was not a period of rapid linguistic development comparable to the fifteenth century, or even the latter part of the twentieth. Many novels are set in a period earlier than that in which they were written. Dickens, Thackeray, Trollope, Kingsley, Eliot, the Brontës, Gaskell and Reade were all born between 1810 and 1820. They sometimes wrote of the pre-Victorian days of their childhood, or of earlier times; so, later, did Hardy and Meredith. There is no evidence that they attempted to reproduce the speech distinctive of those years, or indeed that there were significant differences from the time when they were writing, and it is fair to treat these books in the same way as those given contemporary settings. The deliberate archaism of some historical novels is, of course, another matter. No account is taken of the pseudo-medieval speech attempted in some minor historical novels like Bulwer-Lytton's *The Last of the Barons* (1843): 'And so lose the fairest day this summer hath bestowed on us? Tush! – the more need for pleasaunce to-day, since business must come to-morrow' (8).

The nineteenth century was a time when people became increasingly aware of forms of speech different from those of their immediate circle. Greater mobility and the spread of communication brought more familiarity with other regional and social groups. The complexity of spoken English became apparent, at the same time that the importance of a certain type of pronunciation became more important for social prestige. The understanding between author and reader in the matter of fictional dialogue became more discerning and more demanding.

The effect on the novel was that characters could increasingly be 'placed' by class as well as by idiolect. Cockney speech, for example, was no longer a matter of minor comic characters with a few conventional pointers like the dropped aspirate. Dialect speakers became more important in their own right. The choice of the appropriate register for the personal or social situation was becoming more delicate and subtle. Attention is given to this, and to the specific register of religious speech which pervaded every social class.

The novelists suffered from the same required gentility that seems to have affected legal records. They could not fully reproduce the realities of much that was said. Oaths and overt mention of anything sexual were censored before they were written, by the demands of the critics and the circulating libraries. These things partially changed in the course of the century, not without protest and even persecution. The distinctive usage of women and children can be traced with more difficulty, but some interesting conventions emerge. The aristocracy, threatened but still highly influential, had its own rules of usage; so did other social and professional groups. A different educational system provided frequent allusions to classical and modern literature as a normal support for speech. Despite the growing demand for realism, the novel maintained its own conventions such as the use of educated standard speech for virtuous characters even of a lower social class, and theatrical outburst at moments of high emotion. Finally, some consideration, necessarily selective, is given to the expressed ideas of novelists and critics about the dialogue of fiction.

The period shows a growing resolution by the writers to come closer to representing what they and their readers really heard around them. If they were without the advantages of phonetic skill to describe and depict speech accurately – and how many imaginative writers today have that knowledge? – they had the novelist's power of observation and discernment. The novelists were much exercised by the question of realism in fiction. Concern for the relationship of written dialogue to actual conversation was often expressed, and became stronger after the middle of the century.

I have tried to make sources clear without breaking the text by excessive references. The authorship and date of a novel are given on its first mention and thereafter the title alone is used. I have trusted the intelligence of readers wherever a specific reference seems redundant. For example, if words are quoted as being spoken by David Copperfield, it hardly seems necessary to add *David Copperfield* as the source. Editions of Victorian novels are many. Each substantial quotation is referenced by chapter; when the novel is divided into sections, with new chapter numbering for each, I have added the reference to *Book* or *Part* as appropriate. This period, unlike earlier ones, offers few problems about choice of original or modern spelling. Where the Victorian spelling is different, I have followed it. In quoted material I have also honoured such practices as hyphenating *to-day* and the more copious Victorian mode of punctuation.

Note

1. The principal source of novels in the Victorian period was the circulating library, led by Mudie with an annual subscription of a guinea. Most novels were issued in three volumes at one and half guineas, though cheaper reprints sometimes followed within a few years. Public libraries developed from the middle of the century but tended not to favour fiction; the private libraries attached to churches and educational institutes were generally suspicious of novel reading.

CHAPTER 2
Standard and non-standard speech

Belief in a 'correct' form of speech and regard for it as a point of status became more marked in the nineteenth century than ever before. Anxiety about pronunciation was associated with anxiety about social class at a time when many of the old demarcations were being eroded by a newer type of capitalist economy with its opportunities for sudden rises and catastrophic falls. Outward appearances were becoming less reliable for 'placing' a person in society. G.M. Young writes of the continual fear that the wrong response 'might plant a seed of corruption in the most innocent heart, and the same word or gesture might betray an affinity with the class below' (Young 1936, 2). The compiler of a popular miniature encyclopaedia gives the advice, 'To obtain a good knowledge of pronunciation, it is advisable for the reader to listen to the examples given by good speakers, and by educated persons' (*Enquire Within About Everything* 1891, 65). Another nineteenth-century observer puts the point more specifically:

> The following story sets in a strong light the great difference between the speech of the well-bred and the untaught in England. A servant, who had dropped into a large fortune, asked his master how he was to pass muster in future as a gentleman. The answer was, 'dress in black and hold your tongue'.
> (Moon 1865, 226)

This is the dilemma of Kingsley's noble gamekeeper Tregarva, who explains the hopelessness of ever winning 'a pious and a beautiful lady' because 'you were no gentleman; that you didn't know how to walk, and how to pronounce, and when to speak, and when to keep silent' (*Yeast* 1850). Others were more confident of their linguistic gentility, like the parish clerk who claims, 'I can talk the Queen's English (God bless the Queen!) – and that's more than most of the people about here can do' (Wilkie Collins, *The Woman in White* 1860, Part 3, 9). The acquired standard could fail under stress; this happens to Trollope's parvenu Tifto. ' "I've seen him 'ave his gallops," said the little man, who in his moments of excitement would sometimes fall away from that exact pronunciation which had been one of the studies of his life' (*The Duke's Children* 1880, 17).

Such awareness was not unknown in earlier periods, as English literature abundantly reveals; but like many other aspects of life it took a giant stride in the reign of Victoria. Attention to speech in the earlier eighteenth century was generally more concerned with elocution and careful diction than with the minutiae of pronunciation. Pronunciation was being seriously considered by the last quarter of the century. In 1774 John Walker observed, with some hyperbole, 'our shops swarm with books whose titles announce a standard for pronunciation' (Walker 1774, 22). Orthoepists such as Thomas Sheridan, father of the dramatist, flourished and the way was open for the anxieties of the following century. The new concern about speech is shown in the opinion of Latham:[1]

> There are a vast number of words of which the pronunciation is doubtful, being sounded differently by different persons. For instance the word *neither* is pronounced in three ways: *neither*, *nayther*, and *neether*. To ascertain the proper pronunciation of words is the province of Orth*oepy*. It teaches us to *speak* the words of our language correctly . . . Orthography is less essential to language than orthoepy, since all languages are spoken, whilst but a few languages are written.
>
> (Latham 1862, 445)

Another writer is succinct and confident: 'by accepted usage in speech we understand that which is practised, or approved, consentiently and advertently, by the best writers and speakers of any time' (Hall 1873, 40f). By the end of the century, the linguistic primacy of speech was being asserted, but still as against the prevailing opinion. 'Purity and correctness of the different varieties of spoken English does not depend as popularly thought on the degree of approximation to the written language' (Sweet 1890, vi).

More often, writers on language gave prescriptive guidance about pronunciation and maintained that a particular system was superior to all others. In 1836 Smart's revision of Walker's *Pronouncing Dictionary* declared that 'the common standard dialect is that in which all marks of a particular place of birth and residence are lost and nothing appears to indicate any other habits of intercourse than with the well-bred and well-informed, wherever they may be found' (Smart

1836, xi). Such definition by negative exclusion of regionality and association with upper-class society was widely shared. Richard Garnett in 1859 asserted that 'all agree in calling our standard form of speech the English language, and all provincial variations from it – at least all that assume a specific character – dialects' (Garnett 1859, 42). Ten years later the term 'received pronunciation' was used by the pioneer scholar A.J. Ellis in a slightly more flexible dictum. 'In the present day we may, however, recognise a received pronunciation all over the country, not widely differing in any particular locality, and admitting a certain degree of variety' (Ellis 1869, Part 1, 23). In the last decade of the century, when prescriptive philology was moving slowly towards descriptive linguistics, Henry Sweet noted the historical reality:

> After London English had become the official and literary language of the whole kingdom, it was natural that some dialect in its spoken form should become the general speech of the educated classes, and that as centralisation increased, it should preponderate more and more over the local dialects.   (Sweet 1890, vf)

He had to agree that 'cockney dialect seems very ugly to an educated English man or woman'.

It is generally supposed that the expansion and increased prestige of the English public schools was a principal factor in the imposition of a standard form on those claiming social and educational status. The point may have been somewhat exaggerated through Daniel Jones's famous commendation and use of the pronunciation 'which I believe to be very usually heard in everyday speech in the families of Southern English people who have been educated at the public schools' (Jones 1987, xvii). There is little doubt, however, that the public schools did increasingly foster a certain type of speech which would later be generally known as Received Pronunciation and that boys whose speech deviated markedly from it were brought into line. 'The main agency, undoubtedly, in fixing [this pronunciation] as class speech was the new cult of the public schools' (Williams 1961, 224). 'One of the forces making for the propagation of a standard pronunciation has been the public schools' (Bolton and Crystal 1987, 285). The older generation of masters and even headmasters at these schools often continued to use the pronunciation of their native dialect until late in the century.[2]

The Education Act of 1870 was certainly responsible for an irruption of prescriptive teaching into classes where it had not penetrated before. The new standard passed from universities through training colleges to teachers who regarded it as part of their mission to secure 'correct' speech:

> The emergence of Received Pronunciation (RP) – the outward and visible sign of belonging to the professional middle class – went hand in hand with the rise of an imperial Civil Service and its educational infrastructure. The Education Act of 1870 not only established the English public schools as the melting-pot of upper- and middle-class speech and society, but also started a boom in English preparatory schools . . . The contrast in the English speech of the educated elite before and after the Education Act is startling. Before 1870, many of the most eminent Victorians retained their regional accents throughout their lives . . . By the 1890s, all this had changed. A new generation of post-Education Act schoolmasters would rebuke the boy who said 'loike' for 'like'. Accent levelling was not only applied from above: peer pressure among the schoolboys themselves was a powerful incentive for a new boy to acquire the approved tone.   (McCrum et al. 1987, 23f)

Double standards and a clash between school and home often developed, and for the first time widespread diglossia appeared in England. Even earlier in the century, the notion of correctness was descending from above and causing concern among serious or upwardly mobile speakers of other dialects, a fact which the novelists were quick to notice. Emily Brontë makes the housekeeper Nellie Dean confide to Lockwood that Edgar Linton 'had a sweet, low manner of speaking, and pronounced his words as you do: that's less gruff than we talk here, and softer' (*Wuthering Heights* 1848, 8). George Eliot, particularly sensitive to speech variants, sends Tom Tulliver to a clergyman who confronts him 'not only with a Latin grammar but with a new standard of English pronunciation' and who 'corrected his provincialisms and his deportment in a most playful manner' (*The Mill on the Floss* 1860, Book 2, 1). When Ben Garth finds old Job's dialect amusing and holds that his 'Yo goo . . . is as good as You go', his sister Letty objects to the possible misunderstanding of Job's 'A ship's in the garden instead of a sheep'. This rustic pronunciation is given by Thackeray to the coarse and bucolic Sir Pitt Crawley who talks of 'a "ship" that was to be killed' (*Vanity Fair* 1848, 11). George Eliot's Mrs Garth holds to the view of an older generation that 'these things belong only to pronunciation, which is the least part of grammar' (*Middlemarch* 1872, 24), a view contrary to that of Latham quoted above. It is a slight incident but, like many in the Victorian novel, an insight into changing perspectives.

Mrs Garth's belief in the primacy of grammar over pronunciation was an aspect of the assumption, which endured long after the nineteenth century, that written language was inherently superior to spoken. The exponents of a standard speech often appealed to writing, and especially literature, as a guide. A writer on dialect noted an effect of general education, which in fact was only an escalation of what had been the case since the late sixteenth century: 'there is one written language understood by all, while the inhabitants of different parts may be quite unintelligible to each other *viva voce*' (Elworthy op. cit., xliii; cit. Crowley 1989, 102). Ellis, a leading philologist, could equate literary English with standard speech, saying in his Presidential Address to the Philological Society, 'There is no doubt that the received literary English such as I am using at the present time, is considered the English language pure and simple, and the other forms used in England are considered to be its dialects' (*Transactions of the Philological Society* 1882–4, 21f). Children in schools were taught to read aloud with close regard to the visual signs of the texts. Maggie Tulliver gets her own back on her brother's dismissive 'girls can't learn Latin' by pointing out:

> You don't mind your stops. For you ought to stop twice as long at a semicolon as you do at a comma, and you make the longest stops where there ought to be no stop at all.   (*The Mill on the Floss* Book 2, 2)

Others took a more discerning view of the two realisations of language, and were also aware of the need for realism in fictional dialogue:

> We must distinguish between the English which we speak, and that which we write. Many expressions are not only tolerated but required in conversation, which are not normally put on paper. Thus, for instance, everyone says '*can't*' for *cannot*, '*won't*' for *will not*, '*isn't*' for *is not*, in conversation; but we seldom see these contractions in books, except where a conversation is related. This is a difference which the foreigner is generally slow in apprehending.   (Alford 1864, 68f)

A sense of the increasing international importance of English, connected with its use in the expanding British Empire, may have been another factor in the zeal for an accepted standard. It was in fact a German philologist who suggested that English 'may with all rights be called a world language, and like the English people appears destined hereafter to prevail with a sway more extensive even than its present over all the portions of the globe' (Jacob Grimm, quoted in Trench 1855, 42). Trollope refers to such linguistic patriotism when Wharton, fearing to have the nationally ambivalent Lopez marrying his daughter, reflects that people now do not care whether their sons-in-law have 'the fair skin and bold eyes and uncertain words of an English gentleman, or the swarthy colour and false grimace and glib tongue of some inferior Latin race' (*The Prime Minister* 1876, 14).

Representation of non-standard speech

The effect of such deep and frequently controversial concern about correct speech was a gift to the novelists. In particular, it enhanced the effect of deviant spelling to indicate dialect or other non-standard speech, and it opened ever-widening possibilities for showing social relationships with the minimum of authorial comment through the speech of their characters. Estella's scornful comment on Pip's lexis, 'He calls the knaves, Jacks, this boy' is a well-known example of such succinct social placing (*Great Expectations* 8).

The manner in which non-standard speech was presented derives largely from the attitude to the non-standard speech of London. For the purists, it represented the most debased deviation from correctness. Lady Campbell tells us that Ruskin says 'Provincial dialect is not vulgar, but Cockney dialect is so in a deep degree, because it is the corruption of a finer language continually heard' (Campbell 1898, 48). The American writer George P. Marsh is severe on features which novelists of the time reproduce:

> The emasculation of our once manly and sonorous tongue, by contracting long vowels into short and suppressing short vowels altogether, the crowding of half a dozen syllables into one explosive utterance, the thick indistinguishable articulation, the crazy confusion of the aspirate and silent *h*, all of which characterize the native dialect of London.   (Marsh 1862, 461)

Another writer on pronunciation says of the aspirate, 'its misuse is very much confined to the southern provinces, and not a little to the metropolis' (Lysons 1868, 36). Mrs Oliphant took a poor view of the popularity of literary cockney. 'London is the greatest town in existence, but it is not England, though the dialect of its many vagabonds seems in a fair way for becoming the classic English of our generation' (*Blackwood's Magazine* January 1855). Gissing believed that 'dialect is a very different thing from the bestial jargon which on the lips of the London vulgar passes for English' (*Born in Exile* 1892, Part 7, 3).

For many novelists, however, it was a source of humour and sometimes of pathos. Serious attempts to render cockney speech in writing belong to the discussion of dialect. The representation of non-standard speech generally uses a simplified form of cockney, concentrating on a few features which could be immediately recognised. Even in novels where cockney or other dialect is shown more elaborately, simplified deviance is often used for minor characters. Such representation gives little idea of the actual sound of contemporary speech and was not intended to do so: it is a visual indication of education and social status.

Although individual novelists develop their own special features, there are certain indicators which are commonly used. The dropped aspirate, together with hypercorrection of the wrongly inserted aspirate, is the most common, and one of the easiest to represent visually; examples are found almost every time an uneducated character speaks. Trollope's Quintus Slide, showing no other marked speech deviance, is characterised by the misplaced aspirate alone. He is first introduced as 'a young man under thirty, not remarkable for clean linen, and who always talked of the " 'Ouse" ... though he talked of " 'Ouses" and "horgans", he wrote good English with great rapidity' (*Phineas Finn* 1869, 26). It is a sign of the new age that standard pronunciation rather than literacy is considered the mark of an educated man; earlier in history the judgement would have been reversed. In a later novel he asks Lady Eustace, 'But 'ow do you know?' asserts his respect for 'the very fountain 'ead of truth', tells Lopez 'you can't 'ide your light under a bushel' and invites him to 'go 'and in 'and with me in the matter' (*The Prime Minister* 50, 51). Gissing has Mrs Goby announce herself as being 'of the 'Olloway Road, wife of Mr C.O. Goby, 'aberdasher' (*New Grub Street* 1891, 21). Thackeray's Arthur Pendennis gives linguistic expression to contemporary social barriers when he says of Fanny, 'She dropped her h's, but she was a dear little girl' (*Pendennis* 1850, 54).

Hypercorrection of the aspirate is particularly common among upper servants and others with pretensions to gentility. Major Pendennis's valet announces 'Lady Hagnes Foker's son' and addresses Pendennis as 'Mr Harthur' (*Pendennis* 11, 20). Fanny Squeers exclaims, 'This is the hend, is it?' and Dickens comments, 'who, being excited, aspirated her h's strongly' (*Nicholas Nickleby* 1839, 42). One of Hardy's characters is 'a labouring man known to the world of Welland as Haymoss (the encrusted form of the word Amos, to adopt the phrase of philologists)' (*Two on a Tower* 1882, 1).

The novelists could be sure of a comprehending readership when they used the dropped aspirate to present an uneducated speaker. Dean Hole recalled that during his time at Oxford (c. 1840) 'If a youth omitted the letter *h* in his conversation or construing, he was placed on the *Index Expugatorius*' (Hole 1901, 30). Alford is worth quoting at some length to show the strength of feeling which pronunciation could evoke at this time; he is severe about:

> That worst of all faults, the leaving out of the aspirate where it ought to be, and putting it in where it ought not to be. This is a vulgarism not confined to this or that province of England, nor especially prevalent in one county or another, but common throughout England to persons of low breeding and inferior education, principally to those among the inhabitants of towns. Nothing so surely stamps a man as below the mark in intelligence, self-respect and energy, as this unfortunate habit: in intelligence, because if he were but moderately keen in perception, he would see how it marks him; in self-respect and energy, because if he had these he would long ago have set to work and cured it. Hundreds of stories are current about the absurd consequences of this vulgarism.
>
> (Alford 1864, 38)

A critic of Alford has interest for readers of Dickens:

> We do not agree theoretically with the Dean's remarks on the aspiration of the 'h' in *humble*, though practically we think it advisable to follow the growing usage of the day, and sound the 'h'. It was formerly almost as common to say *umble* as it is to say *onour* and (*h*)*our* ... We believe that the reason why the Clergy have so commonly adopted the practice of sounding the 'h' in *humble* is because educated persons cannot endure the idea of its being said of them that they drop

their 'h's'; directly, therefore, the custom became prevalent of aspirating *humble*, the Clergy at once took it up.

(Moon 1865, 150, quoting *The English Churchman* 28 January 1864)

This suggests that Uriah Heep's reiterated *umble* may be a sign not so much of his low nature as of his aping of a traditional pronunciation which was already moribund. The author of *Enquire within About Everything* in 1891 rules that 'few things point so directly to the want of *cultivation* as the misuse of the letter H by persons in conversation' (74).

A short neutral vowel or *schwa* is much used, especially in unstressed syllables. Many of these would approximate to modern accepted pronunciation and suggest that vowel articulation by educated speakers was more careful then than now. Squeers says 'elbers' for 'elbows' and gives the spelling of *window* as 'winder'. Kenwigs says 'naterally' for 'naturally' and his wife's friend the 'married lady' says 'picter' for 'picture' (*Nicholas Nickleby* 34, 8, 36). This last rendering suggests that the syllable *-ure* was still pronounced with a long vowel by educated speakers; this is supported by the spelling of Mrs Gamp's 'creetur', used also by Bulstrode's servant Mrs Abel (*Middlemarch* 70).

Specific words could be seized upon as social pointers. Alford quotes 'a correspondent' who writes, 'One of the greatest offenders in this matter is a well-known opposition speaker whom I shall not name. The startling way in which he brings out *idear* is enough to make the hair of any one but a well-seasoned Cockney stand on end' (Alford 1864, 47). The Countess of Munster enlists a familiar Old Testament story to make her point about 'the pronunciation of certain words and of certain expressions whereby you know for a fact whether the speaker is a Shibbolethite or a Sibbolethite – *i.e.* whether or not the *crème de la crème* would dub him "vulgar".' She continues with an instance of the word *girl*: 'The higher classes pronounce it as though it were spelt "gairl", whereas the Sibboleths pronounce it as if it were spelt "gurl", or as it is written – "girl" . . . there are many others' (Munster 1904, 176f).

On the other hand, pronunciation once acceptable and polite could be retained after the standard form had changed and become a mark of anxious genteelism. Costigan's friend Mrs Haller describes Pendennis as 'very obleeging' (5), a pronunciation current in the eighteenth century, but by the date of the novel archaic, or at least obsolescent. It may have survived more naturally in provincial speech, for the unaffected Mr Peggotty receives David Copperfield's (1850) fictitious message from his mother with, 'I'm much obleeged to her, I'm sure'(3).[3]

Many common words are given deviant spelling in fiction to suggest lack of education. A nameless apprentice at Wodgate says 'coz' for 'because' (Disraeli, *Sybil* 1845, Book 3, 4). Joseph appeals to 'what Scripture ses' (*Wuthering Heights* 9). A gypsy calls Maggie Tulliver 'pritty' (*The Mill on the Floss* Book 1, 11). Featherstone demands to see 'dockiments' and calls Bulstrode 'a spekilating fellow'; Vincy, whose origins distress his pretentious daughter Rosamond, says 'It'll worret you to death' (*Middlemarch* 12, 26). A second-hand dealer responds to a request to remove furniture 'at once' with 'at wunst?' (*New Grub Street* 19). Some of these renderings, like 'picter', suggest a different standard pronunciation from that of modern RP, where for example *sez* would be a reasonable approximation to the pronunciation of 'says'. The spelling *wot* suggests how most people today pronounce *what*, but it was not always so. As late as 1891 the popular household guide *Enquire Within About Everything* enjoined its readers, 'Be careful to sound the H slightly in such words as *where, when, what, why* – don't say *were, wen, wat, wy*' (78). Interestingly, modern novelists still use some of these spelling conventions to indicate sub-standard speech even though they may represent what would now be acceptable. This can be regarded as 'eye dialect' – 'the somewhat crude presentation of a word in a manner in which it is pronounced anyway, the deliberately inaccurate spelling in such cases conventionally serving rather to point out the character's lack of education, or the way such a person would himself have written the word' (Golding 1985, 9).

Several features may be combined when a stronger indication of an uneducated character is desired. There is no regular pattern and little attempt at consistency: a few pointers suffice and may be combined with standard pronunciation. Such deviance may support the distinctive idiolect of the speaker; Thackeray captures the breathless volubility of Mrs Bolton, while using a number of conventional signals of her lack of education:

'And she went and ast for it at the libery,' Mrs Bolton said, – 'several liberies – and some ad it and it was hout, and some adn't it. And one of the liberies as ad it wouldn't let er ave it without a sovering; and she

adn't one, and she came back a-crying to me – didn't you, Fanny? – and
I gave her a sovering.'   (*Pendennis* 49)

A purist might ask why the personal pronoun is rendered as *er* and *her*
in the same utterance, but this would be to consider too curiously.
Neither Thackeray nor any other novelist of the nineteenth century
was attempting to make a phonemic transcript of speech, but rather to
give through visual signals the information needed by the reader to
form an impression of the character. Further, in a time of uncertainty
and anxiety about correct speech, the aspirate may have come and
gone in utterances of the same speaker. For the reader, all that matters
is that Mrs Bolton is a 'low' character, who helps to further the plot
and gives some comic relief by contrast with the standard speakers.
Henry Kingsley gives credibility to a street urchin describing a brawl,
with a positive orgy of mispronunciation, deviant syntax and non-
standard idiom:

> And the pleece come in, and got gallus well kicked about the head, and
> then they took they to Guy's orspital; and then Miss Flanigan fell out
> of winder into the airy, and then they took she to Guy's orspital; and
> there they is, the whole bilin of 'em in bed together, with their heads
> broke, a-eating of jelly and a-drinking of sherry wind.
>
> (*Ravenshoe* 1862, 41)

Why does *head* keep its aspirate, while *hospital* loses it? Again, the
question is not relevant to the general effect which the novelist
succeeds in creating. The skill and comparative restraint of the
novelists in representing non-standard speech may be seen by contrast
with the work of an amateur reporter. In his autobiography, Dean
Hole recalls the travelling fair of his boyhood with a peep-show of
Waterloo and the showman's commentary: 'Says Blucher to
Vellington, "Vellington, why don't you charge?" Says Vellington to
Blucher, "What's that to you, Mestur Blucher? Do yer think I'm
agoing to be dictated to by the likes of you, on the plains of
Warterloo?" ' (Hole 1901, 150). This is exuberance inspired by
memory of fictional speech, using the traditional cockney v/w
confusion for one proper name but not another, with the
conventional 'yer' for *you* and the forms 'Mestur' and 'Warterloo',
which suggest unspecified deviant pronunciation simply by their
deviant spelling.

Non-standard syntax may act similarly, with little or no deviant pronunciation. Meredith makes the landlady of the 'Dolphin' give her information with grammatical lapses but no phonic deviation: 'It ain't that, but they must be done his particular way, do you see, Mrs Harrington. Laid close on the fire, he say, so as to keep in the juice' (*Evan Harrington* 1861, 26). Mrs Henry Wood has a working-class wife dealing ungrammatically but briskly with her husband: 'There ain't no room for you at the fire, and there ain't no warmth in it; it's but this blessed minute lighted. Sit yourself on that table, again the wall, and then your legs'll be in the dry' (*East Lynne* 1861, 21). The genteel were sensitive about such things; the hack writer Yule rebukes his wife for 'I've forgot the time' with, 'Forgotten, forgotten. Don't go back to that kind of language again' (*New Grub Street* 7). A fuller example of non-standard speech depending mainly on deviant syntax, with only slight suggestions of pronunciation, is the view of Mrs Dollop about the death of Raffles. This is brilliant monologue suggesting the breathless fervour and social jealousies as well as the status of the speaker:

> When a man's been 'ticed to a lone house, and there's them can pay for hospitals and nurses for half the countryside choose to be sitters-up night and day, and nobody to come near but a doctor as is known to stick at nothingk, and as poor as he can hang together, and after that so flushed of money as he can pay off Mr Byles the butcher as his bill has been running on for the best of joints since last Michaelmas was a twelvemonth – I don't want anybody to come and tell me as there's been more going on nor the Prayer-book's got a service for.
>
> (*Middlemarch* 71)

Non-standard language works within the social hierarchy of the time; speech different from that of the more serious or elevated characters is a pointer of status. Servants almost invariably show non-standard features, with greater concentration if they are 'lower' rather than 'higher' in the household. Butler makes Theobald Pontifex's servant John speak with restraint and dignity but with unmistakeable signs of his position in relation to his well-spoken clerical master:

> I've been a good servant to you, and I don't mean to say as you've been a bad master to me, but I do say that if you bear hardly on Master Ernest here I have those in the villages as'll hear on't and let me know;

and if I do hear on't I'll come back and break every bone in your skin,
so there!'   (*The Way of All Flesh* 1903, 41)

Sir Francis Clavering's valet, a 'gentleman's gentleman', has strongly
deviant speech, with comic as well as social effect:

> My lady locked up a'most all the bejewtary afore she went away, and he
> couldn't take away the picters and looking-glasses in a cab: and he
> wouldn't spout the fenders and fire-irons – he ain't so bad as that. But
> he's got money somehow. He's so dam'd imperent when he have.
>   (*Pendennis* 60)

Dickens carries the style of fiction into his report of a coachman's
speech:

> My master's a genelman as wouldn't annoy no genelman if he could
> help it, I'm sure; and my own missis is so afraid of havin' a bit o' fire
> that o' Sundays our little bit of weal or what not, goes to the baker's a
> purpose.   (Forster 1874, I, 197)

A gamekeeper shows vague deviance rather than a rural dialect: 'Oh,
ay, that's the way you young 'uns talk. If he warn't doing mischief,
he'd a been glad to have been doing it, I'll warrant' (*Yeast* 3). So does
a bewildered waiter: 'He said he was 'mercial. So he did. Now he says
as how he's a lawyer. What's a poor man to do?' (Trollope, *Orley Farm*
1862, 9).

Reporters of actual conversations use similar deviant pointers,
perhaps derived from the novelists' practice. Thus Mayhew reports his
interrogation of a housemaid:

> I came from Berkshire, sir, near Windsor; father put me to service some
> years ago, and I've been in London ever since. I'm two and twenty now.
> I've lived in four or five different situations since then. Are followers
> allowed? No, sir, missis don't permit no followers. No, I ain't got no
> perleeceman. Have I got a young man? Well, I have; he's in the army,
> not a hoffisser, but a soldier.   (Mayhew 1862, 119)

The very 'superior' servant, more formal and careful in speech than
her employer, is also encountered, and was a growing phenomenon at
a time of opportunities to 'better' oneself. The lady's maid Parkes says,
'If you will give me your keys, Miss, I will unpack your things, and let
you know when it is time for me to arrange your hair, preparatory to

luncheon.' This brings Gaskell's authorial comment, 'If Lady Harriet used familiar colloquialisms from time to time, she certainly had not learnt it from Parkes, who piqued herself on the correctness of her language' (*Wives and Daughters* 1866, 57).

In the country, social hierarchy was not so firmly established as in the towns and contact between members of different classes was closer. The labouring class indeed was excluded, but there were functions at which the yeomen and the lower middle classes of the small towns would mix with the 'gentry'; the latter might themselves, at least in the early part of the period, have some of the regional accent. Nevertheless, social differences were not forgotten and comedy could be made from them. When Mrs Lookaloft penetrates into Miss Thorne's drawing room at the Ullathorne sports, a single pronoun betrays her position as tradesman's wife and confirms the evidence of her presumption and her costume. Miss Thorne comments on the 'low dresses' of the family and offers to lend something more suitable for outdoors. 'Oh dear no! thank ye, Miss Thorne,' said the mother; 'the girls and myself are quite used to low dresses, when we're out' (*Barchester Towers* 36). At a country ball where some of the local aristocracy are expected, old Mrs Goodenough speaks in robust contrast to the standard speech of the minor gentry around her:

> I should have sent my money, and never stirred out o' doors to-night; for I've seen a many of these here balls, and my lord and my lady too, when they were better worth looking at nor they are now; but every one was talking of the duchess, and the duchess and her diamonds, and I thought I shouldn't like to be behindhand, and never ha' seen neither the duchess nor her diamonds.   (*Wives and Daughters* 26)

In the same society a squire is less formally correct than the aristocracy – 'Well! and so you can come here a-visiting though you have been among the grand folks. I thought you were going to cut us, Miss Molly, when I heard you was gone to the Towers' (ibid. 59). At one point there is authorial comment on his pronunciation: 'my dictionary' (only he called it 'dixonary') 'has gone all wrong' (ibid. 31). This is an example of an accepted pronunciation coming to be considered vulgar, but retained by the rural gentry. In the Regency world of *Vanity Fair* the very correct Miss Jemima Pinkerton gives Becky Sharp Johnson's 'dixonary' (1). In Meredith's *The Ordeal of Richard Feverel* (1859) vulgar and urban Mrs Berry, deserted by her husband, describes herself as one 'that's a widow and not a widow, and haven't got a name for what she is in any Dixonary' (29).

In London the irruption of one class into another is usually less endearing and is a matter for satire rather than sympathy. The kindly Major Pendennis can feel some pity for Mrs Amory although, 'she is not refined, certainly, and calls "Apollo" "Apoller" ' (*Pendennis* 44). Trollope has as sharp an ear for town as for country nuances. Dick Roby's idiom and dropped aspirates betray his origin when he entertains aristocracy and is untroubled by pejorative remarks about his wine:

> ' 'Is lordship is a little out of sorts,' whispered Dick to Lady Monogram.
> 'Very much out of sorts, it seems.'
> 'And the worst of it is there isn't a better glass of wine in London, and 'is lordship knows it.'
> 'I suppose that's what he comes for,' said Lady Monogram, being quite as uncivil in her way as the nobleman.
> ' 'E's like a good many others. He knows where he can get a good dinner. After all there's no attraction like that. Of course, a 'andsome woman won't admit that, Lady Monogram.'   (*The Prime Minister* 10)

Whether the variation of *'e* and *he* in the last speech shows Roby's uncertainty or Trollope's carelessness matters little; the deviance emphasises the social comedy of the situation and the conversational response to it. In the same novel, Sexty Parker's wife contrasts with Emily Wharton, married to Lopez. The men are business partners, matched in cunning but not in background; Mrs Parker's speech conforms to her sentiments:

> What is it but gambling that he and Mr Lopez is a-doing together? Of course, ma'am, I don't know you, and you are different from me. I ain't foolish enough not to know all that. My father stood in Smithfield and sold hay, and you father is a gentleman as has been high up in the Courts all his life. But's it's your husband is a doing this.'   (Ibid. 46)

The mispronunciation of a proper name could exacerbate social difference, as Gissing relates when Mutimer speaks to his 'superior' fiancée Adela. The novelty of having one's Christian name used by a man who is not a relative is also apparent:

> It was unfortunate that Richard did not pronounce the name of his bride elect quite as it sounds on cultured lips. This may have been the

result partly of diffidence; but there was a slurring of the second syllable disagreeably suggestive of vulgarity. It struck on the girl's nerves, and made it more difficult for her to grow accustomed to this form of address from Mutimer.   (*Demos* 1886, Vol. 2, 2)

Even among non-standard speakers, variations in speech can show differences of background or generation. George Moore gives to Esther Waters's mother a more marked deviance than her uneducated and illiterate daughter, who has nevertheless mixed in 'better' company:

'I dunno, dearie; 'tis hard to say what 'e'll do; he's a 'ard man to live with. I've 'ad a terrible time of it lately, and them babies allus coming. Ah, we poor women have more than our right to bear with.'

'Poor mother!' said Esther, and, taking her mother's hand in hers, she passed her arm round her, drew her closer, and kissed her. 'I know what he was; is he any worse now?'   (*Esther Waters* 1894, 13)

Slang

The use of items not universally accepted but limited to a social, occupational or generational section of native speakers is a common feature of language. It is by its nature ephemeral and does not enter into written record except in renderings of real or fictional speech. Occasionally a slang word or phrase is taken into the common core and ceases to excite comment: for if it prosper, who dare call it slang? Swift's famous list of slang words compiled in 1710 reads now as a set of otherwise forgotten and meaningless items, except for *mob* which has long been established as standard.[4] In the nineteenth century, anxiety about speech as a pointer to social rank and breeding caused people to be especially sensitive towards the use of slang.

George Eliot, who often reveals an advanced understanding of linguistic matters, states a fact which many could not or would not accept, and at the same time expresses through dialogue some social truths. Rosamond Vincy tells her mother that 'the pick of them' is 'a vulgar expression' and her mother offers the emendation, 'the most superior young men'. Fred Vincy intervenes:

'Oh, there are so many superior teas and sugars now. Superior is getting to be shopkeepers' slang.'

'Are you beginning to dislike slang, then?' said Rosamond, with mild gravity.

'Only the wrong sort. All choice of words is slang. It marks a class.'

'There is correct English: that is not slang.'

'I beg your pardon: correct English is the slang of prigs who write history and essays. And the strongest slang of all is the slang of poets.'

(*Middlemarch* 12)

The conversation is a reminder that standard language may come to be regarded as slang by association with a particular group. It also reveals the uncertainties of the time, and the fear of being associated with the wrong 'class'.

Slang was not always a downward pointer. There was fashionable slang, disliked by the older members of the class but freely used in relaxed conversation among equals. The word *hipped* in the sense of 'jaded' or 'fed up' ran through the middle of the century. Wrayburn says to Lightwood, 'You are a little hipped, dear fellow . . . you have been too sedentary' (*Our Mutual Friend* Book 3, 10). Chester says, 'You will be hipped. Haredale; you will be miserable, melancholy, utterly wretched' (*Barnaby Rudge* 1841, 27). The vulgar Sexty Parker picks up the fashionable word and uses it to Lopez: 'I was out of sorts,' he said, 'and so d—d hippish I didn't know what I was about' (*The Prime Minister* 30).

The use of slang by educated speakers sometimes upsets their companions. When Newcome says, 'You are always having a shy at Lady Ann and her relations' Maria exclaims, 'A shy! How can you use such vulgar words, Mr Newcome?' (Thackeray, *The Newcomes* 1855, 16). Hardy's Angel Clare, fresh from his dairy experience, says 'that mead was a drop of pretty tipple'. 'Blushing', he explains to his startled brothers that it is 'an expression they use down at Talbothays' (*Tess of the D'Urbervilles* 1891, 26). He might have defended himself by quoting the lapse of Alford, who attacked the use of slang but later 'tells us about some people who had been detained by a tipple' (Moon 1865, 172). However, his brothers, university men, should not have been surprised since it seems to have been undergraduate slang: a hot drink is described as 'not bad tipple' (Thomas Hughes, *Tom Brown at Oxford* 1861, 41). Trollope's Miss Dunstable frequently defies convention in speech as in other things. 'I wonder whether Mrs Proudie will come and put me up to a wrinkle or two', she remarks to the Bishop at his reception. 'The Bishop . . . said that he was sure she would. He never felt at his ease with Miss Dunstable, as he rarely

could ascertain whether or not she was earnest in what she was saying'
(*Framley Parsonage* 1861, 17).

Trollope has an acute ear for the discomfiture caused by slang
among the fashionable. 'Oh, Lily, what a word!' is Mrs Dale's response
to Lily's announcement, 'Major Grantly has – skedaddled' (*Last
Chronicle of Barset* 1867, 31). Lily has a propensity for slang,
expounded at more length in an earlier novel. Here the conversation
of two sisters neatly presents opposing contemporary attitudes to
slang, with their implications about muted female protest. Bell, the
more reserved sister, speaks first:

'I don't like these slang words, Lily.'
　'What slang words?'
'You know what you called Bernard's friend.'
　'Oh, a swell. I fancy I do like slang. I think it awfully jolly, to talk
about things being jolly. Only that I was afraid of your nerves I should
have called him stunning. It's so slow, you know, to use nothing but
words out of a dictionary.'
'I don't think it's nice in talking of gentlemen.'
　　　　　　　　　　　　　　　　　(*The Small House at Allington* 1864, 2)

When Lady Glencora suggests that the Duke might like to 'snub a
man', he says, 'I wish you wouldn't put slang phrases into my mouth,
Cora' (*The Prime Minister* 21).

When the gentry and nobility had their slang, it is not surprising
that arbiters of correct speech felt some confusion. Mrs Humphrey
gets into knots over the proper use of the word *fellow*:

In lowly circles a young man is called 'a fellow', young men 'fellows'. So
it is in good society, but with a distinct difference. It is not very easy to
make this difference clear. Young men of good position refer very
commonly to others of their acquaintance as 'the fellows', but they
would not use the word to describe young men generally. Women,
young and old, of the lower classes, speak of young men generally as
'fellows', but gentlewomen never do so. A lady never uses the
expression 'a girl and a fellow'. At the same time she very frequently
speaks of 'young fellows'. I am aware that there is a want of clearness in
all this, but it is matter among many others that can only be acquired
by being accustomed to the usages of good society.
　　　　　　　　　　　　　　　　　　　　　　(Humphrey 1897, 140f)

The Countess of Munster predictably castigates the use of slang, especially by women:

> What more detestable, more coarsely vulgar, than the jargon of the present day called 'slang' indulged in by women and girls of all classes? What is more hurtful to the English language, and to every sense of reverence and refinement? What about that dreadful word, 'ripping', *opening up*, as it does such unpleasant, disgusting thoughts?
>
> (Munster 1904, 178)

The emphasis is that of the Countess: what *can* she have been thinking of?

As with other forms of non-standard speech, novelists often give a character a slang word as a single pointer to status. 'Why this is the muff that called on me in Hell-house Yard three years ago' says Hatton when he sees Morley (*Sybil* Book 6, 9). Hardy's Arabella, contemplating her new marriage, is pleased to announce that she will be 'spliced by English law' (*Jude the Obscure* 1895, Part 5, 2). Esther Waters tells Fred Parsons, 'you can take your hook when you like' and in the same novel Sarah, fearing an informer on William's illegal bookmaking, says, 'It's very hard to keep it dark; someone's sure to crab it and bring the police down on you' (*Esther Waters* 23, 34). Sometimes working-class slang is clearly derived from familiar occupational or other experience. When two men worked on a two-handed saw in a sawpit, the one above directed the operation and also escaped the continual deluge of sawdust. Mantalini describes the 'gentlemanly' Pyke as 'Demnition pleasant and a tip-top sawyer' (*Nicholas Nickleby* 34), and Fagin fiercely defends the Artful Dodger after his arrest – 'wasn't he always top-sawyer among you all?' (*Oliver Twist* 1838, 43).

A word used in speech by several novelists may be considered a malapropism rather than slang, but its currency suggests that it was a regular lexical item among the uneducated. 'Fondling' for *foundling* is used by Mr Kenwigs, despairing of his children's future, 'Take 'em away to the Fondling' ('hospital'; *Nicholas Nickleby* 36). Isabella Linton is called 'you naughty fondling' by her mother (*Wuthering Heights* 10), and Solomon Featherstone vows that he will not leave his money 'to fondlings from Africay' (*Middlemarch* 35).

Much slang was derived from the thieves' cant which Fagin and his associates use freely. It is naturally a feature of criminal characters, though sometimes used by others ignorant of its origin. Fagin has to explain to Claypole the 'kinchin lay' – snatching money from children; he fears that the Dodger will get a 'lagging' and become a 'lifer' and is interrupted before he can 'translate these mysterious expressions into the vulgar tongue' as meaning transportation for life (43). He rejoices that his executed confederates 'never peached upon old Fagin' (8), a word used by a country poacher later in the century who 'an't the chap to peach' (*The Ordeal of Richard Feverel* 6). A street boy speaks of an acquaintance who 'goes out cly-faking, and such. He's a prig, and a smart one too'. A plea for enlightenment on 'cly-faking' brings 'a-prigging of wipes, and sneeze-boxes, and ridicules'; his interlocutor 'was not so ignorant of slang as not to understand what his little friend meant now' (Henry Kingsley, *Ravenshoe* 35).[5] The accuracy of the novelists' use of criminal slang is borne out when we remember the apple-woman on London Bridge encountered by George Borrow who promised him, 'If you have any clies to sell at any time, I'll buy them of you; all safe with me; I never peach' (*Lavengro* 1851, 31). The shady boatman who rows Mary Barton in pursuit of Jem's ship uses the criminal 'blunt' for money – 'some folks say they've no more blunt, when all the while they've getten a mint' (Gaskell, *Mary Barton* 1848, 28).

More educated characters use slang in familiar conversation, often as part of the latest fashion. The use of *bunkum* in the sense of insincere talk is recorded from 1862; Arthur Fletcher says to Emily in *The Prime Minister* (1875), 'I don't want to talk buncum; I only want you to believe me' (17). Words to suggest that what the other person says is rubbish are always popular and Victorian slang had a good selection. Jasper Milvain calls his sister's opinion 'twaddle' and then 'bosh' (*New Grub Street* 33). Little Jack asks whether William is really his father – 'No humbug, you know' and is answered 'I'm not humbugging, Jack. I'm your father right enough' (*Esther Waters* 26). None of these words seems to cause offence in friendly company, but one 'commercial gentleman' is affronted by another telling him that 'the most of what you says is gammon' and reiterating the word (*Orley Farm* 9).

Some words seem to have been particular favourites and to have endured through the period. An example is 'scrape', still meaningful today among the older generation though perhaps not the younger, which seems to have bridged the generations in informal talk. It is used by an undergraduate at Oxford in the 1840s who has 'not known how to get out of the scrape' (*Loss and Gain* Part 1, 4); by a 'forward' provincial girl, 'you know what a scrape I am in' (*Wives and Daughters* 43); by a dissolute young man, 'I knew I should get into scrapes there' (Dickens, *Hard Times* 1854, Book 2, 3); by a fashionable and travelled young man, 'I can't bear the idea of getting the poor girl into a scrape' (Collins, *The Moonstone* 1868, 11); by a young man in a serious Tractarian family, 'tell me what you think I had better do about this scrape' and a middle-aged man in the same one, 'He was pretty considerably shocked to find he had brought you into such a scrape' (Yonge, *The Heir of Redclyffe* 1853, 10, 25); by an elderly lawyer, 'You seem to have got into some scrape down there' (*The Prime Minister* 35); by a young woman anxious for her sister, 'Now, Dodo, do listen to what James says, else you will be getting into a scrape' (*Middlemarch* 72); and effectively by Hardy who makes Sue Bridehead change register from formal to slang as emotion prevails over dignity: 'My curiosity to hunt up a new sensation always leads me into these scrapes' (*Jude the Obscure* Part 3, 7).

Speakers of more than one generation use 'bang' or 'bang-up' to show enthusiasm for the quality of an event or experience. Hardy's Grandfather Cantle recalls his days in the Volunteers, the 'Bang-up Locals', and Humphrey argues that the circumstances of Tamsin's marriage preclude 'a banging wedding' (*The Return of the Native*, 1878, Book 1, 3). An unnamed servant describes Bella Wilfer riding with her father as 'a slap-up gal in a bang-up chariot' (*Our Mutual Friend* Book 2, 8) and Bob Jakins says of the books he buys for Maggie that 'they banged iverything for picturs' (*The Mill on the Floss* Book 4, 3). 'Screw' has a sense different from its modern taboo slang one;[6] it can refer to a poor-quality horse, and by analogy to a man of inferior social status. 'If you had a pure-blood Arab barb would you cross him with a screw?' Sir Austin asks when his son's marriage is discussed (*The Ordeal of Richard Feverel* 17), and Butler's Anthea fears that she will choose as her heir 'some nice-looking, well-dressed screw with gentlemanly manners which will take me in' (*The Way of All Flesh* 33). Anyone regarded as weak and foolish is a 'spooney': a 'stupid old spooney' who falls in love (*Pendennis* 28), a girl whose brother laughs at her for crying (*The Mill on the Floss* Book 1, 7), or a lawyer's client who is too frank about the pliant character of a witness (*Great Expectations* 20).

These few examples give an idea of how slang words are used by speakers of different ages and backgrounds, and could be multiplied many times. Victorian slang is a rich field for the historical linguist.

Many slang expressions, then as always, had an ephemeral popularity
and more must have been lost than recorded. Trollope captures one in
Doctor Thorne (1858) which does not seem to have found its way into
dictionaries of slang, as a facetious use of a current formal word. Frank
Gresham first puzzles his aunt with the well-known Oxford use of
'plucked' for examination failure, and then speaks of a 'set of men
who did nothing but smoke and drink beer. Malthusians we call
them'. To her astonished, 'Malthusians!' he replies, ' "Malt" you
know, aunt, and "use"; meaning they drink beer' (5).

The novelists make judicious use of slang to show social or
situational relationships. Respectable readers had the satisfaction of
vicariously entering questionable areas of language. Trollope's Charley
Tudor, writing a novel, reflects on the need to 'touch up' the reader
with 'a chapter of horrors, then another of fun, then a little love or a
little slang, or something of that sort' (*The Three Clerks* 1857, 19).
Use of slang can be a guide to character. Tom Gradgrind, especially in
conversation with Harthouse, tries to show himself as up to date and
'fly' in his language (*Hard Times* Book 2, 3). In a lighter book, Lupin
Pooter puts himself in a similar role later in the century when he
admits that he has 'got the chuck' from his job and exclaims 'Good
biz!' when offered a new one (Grossmith, *The Diary of a Nobody* 1892,
6, 7). Comic misunderstanding between the generations is frequent in
this story. Mr Pooter is puzzled by his son's comment that where he
lives is 'a bit off', and wonders if he means 'far off' geographically.
Sympathy for a hangover voiced as 'what priced head have you this
morning?' is responded to with 'I told him he might just as well speak
to me in Dutch'. Eventually he says, 'I don't understand your slang,
and at my time of life have no desire to learn it' (23, 10, 21).

Dickens gives a more sombre example of misunderstanding,
between classes rather than generations, in the disguised Lady
Dedlock's encounter with Jo:

> 'I am fly', says Jo. 'But fen larks, you know! Stow hooking it!'
> 'What does the horrible creature mean?' exclaims the servant,
> recoiling from him.
> 'Stow cutting away, you know!' says Jo.
> 'I don't understand you.'   (*Bleak House* 1853, 16)

Used at the wrong time or to the wrong person, slang can cause offence in a society so conscious of social niceties and jealous for respect. Frederick Aylmer tells his mother that if his wife thought she was being bullied 'she would turn rusty at once'. The reaction is strong: 'Turn rusty! What am I to think of a young lady who is prepared to turn rusty – at once too, because she is cautioned by the mother of the man she professes to love against an improper acquaintance?' (Trollope, *The Belton Estate* 1866, 17). The annoyance here is caused as much by the low nature of the slang as by the message; it is servants' talk, as when a footman snubbed for asking personal questions replies, 'you needn't turn so rusty' (*Esther Waters* 15). A stewardess who calls a passenger 'honey' escapes rebuke, presumably through the disabling effects of seasickness (Charlotte Brontë, *Villette* 1853, 6).

Sensitivity is not found among the upper class alone; Pooter objects to Lupin's slang but is surprised to be rebuked by his wife who 'begged me not to use the expression "Good old", but to leave it to Mr Stillbrook and other *gentlemen* of his type', Stillbrook being a 'cad' of their acquaintance (5). Objections are voiced below the genteel lower middle class, by pretentious servants: Lightfoot's linguistic lack of proper respect rouses Morgan to say: 'Don't call Major Pendennis an old cove, if you'll 'ave the goodness, Lightfoot, and don't call *me* an old cove nether. Such words aren't used in society' (*Pendennis* 60). Morgan seems to have a point; the Artful Dodger draws Oliver's attention to Mr Brownlow as 'that old cove by the book-stall' and in *Martin Chuzzlewit* (1844) 'the youngest gentleman' says, "I knew a cove" – he used that familiar epithet in his agitation, but corrected himself, by adding, 'a gentleman of property, I mean' (10). When Silas Wegg asks when Venus's marriage is to 'come off', the response is, 'I cannot permit it to be put in the form of a Flight' (*Our Mutual Friend* Book 4, 14).

Foreign speakers

When foreign speakers appear in novels they are seldom shown with much subtlety. They are usually minor persons in the plot, comic or sinister, reflecting the British view that imperfect speaking of English shows inferiority of character. The devices that show their speech are those used for other non-standard speakers of English: adapted spelling, punctuation to show elision or omission, with lexical and syntactic deviance. There is, again, little attempt at a complete or consistent rendering. Foreign characters who make only a brief appearance do not need elaborate treatment. They may be purely comic, like Dickens's Count Smorltork, of uncertain nationality, who has been 'ver long time' in England and has a 'Large book at home – full of notes – music, picture, science, poetry, politic; all tings' (*Pickwick Papers* 1837, 15). The effect may be to heighten pathos, as when Mary Barton in her distress meets an Italian boy begging who says 'in his pretty broken English, the word "Hungry! so hungry!" ' (20). Broken English may reinforce a foreign setting, as when a customs official tells Lucy Snowe, 'All right! haf your tronc soon' (*Villette* 7), or a foreign character in England, as when Foker's valet asks 'At what dime sall I order de drag, sir, to be to Miss Pingney's door, sir?' (*Pendennis* 39).

A foreigner may be introduced to make a point about British attitudes; the best-known example is Podsnap's patronising tone to the 'foreign gentleman' whose conversation is limited to short phrases – 'Mais yees; I know eem'. Podsnap speaks to him with loud emphasis, shown in the text by capital initial letters; the foreigner at one point produces a perfect sentence, speaking more for the author than for himself, when he replies to Podsnap's praises of what Providence has bestowed on England with 'It was a little particular of Providence . . . for the frontier is not large' (*Our Mutual Friend* 11).

Foreign characters who are more fully developed may not show such strong deviance. An example is Rigaud in *Little Dorrit* (1857), whose speech is appropriate for his villainy rather than his foreign origin:

> I am just landed from the packet-boat, madam, and have been delayed
> by the weather: the infernal weather! In consequence of this, madam,
> some necessary business that I should otherwise have transacted here
> within the regular hours (necessary business because money-business),
> still remains to be done.   (29)

One of the few major foreign characters in Victorian fiction is Count Fosco in *The Woman in White*. Collins saves himself the work of creating deviant spelling and syntax for his many speeches by the statement of Marian Halcombe:

> There are times when it is almost impossible to detect, by his accent,
> that he is not a countryman of our own; and as for fluency, there are

very few born Englishmen who can talk with as few stoppages and repetitions as the Count. He may construct his sentences, more or less, in the foreign way; but I have never yet heard him use a wrong expression, or hesitate for a moment in his choice of a word.

(Part 2, 1)

Collins cleverly prepares the way for Fosco's perfect English by earlier introducing a minor Italian character, Pesca, whose speech shows foreign characteristics.

Very slight deviance with a sprinkling of foreign phrases may serve as a pointer; Thackeray's French chef Alcide says:

At her accustomed hour, and instead of the rude *gigot à l'eau* which was ordinarily served at her too simple table, I sent her up a little *potage a la Reine* – *à la Reine Blanche* I called it, – as white as her own tint – and confectioned with the most fragrant cream and almonds.

(*Pendennis* 23)

Hortense, longer resident in England, shows minimal deviance, just enough to give credibility to her French nationality when she speaks to Esther:

Assuredly; mademoiselle, I am thankful for your politeness. Mademoiselle, I have an inexpressible desire to find service with a young lady who is good, accomplished, beautiful. You are good, accomplished, and beautiful as an angel. Ah, could I have the honour of being your domestic!   (*Bleak House* 23)

A foreigner who is not designed to be comic or villainous may be credited with almost standard native English, perhaps with authorial comment about accent. A Pole, sleeping rough in London, speaks 'tolerable English, but with a marked accent' and shows no deviance in his conversation (*Sybil* Book 5, 7). A German painter in Rome is noted for 'his confident English' (*Middlemarch* 22). Claude Mellot's French wife has 'an accent prettily tinged with French' (*Yeast* 15) and Osborne Hamley's widow in *Wives and Daughters* speaks with neither deviance nor comment. G.H. Lewes deplored Charlotte Brontë's inconsistency in *Shirley*: 'When Gerald Moore and his sister talk in French, which the authoress translates, it is surely not allowable to leave scraps of French in the translation' (*Edinburgh Review* January 1850).

Notes

1. R.G. Latham (1812–88) was Professor of English Language and Literature at University College, London. He wrote a number of works on philology and ethnology and edited a revised version of Johnson's *Dictionary*.

2. Frederick Temple, Headmaster of Rugby and later Archbishop of Canterbury, had 'a marked provincial accent'. See Honey (1977, 231f) for this and other examples.

3. Pope rhymes *obliged* and *besieged* (Epistle to Dr Arbuthnot 207f). Later, however, the Prince Regent was advised by the actor Kemble that 'It would become your royal mouth much better to say, *oblige* me than *obleege*' (Coleridge, *Table Talk* 29 December 1822).

4. Swift wrote in the *Tatler* September 1710. His objection was particularly to slang created by reducing a word to its first syllable, 'when we are already overloaded with monosyllables, which are the disgrace of our language'.

5. The stolen articles were handkerchiefs, snuff-boxes and reticules – the main quarry of Fagin's boys. The language is a nice mixture of slang and malapropism.

6. The sexual meaning is also attested from the eighteenth century; see Partridge (1961 s.v.). Unsurprisingly, I have not come across this usage in Victorian fictional dialogue.

CHAPTER 3
Dialect

When the Victorian novelists provided some of their characters with speech that was distinctive of certain regions, they were following a long-established literary tradition. Awareness of dialect variations had been growing ever since the language of London and its environs had been taken as a literary standard from the late sixteenth century. The representation of dialect goes back even earlier; Chaucer gave some northern forms to the Cambridge undergraduates in the *Reeve's Tale*, and expressed at the end of *Troilus and Criseyde* his anxiety about the diversity of current English. Such disquiet increased in the following century, and was voiced by Caxton in his anecdote about a misunderstanding in a request for eggs which culminates in the despairing question, 'Loo! what sholde a man in thyse days now wryte, egges or eyren?'.[1] A hundred years later, regional variations could be treated in literature as sub-standard and comic, as Shakespeare represents the Welsh English of Hugh Evans in *The Merry Wives of Windsor* and Fluellen in *Henry V*, and gives the disguised Edgar in *King Lear* south-western rustic speech already accepted as a stage convention. At the same time, people of unchallenged social status were not despised for keeping the characteristics of their locality. John Aubrey relates that Walter Raleigh spoke broad Devon all his life.

The actor could supply such regional pointers as the stage might require. With the growth of the novel, it was only the invention of the author that could suggest regional speech. The eighteenth-century writers did not meet the challenge with great subtlety. As the concept of standard English in speech as well as writing developed, it became easier to show by a few visual pointers that a character deviated from the norm. Among the major novelists, Smollett was the one most interested in language variation, but he did not use dialect in any imaginative depth. When, for example, he presents a minor character with a northern accent, the odd mixture of deviant spellings simply creates a comically alien effect as background for the southward journey of his principals. 'Here's a poor lad that's willing to make attoonement for his offence; and an that woant't satisfy yaw, offers to fight yaw fairly' (*Roderick Random* 1748, 11). The misspellings of characters like Tabitha Bramble in the epistolary *Humphrey Clinker* 1771, again suggest a lack of education and sophistication rather than distinctive speech. The same may be said of the malapropisms and irregular spellings given to Fielding's 'low' characters.[2]

It was Walter Scott who made dialect speech in fiction important, and not invariably comic. Scots was something of a special case, a variety rather than a dialect of English, already known in the dominant metropolis by the work of Burns and Ramsey as well as by the presence of a substantial number of visitors from Scotland. Scott knew that his main readership was English and his deviant spelling aimed at being intelligible rather than fully representational. He brought to fiction something which the Victorian writers were to develop more fully: a distinction between the social and educational levels of characters from the same locality. Henceforth dialect could not only place a character regionally but could also show register and relationships within that region. Thus in *Old Mortality* (1816) Lady Margaret is clearly identified with the people among whom she lives and set apart from the more anglicised aristocracy. 'How mean ye by that, ye auld fule woman? – D'ye think that I order ony thing against conscience?' (7). But she is also different from the peasants like Cuddy with his much broader speech:

> Sae get up, mither, and sort your things to gang away; for since sae it is that gang we maun, I wad like ill to wait till Mr Harrison and auld Gudyill cam to pu' us out by the lug and the horn. (7)

Scott gave new credibility to fictional dialect, as he helped to make novel reading respectable. His influence was catalytic, not definitive. Dialect found its place in serious fiction, as economic changes gave national importance to areas previously remote and little regarded and as social and physical mobility made people more fully aware of the many varieties of English, and the consequent difficulties of communication. Yet, for many, knowledge of regional dialect was more often from literature than from experience; Lady Harriet cannot recollect the Irish word she wants but is sure that Molly Gibson's sharing of her ignorance 'shows you've never read Miss Edgeworth's tales . . . If you had, you'd have recollected that there was such a word, even if you didn't remember what it was' (*Wives and Daughters* 14).[3] Literature was sometimes easier to manage than life; Earle observed, 'every Englishman knows that it is comparatively easy to understand the dialects in print, but often quite impossible in conversation' (Earle 1873, 98). While deviant spelling continued to be used for social rather than specifically local differentiation, writers began to treat more seriously the speech of the areas in which their stories were placed.

Although the novelists were not dialectologists, they were aware of the new scholarly interest in dialect which was developing. Their own experience gave them pride in local speech and they welcomed the support of those whose interest was linguistic and historical rather than imaginative. The champions of regional dialects were explaining that these were not debased and inferior forms of speech but historical survivals with as good an ancestry as the particular dialect which had come to be accepted as the standard. Dialect could be seen as an aspect of the nostalgia for a vanished past which took many forms in the Victorian mind.

Serious study of dialect developed in the nineteenth century. Earlier attempts like Alexander Gil's *Logonomia Anglica* (1619) were handicapped by lack of general linguistic theory. Although dialect words were frequently included in dictionaries, and glossaries for specific areas were produced in the eighteenth and early nineteenth centuries, the first writer to give serious attention to historical phonology was A.J. Ellis, who included current English dialects in his *Early English Pronunciation* (1869–74). Ellis undertook systematic investigation in the field, aided by a large band of volunteers including the French Crown Prince Louis Bonaparte, who himself tried rendering the Song of Solomon in Yorkshire dialects. In 1889 Ellis published the final version of his researches as *The Existing Phonology of English Dialects*. By this time the English Dialect Society, founded in 1873 on the initiative of W.A. Wright with W.W. Skeat as its first director, was well established and had published a number of monographs. In 1895 Joseph Wright began work on the *English Dialect Dictionary*, the six volumes of which appeared between 1898 and 1905.

Although scientific English dialectology developed after the serious treatment of regional speech in fiction was well established, the growing interest in dialect worked together with the concern of the novelists to present sympathetically the parts of the country which

they knew and loved. The essential goodness and underlying nobility
of simple people could be supported by showing them as heirs of a
long national tradition, preserving in their speech forms which were
archaic in standard use but which had an honourable and often
cultivated ancestry. Elizabeth Gaskell supplemented her empirical
observation with the work of her husband, the Unitarian minister
William Gaskell, whose *Two Lectures on the Lancashire Dialect* she
appended to the fifth edition of *Mary Barton* in 1854. Throughout this
novel she is at pains to give the credentials of Lancashire usage which
might seem odd or barbaric to the southern reader. Often it is a
simple gloss on a word or phrase, but her footnotes sometimes adduce
a literary use. Thus Alice Wilson's 'poor lile fellow' has the comment,
'a north country word for "little". "Wit *leil* labour to live." – *Piers
Ploughman*' (7). When John Barton recalls 'dree work' on his travels,
the reader is informed, ' "Dree", long and tedious. Anglo-Saxon,
"dreogan", to suffer, to endure'(9).

Thomas Hardy's pride in the Old English antecedents of dialect
was even stronger. He learned much from William Barnes, the
clergyman and schoolmaster who wrote poems in Dorset dialect, with
ingenious spelling and punctuation (including a liberal use of the
diaeresis that often makes his texts as opaque as Emily Brontë's
unrevised renderings of Joseph). Barnes was an extreme Saxonist,
whose wish to eliminate the Romance and classical elements in
English went to the length of offering coinages like *kinlore* for
'genealogy' and *wheel-saddle* for 'bicycle'. Hardy's obituary of Barnes
contained a comment with which many other regional novelists
would have agreed:

> In the systematic study of his native dialect . . . he has shown the
> world that far from being, as popularly supposed, a corruption of correct
> English, it is a distinct branch of Teutonic speech, regular in declension
> and conjugation, and richer in many classes of words than any other
> tongue known to him.   (Orel 1967, 101)

The Saxonists had support from John Earle who asserted, with the
confidence proper to an Oxford Professor of Anglo-Saxon, 'the great
characteristic which distinguishes all the dialects from the King's
English is this – they are comparatively unaltered by French influence'
(Earle 1873, 96). Latham, however, observed more sceptically, 'The
evidence of natives is always to be taken with caution. Every patriotic

provincial claims the greatest amount of Anglo-Saxon for his own dialect' (Latham 1862, 347).

Cockney

The cockney speech of London had for long lent some of its salient features to the presentation of uneducated characters in fiction. By the early Victorian period it was also recognised as the more specifically London dialect, regionally distinct and already subject to new pressures and changes. The metropolitan dominance of London remained throughout the century, even while the regions became more important, and London continued to be a favoured setting for fiction. The life of its people outside the fashionable milieu, their culture patterns and the degree of their social and intellectual deprivation were all increasingly matters of concern.

Their speech, on the other hand, was little regarded until late in the century and was usually dismissed as a deviant and slovenly form of English. Interest in recording it as evidence of older usage came later than the corresponding study of regional dialects. Later analysts would recognise certain salient phonemic features:

1   Nasalisation of vowels, resulting from minimal lip movement, with a tendency to move back vowels to a central position. This gives such results as the sound of *nice* approximating to 'noice' and *father* as 'fawther'.

2   Glottal stop replacing /t/ and /k/ between vowels, to make *butter* sound like 'bu'er'.

3   After vowel sounds /l/ sometimes moves close to /u/, so that *till* is pronounced /tiu/.

4   The two sounds of the dental *th-* are fronted to /f/ and /v/: *think* as 'fink', *though* as 'vough'.

5   The aspirate is dropped to make *house* into 'ouse', but also is sometimes inserted incorrectly to pronounce *air* as 'hair'.

6   The sounds of initial *v* and *w* are confused.

It will appear from the examples of written cockney below, that neither novelists nor social observers attempted to do much with the first four of these features. The dropped or misplaced aspirate is a constant signal. The v/w confusion, which is regularly exploited,

needs closer scrutiny. Writers generally depend on grammatical
deviance, and the suggestion of unfamiliar speech through deliberate
misspelling, which is seldom consistent for long.

Dickens was the most extensive and most successful depicter of
cockney speech, but he was not an innovator except in the blending
of cockney characteristics with his own gift for memorable idiolects.
Surtees and Egan represented cockney speech but, like the
eighteenth-century novelists, were interested mainly in its comic and
localising qualities. As late as 1853 Surtees gives the horse-dealer
Buckram, somewhere on the rural edge of London, speech which
depends on some outrageous spellings and such popularly accepted
cockney features as the dropped aspirate, emphasised by the strong
form of the indefinite article:

> I've an unkimmon nice oss, and **an oss** in hevery respect werry like
> your work, but he's an oss I'll candidly state, I wouldn't put in every
> one's 'ands, for in fust place, he's werry waluerous, and in the second,
> he requires an ossman to ride.   (*Mr Sponge's Sporting Tour* 1853, 3)

The music hall and the melodrama made cockney a feature of public
entertainment, and their popularity brought a demand for published
scripts with an attempt at visual representation. Cartoons and
illustrated jokes, from popular broadsides to *Punch*, were another
source of visible speech. Serious observers such as Mayhew tried to
convey to the readers the effect of what they had heard. It is difficult
to disentangle the various lines of influence. The debt was probably
reciprocal, all writers working within a convention which had evolved
and which fulfilled expectations without aiming at a consistent
transcription. While some were concerned only to exploit the comic
possibilities of cockney, Dickens and others saw their Londoners as
individuals with a shared culture of their own.

Certainly Dickens is not wholly consistent. His training in
shorthand, although the system he used was less phonetic than later
ones, had helped to accustom his naturally acute ear to the sounds of
speech. His early life had brought him into close and sometimes
traumatic contact with the lower side of London. In his first popular
success, *The Pickwick Papers*, one of the most successful characters was
Mr Pickwick's servant Sam Weller. Sam is an original but he is not
the original literary cockney. His most famous speech characteristic,
the transference of *v* and *w*, was already considered to be veritable

cockney; spellings suggesting it can be traced back much earlier.[4] In the eighteenth century Thomas Sheridan regarded the confusion as one of the reprehensible marks of cockney:

> How easy it would be to change the cockney pronunciation, by making use of a proper method! The chief difference lies in the manner of pronouncing the v, or u consonant as it is commonly called, and the w; which they frequently interchangeably use for each other. Thus they call veal weal, vinegar winegar. On the other hand they call winter vinter, well vell. Tho' the converting the *w* into a *v* is not so common as the changing the *v* into a *w*.   (Sheridan 1762, 54)

It is questionable whether cockney speakers regularly transposed the two sounds. Possibly London speech produced an intermediate sound, a labio-dental frictionless sound or a voiced bi-labial fricative, unfamiliar to speakers of standard English and heard as a more familiar sound misplaced; such adjustment to the known is common in interpreting sounds outside one's own system (Jespersen 1909, 385f, Chapman 1984, 66f). Certainly Dickens often uses this device; Sam Weller speaks:

> Look here, Sir; here's a oyster stall to every half-dozen houses – the street's lined vith 'em. Blessed if I don't think that ven a man's wery poor, he rushes out of his lodgings, and eats oysters in reg'lar desperation.   (*Pickwick Papers* 22)

The other deviant representations in this extract, *'em* and *reg'lar*, are purely visual suggestions of sub-standard speech. They would certainly be heard in ordinary rapid speech today, and probably at the time of writing. Comments by purists about slurred and slovenly speech suggest that it was not uncommon. It was one of the habits which Bulwer-Lytton, a novelist who also gave his views on speech more directly, deprecated among the aristocracy, who neglected 'the regular and polished smoothness of conversation' (Bulwer-Lytton 1833, Vol. 1, 156f). Mrs Humphrey, a writer on etiquette at the end of the century, took a very dim view of it: 'It is good manners to articulate distinctly, and bad manners to neglect to do so. A man need not exactly take lessons in elocution (though they would not be amiss), but he can teach himself to pronounce clearly' (Humphrey 1897, 13). Gissing comments on Mutimer's non-standard pronunciation of his fiancée's name 'Adela': 'there was a slurring of the second syllable disagreeably suggestive of vulgarity' (*Demos* Book 2, 2).[5] Both Sam Weller and his father Tony share these and other cockney characteristics, with some differentiation for the older man, who also draws upon the register of the coach trade.

Dickens was well aware of variations in cockney speech. He represented subtle nuances which to many would have been lost in a general assumption about uneducated Londoners. Mr Kenwigs shows genteel cockney by the *v/w* confusion in otherwise standard speech: 'A man in public life expects to be sneered at – it is the fault of his elewated sitiwation, not of himself' (*Nicholas Nickleby* 14). At the lower extreme is Mrs Gamp, who combines cockney features with her own inimitable idiolect. Again, her speech is created by a few recurring features, with the particular trick of using an affricate sound in some final positions after a long vowel. 'Poor sweet creetur, there she goes, like a lamb to the sacrifige! If there's any illness when that wessel gets to sea . . . it's murder, and I'm the witness for the persecution' (*Martin Chuzzlewit* 1844, 40). This is magnificent in context but does not bear close phonetic analysis. The *v/w* transposition appears in *wessel* but not in *witness*; the spelling of *creetur* suggests a visual rather than a phonic difference from the standard. The spelling of *sacrifige* is a feature of the Gamp idiolect, with many forms like 'excuge', 'suppoge'. This, like much Victorian non-standard speech, is a survival from earlier upper-class pronunciation which perhaps has an additional function for this character if it is correct that 'Dickens extended its application here to underline a certain thickness of speech on the part of the drink-sodden Mrs Gamp' (Golding 1985, 109). Another possibility is that it is only 'a speech defect, a sort of impediment with which some people are afflicted' (Franklyn 1953, 232). It is found elsewhere in fiction and perhaps was not confined to London. Disraeli makes a north-country woman say, 'I don't care too much for a good squeedge' (*Sybil* Book 3, 3)

The effect is also given, here and elsewhere, by malapropism, associated with uneducated London speech as early as Shakespeare's Mistress Quickly (*2 Henry IV*) with her 'conformities' for 'infirmities', and Elbow's 'respected' for 'suspected' (*Measure for Measure*). Dickens's frequent claim that he did not exaggerate is supported by factual reporting in this matter as in others. Mayhew records the comment of a granary worker on the rats, 'Great black fellows as would frighten a lady into asterisks to see of a sudden' (Mayhew 1862,

Vol. 2, 431). Apart from malapropisms and slang words, Dickens uses comparatively little deviant lexis or syntax in rendering cockney speech, but depends on signals of pronunciation. One feature of Mrs Gamp's syntax is the change to a relative clause beginning with *which* without clear antecedent: 'As a good friend of mine has frequent made remark to me, which her name, my love, is Mrs Harris' (40). This would sound like a bizarre idiolect invented by Dickens, but there is the evidence of another cockney woman, Munby's servant-wife Hannah, whom he reports as speaking of the marriage of a housemaid to a 'gentleman' as witnessed by 'Davies, a nurse who knows the cook as lived with her – which her name was Betsy Wade' (Hudson 1972, 45).

While Dickens never ceased to exploit the comic possibilities of cockney, the deeper seriousness of his later novels found a tragic sense in its contrast with the speech of more privileged Londoners. Mr Pickwick is puzzled by Sam Weller's tale of how a barmaid was bribed 'to hocus the brandy and water of fourteen unpolled electors':

> 'What do you mean by 'hocussing' brandy and water?' inquired Mr Pickwick.
> 'Puttin' laud'num in it,' replied Sam.
>
> (*Pickwick Papers* 13)

This carries a very different message about the mutual incomprehension between the 'two nations' from Lady Dedlock's meeting with Jo, discussed in the previous chapter.

Accepting that Dickens was not attempting a close and consistent transcription of cockney speech, and setting aside his genius for idiolect, how accurate was his presentation? It is generally agreed that there is evidence of a change in cockney speech between 1850 and 1880, with the disappearance of some of the characteristics which he uses, such as the *v/w* confusion (Matthews 1938, 159ff).[6] Indeed, Dickens may have been recording usage which was already becoming old-fashioned as early as the 1830s. In the absence of precise linguistic record, it is hard to be certain; the evidence of reporters like Mayhew is inconclusive in this respect since they too followed many of the accepted conventions. Contemporary criticism was not so much of his accuracy in matters of cockney deviance, but of his creating characters with knowledge and abilities beyond their station. A critic of *Pickwick Papers* in the *Quarterly Review* of October 1837 complained:

> The Wellers, father and son, both talk a language and employ allusions
> utterly irreconcilable with their habits and station, and we constantly
> detect both in the nice and even critical use of words and images
> borrowed from sources wholly inaccessible to them.

This perhaps may be granted, though it misconceives the
imaginative art of fiction in defence of a stolid realism. In other ways
Dickens's observation may once again be vindicated, and it is worth
pursuing a single word to show how formal record of the language can
illuminate fictional speech. He gives Londoners the pronunciation
'cowcumber' for *cucumber*, which was standard until the beginning of
the nineteenth century. Walker's *Critical Pronouncing Dictionary* 1791
accepts the new *cucumber* as following the spelling, but prefers the
older *cowcumber*. In 1836 R.B. Smart in *Walker Remodelled* ruled that
'no well-taught person, except of the old school, now says *cow-cumber*
. . . although any other pronunciation . . . would have been pedantic
thirty years ago' (*O.E.D. s.v. cucumber*). Lord John Russell
(1792–1878) 'like other high-bred people of his time . . . talked of
"cowcumbers" and "laylocks" [lilacs], called a woman a '"ooman", and
was "much obleeged" where a degenerate age is content to be obliged'
(Russell 1898, 14). Bulwer-Lytton accepted grudgingly that 'cucumber
may receive its final exactness of pronunciation from the prosodiacal
fiat of my Lord Hertford' (Bulwer 1833, Vol. 1, 156). Mrs Gamp who
asks if there is 'such a thing as a cowcumber in the 'ouse', and
Inspector Bucket who calls Mrs Snagsby a 'little pickled cowcumber'
might seem to be anachronistic (*Martin Chuzzlewit* 25, *Bleak House*
54). Alford, however, gives evidence that it was still an option for
educated speakers even later. He records disagreement about whether
the first syllable of *cucumber* should be pronounced *coo, cow* or *kew* :

> The point is one warmly debated: so warmly in certain circles that
> when I had a house full of pupils, we were driven to legislation on it,
> merely to keep the peace of the household. Whenever the unfortunate
> word occurred at table, which was almost every day during the summer
> months, a fierce fray invariably set in. At last we abated the nuisance
> by enacting, that in future the debateable first syllable should be
> dropped, and the article be called for under the undebateable name of
> '*cumber*'.   (Alford 1864, 51)

As a cockney pronunciation it is witnessed as late as 1891, when a
policeman is reported as calling for 'a bit o' pickled sallamon and a

cowcumber' (*Enquire Within About Everything* 68). This brief case-study of a single word – and it could be paralleled many times for others – reveals two matters of interest. The Victorians were greatly concerned about the 'correct' pronunciation of disputed words, and forms which had been aristocratic in the previous generation sometimes lingered on in cockney speech.

There is little firm evidence of actual cockney speech at this time. The recorders of real conversations were no more skilled in the niceties of phonology than the novelists, and indeed lacked their interpretative skills. It is clear that a few conventional pointers such as the dropped or misplaced aspirate, the *v/w* confusion, some non-standard vowel sounds and grammatical deviances were accepted as representing cockney. Mayhew generally makes little attempt to show the phonic and prosodic features of those whom he interviewed; occasionally he plunges into representation; a beggar is relating a conversation about the workhouse:

> Jem he says, 'It's a great hinstitooshin, Enery', says he, for you see Jem was a bit of a scollard [scholar], and could talk just like a book. 'I don't know about a hinstitooshin, Jem,' says I, 'but what I does know is that a man might do wuss nor goe in there and have his grub and his baccy regular, without nought to stress him, like them old chaps.' Somehow or other that 'ere conversation came across me, and off I started to the work'ouse'.
>
> (Mayhew 1862, 401)

This is certainly not an accurate transcript of pronunciation. The aspirate is sometimes dropped and sometimes retained; the spelling of *goe* does not seem to show a deviant sound, but simply suggests illiteracy. Kirwan goes into an orgy of misplaced aspirates and bi-labials in reporting a young pickpocket at an impromptu entertainment in the East End:

> I am sorry, me blokes, that my voice is so werry much out of tune in singing at Her Majesty's Hopera in the Haymarket, but howsumbever, as I have given hup my hengagement at that 'ouse, I'll fake you a few werses to show wot I wonce wos when I wos in voice.
>
> (Kirwan 1870, 37)

Surely no speaker ever added so many aspirates and dropped only one, but again such analysis is beside the point. The tone of the conversation has a ring of truth. This is the idiom of the Artful

Dodger outfacing the magistrates; the sensation of non-standard speech is secondary to the comic effrontery of the cockney street-boy which Kirwan's record shows that Dickens could take from life:

> I shall thank the madg'strates to dispose of this here little affair, and not to keep me while they read the paper, for I've got an appointment with a genelman in the City, and as I'm a man of my word and wery punctual in business affairs, he'll go away if I ain't there to my time.
>
> (*Oliver Twist* 43)

Greenwood gives a lively account of a cab-driver explaining that his horse has only three good legs:

> 'Ah, if you count that thing in the off side she's got four; but I don't call that a leg, it's only a swinger, and been nothing but a swinger this nine years, to my knowledge,' said Mr. Barlow. 'It's awfully agin her, that leg is . . . Her appetite's all that can be desired, and a jolly sight more than is conwenient sometimes, . . . but it's that leg that beats her. Oftentimes when we've had a run o' luck, I've got it into my 'art to stand a quartern of beans to the old gal, but I daresent; they get into them three sound legs of hers and make her so sarsy that she'd forget to be keerful of her lame pin, and lay herself up.'
>
> (Greenwood 1881, 108f)

This cockney cabman is surely kin to the one who drives Mr Pickwick to the Golden Cross:

> He always falls down when he's took out of the cab . . . but when he's in it, we bears him up werry tight, and takes him in werry short, so as he can't werry well fall down, and we've got a pair o' precious large wheels on; so ven he does move, they run after him, and he must go on – he can't help it.   (*Pickwick Papers* 2)

The success of Dickens in reproducing cockney speech is not a matter of pronunciation so much as idiom and spirit, and the evidence is that he brings before his readers the reality of the lower strata of London life. There is little deviant syntax and, except for malapropisms, little deviant lexis, in his representations.

Moore and Gissing take a more sombre view of the cockney. There is less humour and more compassion, as when Moore makes Esther's mother say, 'I dunno, dearie; 'tis hard to say what 'e'll do; he's a 'ard man to live with. I've 'ad a terrible time of it lately, and them babies allus coming. Ah, we poor women have more than our right to bear with' (*Esther Waters* 13). Gissing's Mrs Peckover is venal but not comic or contemptible when she speaks of the child she has fostered:

> Her cirkinstances has been peculiar; that you'll understand, I'm sure. But I done my best to take the place of the mother as is gone to a better world. An' now that she's layin' ill, I'm sure no mother could feel it more.   (*The Nether World* 1889, 5)

Through the novel, cockney became a literary dialect. In various degrees of deviation, it was used to convey the low life of London and also to present sub-standard speakers in contrast to the unmarked norm of fictional dialogue.

Regional dialect

Apart from Dickens, the greatest novelists of the period did not concern themselves with the details of the London poor. Such characters remain incidental to the main plot, with its cast of characters who show no special types of pronunciation. Other dialects, however, received more careful attention than ever before. The treatment of dialect in the regional novel is generally different from that of vaguely cockney speech. The concern is not only to show the difference between social classes, although this point can be developed for both comic and tragic potential. There is also the desire to convey the distinctive qualities of provincial life, to give shared human dimension to regions which for centuries had been little regarded in the mainstream of English literature.

Serious regionalism in the novel is distinct from the visits of provincial characters to London, and the temporary excursion of Londoners to other parts. These are treated briefly, with few linguistic pointers, giving an effect of surface difference rather than a meeting of cultures. Yet such brief encounters in fiction reflect a truth of life. The railway had increased national mobility in a couple of decades; people were hearing other forms of speech for themselves and not meeting them only as written conventions. By the 1840s when the novel was beginning its greatest years, the social geography of Britain was becoming more widely known. Readers were forced to acknowledge that what seemed normal to them was not the criterion for all their compatriots. John Barton from Manchester takes a poor view of London speech when he encounters a policeman: "You're frightening them horses," says he, in his mincing way (for Londoners are mostly all tongue-tied, and can't say their a's and u's properly)' (*Mary Barton* 9). The same sentiment is shared by Yorke in Charlotte Brontë's *Shirley* (1849), who asserted that 'A Yorkshire burr was as much better than a cockney's lisp, as a bull's bellow than a raton's squeak'(4).

Later in the century Hardy's Gwendoline Chickerel from Dorset has a lexical difficulty with a London greengrocer where 'they sweared me down that they hadn't got such things as chippols in the shop, and had never heard of them in their lives'. Her more sophisticated sister Ethelberta explains, 'they call them young onions here' (*The Hand of Ethelberta* 1876, 23). The episode illustrates the occasional mutual incomprehension between regions, and it has a pragmatic role in the novel by showing how far Ethelberta has moved from her simple family.[7]

In the other direction, Lancelot Smith finds that the speech of rural England is alien to him when he goes to a village fair in Hampshire. 'Lancelot tried to listen to the conversation of the men round him. To his astonishment he hardly understood a word of it. It was half articulate, nasal, guttural, made up almost entirely of vowels, like the speech of savages' (*Yeast* 13). His incomprehension must have been a common experience among the middle-class Victorians who tried to make contact with those whose lives they wanted to improve; one writer on the language observes '[that] the language of the uneducated should be unintelligible to the educated is again a thing to be expected' (Lysons 1868, 45). The effect of the provincial on the Londoner is not always so extreme. Nicholas Nickleby's reconciliation with John Browdie is not hampered by the latter's Yorkshire dialect:

> Beatten the schoolmeaster! Ho! ho! ho! Beatten the schoolmeaster! Who ever heard o' the loike of that noo! Giv' us thee hond agean, yoongster. Beatten a schoolmeaster! Dang it, I loove thee for't.
>
> (*Nicholas Nickleby* 13)

This is more impressionistic than convincing, but it serves its purpose at this moment in the novel. The lengthened vowels have the hypnotic effect that Dickens knew how to produce by many devices of repetition and accumulation. The deviant spelling of *give* suggests nothing about the pronunciation but gives an extra effect of difference from expectation. In his preface to a new edition of the novel in 1848, Dickens relates his conversation with a Yorkshireman who gave him information about the notorious 'Yorkshire schools', and admitting that 'I descry a faint reflection of him in John Browdie'. The report of this man's speech is much broader than that of Browdie himself:

> Weel, Misther, we've been vary pleasant toogether, and ar'll spak' my moind tiv 'ee. Dinnot let the weedur send her lattle boy to yan o' our school-measthers while there's a harse to hoold in a' Lunnon, or a goother [gutter] to lie asleep in!

It seems that Dickens consciously restrained his attempt to reproduce dialect speech in the interest of readers who would become impatient at written dialect which was too opaque in its deviance.

Other writers are often content with a very brief suggestion of dialect. Thackeray uses a few conventional pointers for Costigan's Irish speech – 'I marked ye in the thayater last night during me daughter's perfawrumance; and missed ye on my return' (*Pendennis* 49). This is well enough, for Costigan's origin is not very material to the plot except to suggest a world alien to Pendennis and the intemperate fecklessness calumniously associated with the Irish at the time. The audacious deviance of *perfawrumance* in itself is enough to compel the reader's belief. Sometimes a single word or phrase is sufficient to place the speaker. Butler's north-country tinker Shaw is given no deviant spellings in his speech, but on his first appearance is reported as saying that 'he was rather throng just now' (*The Way of All Flesh* 59). In the same novel a coachman 'who was from the north country' is given a few more pointers – 'Take it, my lass, take what thou canst get whiles thou canst get it' (39), but when a longer passage of dialogue includes another northern speaker, Butler dodges the challenge with 'he said in a broad northern accent which I will not attempt to reproduce' (41). Wilkie Collins similarly evades the issue, with more than a hint of a southerner's collusion with the assumed standard speech of his readers:

> I translate Mrs Yolland out of the Yorkshire language into the English language. When I tell you that the all-accomplished Cuff was every now and then puzzled to understand her until I helped him, you will draw your own conclusions as to what your state of mind would be if I reported her in her native tongue.   (*The Moonstone* 14)

Dickens makes use of the first-person narrator to gloss a dialect word for the reader: ' "Cheer up, old mawther!" (Mr Peggotty meant old girl)' (*David Copperfield* 3).

In such episodes the novelists neither intended nor were expected to provide full and consistent dialect speech; the effect of deviance was enough. The approach is different when the novel is set entirely or mainly in a particular region. Dialect is still often incomplete and impressionistic, but it serves a more serious purpose. The standardisation of literary English left no tradition of writing in regional forms of language comparable to that which prevailed in France and Italy. Written representation of dialect was not, however, confined to dialogue in fiction and drama. There was, particularly in the north of England, a good deal of dialect writing asserting its own identity through visual deviation. The growing move towards uniformity in speech as well as writing brought concern to preserve local forms. When Elizabeth Gaskell brought Lancashire speech into the novel, less famous contemporaries like Edwin Waugh, James Staton and Benjamin Brierly were versifying Lancashire dialect, often as a vehicle of radical protest.[8] The novel of social concern had associate texts in which the 'Condition of England' was debated in non-standard English.

Popular literature, designed mainly for local attention, often used elaborately deviant spelling and punctuation, which would have the same effect on the uninitiated as Mrs Yolland's speech on Sergeant Cuff. Novelists who wished to show dialect speech did so by similarly breaking the convention which equated standard written English with speech showing no strong regional or class features. Even if they had desired a consistent and accurate representation, it would have been impossible within the limits of the regular alphabet and its conventional sound-values. The novelists were not skilled in phonetics, a science still rudimentary during the great days of Victorian fiction. Nor were they dialectologists, though some of them were interested in more serious contemporary studies of dialect. They worked by impression and suggestion, trusting in the effect of visual deviance to convey a sense of auditory difference. Visual representation of sound is an area of study still developing, and much work remains to be done on the relationship between texts and actual speech. The present concern is not with accuracy of transcription but with the use of dialect to develop character, to show relationships and to convey changing moods. Yet sometimes the novelists were in danger of defeating their own purpose, of hindering communication by excess of realism. The desire to create an effect of strangeness had to be tempered by concessions to the ordinary reader. Degrees of intensity within a dialect were to be shown, but without deviating too far from the normal convention of the written code. The efforts of the popular ballad writers stood as a warning as well as an example.

It was a warning which was usually but not always heeded. While Dickens modified his sense of Yorkshire speech in creating John Browdie, Emily Brontë gave fuller rein to Joseph in *Wuthering Heights*.[9] His speech was too difficult for some readers; Charlotte modified it in places for the second edition but did not escape censure for her own *Shirley* (1849) which G.H. Lewes said would be 'unintelligible for most people, for it is half in French and half in broad Yorkshire' (*Fraser's Magazine* XL, December 1849, 693). The same objection was made to Hardy, 'whose strange knowledge of the dialectical peculiarities of certain districts has tempted him to write whole conversations which are, to the ordinary reader, nothing but a series of linguistic puzzles' (*Spectator* 8 October 1881). Hardy, not alone among authors, suffered from diametrically opposed criticisms. Three years before the *Spectator* review he was accused by an *Athenaeum* reviewer of artificiality in *The Return of the Native* by creating characters who 'talk as no people ever talk now'. His reply showed that by the 1870s novelists were aware of the implications of what they were doing in rendering deviant speech in written form:

> An author may be said to fairly convey the spirit of intelligent peasant talk if he retains the idiom, compass and characteristic expressions, although he may not cumber the page with obsolete pronunciations of the purely English words, and with mispronunciations of those derived from Latin and Greek. In the printing of standard speech hardly any phonetic principle at all is observed; and if a writer attempts to exhibit on paper the precise accents of a rustic speaker he disturbs the proper balance of a true representation by unduly insisting upon the grotesque element, thus directing attention to a point of inferior interest, and diverting it from the speaker's meaning.
>
> (*Athenaeum* 30 November 1878)

Although complaints of both artificiality and opacity were frequent, they did not prevent novels with a strong dialect element being accepted and esteemed. The most notable change from the 1840s onwards was that dialect was no longer used exclusively for comedy or to present a 'low' character in a more educated context. Scott's example, accompanied and partly anticipated by the Irish novels of Maria Edgeworth, was followed by a more dignified treatment of dialect in fiction. Regional novelists regarded dialect speech as an important part of their creation. Elizabeth Gaskell peoples *Sylvia's Lovers* (1863) almost entirely with dialect speakers. George Eliot wrote to John Blackwood that Lytton 'thinks the two defects of "Adam Bede" are the dialect and Adam's marriage with Dinah; but of course I would rather have my teeth drawn than give up either' (Haight 1954–6, III, 264; 23 February 1860).

Received Victorian wisdom stressed the basic honesty and goodness of the uneducated poor. It was an emphasis which was socially acceptable, held often in happy association with the belief that poverty was part of the nature of things and tended to be the fault of the poor. Yet the use of dialect in the mouths of virtuous and even heroic characters was neither a mere concession to complacency, nor a late manifestation of the pastoral idyll. Writers like Gaskell, Eliot and Hardy had lived among those whom they depicted and knew them for the good and the bad that was in them as much as in dwellers in different regions and social strata. By no means radical in political terms, they shared by experience and knowledge in the growing tide of disquiet and protest about social conditions in both town and country. They would feel sympathy, though also anxiety, for the spirit expressed in local ballads and in the popular melodrama. In the latter the hero and heroine were of humble birth, the villain usually of higher social level, ranging from the wicked squire early in the century to the equally wicked capitalist employer towards the end. The same confrontation appears in the relationship between Tess and Alec in *Tess of the D'Urbervilles* and between Arthur Donnithorne and Hetty Sorrel in Eliot's *Adam Bede* (1859). It is reflected in their speech, through style and phonation rather than dialect:

> 'Yes, sir,' Hetty answered, with a tremulous, almost whispering voice.
> She didn't know how to speak to a gentleman like Mr Arthur, and her
> very vanity made her more coy of speech.   (*Adam Bede* 12)

Confident in the dignity and antiquity of dialect, novelists were able to show that it was not uniform but reflected social niceties and personal relationships as faithfully as standard speech. The most interesting aspect of dialect speech in Victorian fiction is not the methodology used to reproduce local features but the pragmatic use of dialect to show the underlying realities of situations. Growing anxieties about social class and aspirations to higher status, revealed a hierarchy among those in town or country who might seem to the privileged to be uniform in their poverty. The 'swarry' [soiree] at Bath, which Dickens describes in *Pickwick Papers*, is an entertaining but not very subtle comment on the ranking of servants according to their masters' positions. Novelists who were closer to those of whom they wrote could show by patterns of speech that dialect speakers were far from identical. Whether the representations reflect heard reality is not important: they convey what the reader needs to know about comparative status. The rural poor on the outskirts of Miss Thorne's entertainment speak in a vaguely southern dialect as they comment on those who have thrust themselves inside: 'I do tell 'ee plainly – face to face – she be there in madam's drawing-room; herself and Gussy, and them two walloping gals, dressed up to their very eyeses' (*Barchester Towers* 39).

In the closed society at Wuthering Heights, Heathcliff speaks standard English. Zillah, the housekeeper, uses Yorkshire dialect in a modified and intelligible form:

> 'Well, Mr Earnshaw,' she cried, 'I wonder what you'll have agait next! Are we going to murder folk on our very doorstones! I see this house will never do for me – look to the poor lad, he's fair choking! Wisht, wisht! you mun'n't go on so. Come in, and I'll cure that: there now, hold ye still.' (2)

The servant Joseph speaks in a manner which is less accessible and suggests a more primitive and submerged member of the strange household:

> Aw wonder how yah can faishion to stand thear i' idleness un war, when all on 'ems goan out! Bud yah're a nowt and it's no good talking – yah'll niver mend o' yer ill ways, but goa raight to the t' devil, like yer mother afore ye! (Ibid.)

The contrast between employers and servants, a daily reality of Victorian life, is frequently shown through dialect. In *The Woodlanders* (1887) Giles has hardly any Dorset features in speaking to his servant Creedy, but the latter replies in broad dialect: 'This is a bruckle het [misfortune], maister, I'm much afeard! Who'd ha' thought they'd ha'

come so soon!' (9). Those who occupy positions of respect in the local
hierarchy are similarly marked in speech. When John Barton is being
briefed for his visit to London with a statement of grievances, his
fellow workmen are shown as strong Lancashire speakers:

> Tell 'em our minds; how we're thinking we've been clemmed [starved]
> long enough, and we donnot see whatten good they'n been doing, if
> they can't give us what we're all crying for sin' the day we were born.
>
> (*Mary Barton* 8)

In the same debate 'a pompous, careful-speaking man' shows
grammatical deviance but no specifically local pointers of lexis or
pronunciation:

> I've one plan I wish to tell John Barton . . . and I should like him for to
> lay it afore the honourable house. My mother comed out of
> Oxfordshire, and were under laundry-maid in Sir Francis Dashwood's
> family; and when we were little ones, she'd tell us stories of their
> grandeur.

Speech contrast is used effectively in *The Mayor of Casterbridge*
(1886), a novel which yields a great deal of interest in comparative
dialect (Chapman, 1989). A minor character who is a magistrate gives
his orders in standard speech, and is answered in dialect by the
illiterate constable, Stubberd:

> What can we poor lammigers [wretches, lit. 'cripples'] do against such a
> multitude? . . . 'Tis tempting them to commit *felo de se* upon us, and
> that would be the death of the perpetrators; and we wouldn't be the
> cause of a fellow creature's death on no account, not we! (39)

In 'polite' English society the real equivalent of Mr Grower the
magistrate would not have been highly esteemed and would have had
a detectable Dorset accent. Hardy is concerned with his relationship
to Stubberd, not with his national status, so he foregrounds the
constable's speech with deviant syntax, dialect lexis and the
malapropism of *felo de se*, suicide, used for murder. The reader is
enlightened within the world of the text and is not meant to
speculate about wider social implications.

The novelists were not trying to transport the reader into a total
experience of regional life. Much that would have seemed unfamiliar

to a London ear in Dorset, Lancashire or Warwickshire is passed over. Mr Riley in *The Mill on the Floss* speaks without any traces of deviance as a man respected by the Tullivers and not as a man of high status and education.   When Jude and Sue stay overnight in a labourer's cottage, Sue can say, 'I like reading and all that, but I crave to get back to the life of my infancy and its freedom', while their host is placed socially by his speech, 'You can stay here, you know, over the night – can't 'em, mother? The place is welcome to ye. 'Tis hard lying, rather, but volk may do worse.' (*Jude the Obscure* Part 3, 2). They would certainly have had Dorset accents, which Sue's residence at a provincial training college might have modified but would not have destroyed. Their standard speech contrasts their tragic sensitivity with the more placid temperaments of the Wessex 'workfolk'. It is also influenced by the convention that sympathetic major characters in novels use standard speech, a matter to be considered more fully later. In terms of content rather than pronunciation, there are passages where the reader sympathises with Edmund Gosse's criticism 'Sue and Jude talk a sort of University Extension jargon that breaks the heart' (*Cosmopolis* January 1896).

In *The Mayor of Casterbridge* the changing status of Henchard is revealed in his speech. When he first appears he is poor and wandering, a man who in reality would have had a strong Dorset accent. His potential strength of character and his centrality in the novel is shown by contrast with a countryman whom he meets; in practice there would have been no discernible difference between them, but Henchard shows very little deviance:

> Then is there any house to let – a little small new cottage just a builded, or such like?
> Pulling down is more the nater of Weydon. There were five houses cleared away lass year, and three this; and the volk nowhere to go – no, not so much as a thatched hurdle. (1)

Henchard uses the irregular past form *builded*, with the archaic but not originally dialectal prefix *a*; the suffix -ed added to the infinitive of a verb is common in both Hardy and Barnes as a Dorset usage. His 'such like' is broadly sub-standard for the period rather than regional. The anonymous countryman shows deviant pronunciation with *nater*, the elided form *lass* for 'last' and the distinctive *volk* for 'folk'. Voicing of initial /f/ and /s/ developed in south-western English before the

Conquest and came to be regarded as a shibboleth of rustic dialect. It appears in Edgar's *vurther* and *vortnight* in (*King Lear* IV, vi) mentioned above and is still the staple of cartoonists and comedians.

When Henchard becomes mayor many years later his speech shows hardly any dialect traces. His upward mobility causes him to castigate his supposed daughter for her use of dialect:

'Bide where you be!' he echoed sharply. 'Good God, are you only fit to carry wash to a pig-trough that ye use such words as those?' (20)

Only the form *ye* betrays a regional speaker; but when Henchard falls from prosperity and is working again as a journeyman his speech shows how local people now regard him and the dialect pointers are more apparent; the recessive effect of trauma may also be indicated:

A fellow of his age going to be Mayor, indeed! . . . But 'tis her money that floats en upward. Ha-ha – how cust odd it is! Here be I, his former master, working for him as man, and he the man standing as master. (32)

Comparative social status between husband and wife, a frequent theme with Hardy, can be shown by speech; Mrs Dewey is scornful of her husband's lexis, while at the same time showing the contrast of her own position with that of the standard speaker: 'Talking about "taties" to Michael in such a work-folk way. Well, 'tis what I was never brought up to! With our family 'twas never less than "taters", and very often "pertatoes" outright' (*Under the Greenwood Tree* 1872, 8).

The generation gap can also reveal aspirations towards standard speech. Grace Melbury in *The Woodlanders*, returned from her boarding school, speaks differently from her father, who is himself 'superior' to his workmen and servants in language. Dewey is in trouble with his daughter as well as his wife for saying 'thou'. Tom and Maggie Tulliver do not speak in the dialect of their parents, even in their early years: again their later importance in the novel is a factor in the author's presentation.

Dialect is usually strongest when it shows social contrasts or sets characters apart as comic or markedly out of their normal social context. The older tradition of humorous dialect survived through the years of more serious application. The reader's amusement is directed to both dialect and standard speakers when the clergyman Torkingham reacts to the choir's rendering, 'The Lard looked down vrom Heav'ns high tower' with, 'that's where we are so defective – the pronunciation' and gets them to produce instead, 'The Lawd look'd down from Heav'ns high towah' (*Two on a Tower* 2).

Sometimes a single deviant item is enough to suggest dialect speech. The device is most often used when a dialect speaker is introduced briefly into an alien situation, or when a travelling Londoner makes a casual regional encounter. It may appear in a novel where dialect is prominent, perhaps to hint at the local speech in an 'educated' character and remind the reader that most speakers in the area might sound strange to an unaccustomed ear. Thus Catherine exclaims, 'I'm tired – I'm *stalled*' (*Wuthering Heights* 31). A character using the convention of standard speech by reason of virtue and importance in the plot may give a reminder of dialect status, as when Mary Barton says to Mrs Wilson, 'Let me do that for you. I'm sure you mun be tired', and exclaims to Jem, 'tell me what to say when they question me; I shall be so gloppened [terrified], I shall not know what to answer' (*Mary Barton* 20, 23).

Conversely, the novelist may make a bolder attempt at an alien dialect, not always to the best effect of realism. Dickens is less reliable away from London speech; his Coketown workers show massive deviance which is difficult to equate with a heard way of speaking. When Stephen Blackpool speaks, the effect on the reader is not of precise Lancashire dialect so much as the image of an honest man limited by locality and lack of opportunity:

> Sir, I canna, wi' my little learning an my common way, tell the genelman what will better aw this – though some working-men o' this town could, above my powers – but I can tell him what I know will never do 't. The strong hand will never do 't. Vict'ry and triumph will never do 't. (*Hard Times* Book 2, 5)

Disraeli is even less sure of his ground when he enters the northern world in *Sybil*. His principal characters use standard speech; single dialect pointers include 'squeedge', and 'coz' for 'because' which can be taken as broadly deviant without regional placing (Book 3, 3, 4).[10] Disraeli transplants the regular cockney *v/w* confusion to the north with 'wittals', 'feeds on weal', 'wery'. Otherwise he is content with northern hints for a farmer – 'You wunna find them much changed' (Book 2, 4) or broad and eclectic deviance with occasional northern lexis for the semi-comic poor – 'I should think he wor; as

bloody-a-hearted butty as ever jingled' (Book 3, 1). Disraeli's father
questioned whether he knew anything about dukes; he certainly seems
to have known little about the speech of the northern poor, but he
makes his point of the 'Two Nations' with good effect.

When dialect characters are together without the presence of
strangers, their speech may be represented less broadly. The
assumption is that they are not 'hearing' any deviance among
themselves but are conversing as easily as a group of standard
speakers. This is general, for example, among the Tullivers and their
extended family. In *The Mayor of Casterbridge* Henchard talks with his
returned wife Susan and Elizabeth-Jane, or with Farfrae in the days of
their friendship, without any of them showing dialect except a few
traces such as *ye*. Yet the very intimacy and lack of self-consciousness
in dialect can support alienation from the main action. Hardy's 'rustic
chorus' generally converse in marked dialect, and are set apart as
commentators aware of the tragic action but not directly involved in
it. This appears in the talk at the malthouse in *Far from the Madding
Crowd* or the frequent comments of the working population in *The
Mayor of Casterbridge*. The comment of Mother Cuxsom on the death
of Susan Henchard gains choric quality from the strangeness which
foregrounds it: 'And all her shining keys will be took from her, and
her cupboards opened; and little things a' didn't wish seen, anybody
will see; and her wishes and ways will be as nothing' (*The Mayor of
Casterbridge* 18).[11]

If dialect is consciously suppressed to give a genteel effect in
standard company, shared intimacy may bring it out more strongly. In
Pendennis Costigan and his daughter put on a show in the presence of
others, but when they are alone the Irish quality is allowed full play.
Emily Costigan has one voice for Major Pendennis – 'He's very well,
in spite of his weight, now he's young, but he's no conversation' – but
alone with her father and Bows she makes her origins clear: 'Ye
wouldn't be for not sending the poor boy his letters back? Them
letters and pomes [poems] is mine' (11, 12).

Dialect may be manipulated not only to show social and personal
relationships but also to present individual character. Regional speech
pointers are often increased when the speaker is under emotional
pressure. The Costigan family show their Irish background not only in
intimate talk but also when roused. Captain Costigan becomes a
caricature of a stage Irishman when refused admission to Vauxhall
Gardens:

> Don't be froightened, me dear madam, I'm not going to quarl with this
> gintleman, at anyreet before leedies. Will ye go, sir, and desire Mr
> Hodgen (whose orther I keem in with, and he's me most intemate
> friend, and I know he's goan to sing the 'Body Snatcher' here
> to-noight), with Captain Costigan's compliments, to stip out and let in
> the leedies.   (Pendennis 46)

Kingsley dresses a stock stage Irishman to show the impact of an Irish
Protestant clergyman, O'Blareaway, on an English rural setting: 'The
top of the morning to ye, Mr Smith. Ye haven't such a thing as a
cegar about ye? I've been preaching to school-children till me throat's
as dry as the slave of a lime-burner's coat' (Yeast 10).

John Barton, whose speech is marked mainly by deviant syntax and
omitted letters, shows a closer distribution of these features when he is
angered by Henry Carson's caricature of the delegation:

> It makes me more than sad, it makes my heart burn within me, to see
> that folk can make a jest of earnest men; of chaps, who comed to ask
> for a bit o' fire for th' old granny, as shivers in the cold; for a bit o'
> bedding and warm clothing for the poor wife as lies in labour on the
> damp flags; and for victuals for the childer, whose little voices are
> getting too faint and weak to cry aloud wi' hunger.   (Mary Barton 16)

The combination of dialect features with rhetorical and balanced
phraseology should not be stigmatised as unnatural. In times of crisis
the speaker takes on a wider and more representative role. Mrs
Tulliver has a similar combination of more marked dialect and
articulate expression when she is losing her home:

> To think o' these cloths as I spun myself . . . and Job Haxey wove
> 'em, and brought the piece home on his back, as I remember standing
> at the door and seeing him come, before I ever thought o' marrying
> your father! And the pattern as I chose myself – and bleached so
> beautiful, and I marked 'em as nobody ever saw such marking – they
> must cut the cloth to get it out, for it's a particular stitch. And they're
> all to be sold – and go to strange people's houses, and perhaps be cut
> with the knives, and wore out before I'm dead.
>   (The Mill on the Floss Book 3, 2)

Hardy is particularly sensitive to the role of dialect in heightened
emotion. When Tess comes home after her disastrous wedding night,
she breaks into stronger dialect than is usual with her – 'I don't know

how to tell 'ee, mother . . . that's where my misery do lie' (*Tess of the D'Urbervilles* 38). Gabriel Oak, usually given the almost standard speech of a 'superior' countryman who is also a sympathetic leading character, changes his speech in passionate talk with Bathsheba:

> If wild heat had to do wi' it, making ye long to overcome the awkwardness about your husband's vanishing, it mid be wrong; but a cold-hearted argument to oblige a man seems different, somehow. The real sin, ma'am, in my mind, lies in thinking of ever wedding wi' a man you don't love honest and true. (*Far from the Madding Crowd* 1874, 51)

Eliot records and comments on similar intensifying of dialect in emotion:

> 'Donna thee sit up, mother,' said Adam, in a gentle tone. He had worked off his anger now, and whenever he wished to be especially kind to his mother, he fell into his strongest native accent and dialect, with which at other times his speech was less deeply tinged.
> (*Adam Bede* Book 1, 4)

Reversion into stronger dialect can occur under emotional pressure when the standard form is an acquired characteristic, and in other cases of diglossia. When a novelist describes the regional speakers in a shared local situation, the change suggests the tension which would be felt by all parties to the conversation and would show itself in face and tone as much as in the specific features which can be graphologically realised. Conversely, a minor dialect character can take on more or less standard speech for the sake of the fictional situation. A fine example is the furmity woman in *The Mayor of Casterbridge* who reveals Henchard's past when he is sitting as a magistrate. In the role of Nemesis she loses nearly all her dialect characteristics and gives her evidence in clear narrative.

By the end of the century, the spread of education and the concomitant regard for standard speech made it possible to give direct credibility to what novelists had already been doing without comment:

> Mrs. Durbeyfield habitually spoke the dialect; her daughter, who had passed the Sixth Standard in the National School under a London-trained mistress, spoke two languages; the dialect at home, more or less; ordinary English abroad and to persons of quality.
> (*Tess of the D'Urbervilles* Book 1, 3)

Hardy's first thought, in the serial version of the novel, is closer to fictional practice in saying that Tess spoke dialect 'only when excited by joy, surprise, or grief'. His treatment of the character is borne out by the observation made to the English Dialect Society in 1888, a few years before the novel, that as a result of general schooling:

> At the present moment our people are learning two distinct tongues – distinct in pronunciation, in grammar and in syntax. A child, who in class or even at home can read correctly, giving accents, aspirates (painfully), intonation, and all the rest of it, according to rule, will at home, and among his fellows, go back to his vernacular, and never even deviate into the right path he has been taught at school.
>
> (F. Elworthy, *The Dialect of West Somerset* 1875–6, xliv; cit Crowley 1989, 159)

The phenomenon is now well known to linguists under the name of *diglossia*. Two varieties of a language are used by the same speakers, the 'high' form in written usage and formal speech, the 'low' in relaxed and informal situations (Ferguson 1959). Hardy's comment on the speech of Tess accords with the finding of modern dialectology that 'people who are known to be bidialectal do actually control the two dialects, using one of them in special circumstances, such as when visiting a speaker with a similar 'home' background, and using the other for daily social and business affairs' (Chambers and Trudgill 1980, 146). Charlotte Brontë attributes diglossia to Yorke in *Shirley*. When he speaks in standard form immediately after Yorkshire dialect, she comments in words that say much about the contemporary uncertainties of class and the shifting of social positions:

> It will have been remarked that Mr Yorke varied a little in his phraseology; now he spoke broad Yorkshire. And anon he expressed himself in very pure English. His manner was liable to equal alterations; he could be polite and affable, and he could be blunt and rough. His station then you could not easily determine by his speech or demeanour. (3)

Throughout the years of greater sophistication, dialect was still used in the old way to foreground the comedy of simple characters such as Hardy's William Worm:

> Would ye mind coming round by the back way? The front door is got stuck wi' the wet, as he will do sometimes; and the Turk can't open

en. I know I am only a poor wambling man that 'ill never pay the Lord
for my making, sir; but I can show the way in, sir.

(*A Pair of Blue Eyes* 1873, 2)

Nevertheless, some of the major Victorian novelists used dialect to
give tragic stature to the simple and unlettered. They brought into
literary fiction the appeal which local balladists had made in their
dialect songs of protest, and created scenes which made the reader
respond to the written signs of deviant speech not with amusement
but with the sympathy of shared humanity.

Notes

1. Preface to *Eynedos* 1490. Caxton tells of a merchant whose request for
    'eggys' was thought to be a French word; he comments that 'comyn
    englysshe that is spoken in one shyre varyeth from another'.

2. For example, Squire Western in *Tom Jones* (1749).

3. Maria Edgeworth (1768–1849) is often regarded as the pioneer of the
    'regional novel' with her tales of Irish life.

4. See Davies (1934) for examples, especially of *w* for words normally
    beginning with *v*. It must be remembered that the irregular state of
    orthography before the late seventeenth century makes it unwise to draw
    any firm conclusions about the relationship between writing and speech,
    but the evidence is interesting. The nineteenth-century transposition 'did
    certainly exist, but it is wrong to suppose that it was anything like as
    marked and as frequent as Dickens makes it in the mouth of Sam Weller'
    (Franklyn 1953, 23).

5. The fact that nineteenth-century purists objected to slurring in speech
    suggests that it was often heard. Elision and weakening are censured by
    B.H. Smart in *Walker Remodelled: A New Critical Pronouncing Dictionary
    of the English Language* (1836). However, the struggle between perfection
    and reality had been going on for a long time. In *The Gouernour* (1531)
    Thomas Elyot recommended that those who attended on a nobleman's
    infant son should 'speke none englisshe but that which is cleane, polite,
    perfectly and articulately pronounced, omitting no lettre or sillable, as
    folishe women oftentimes do of a wantonesse whereby diuers noble men
    and gentlemennes chyldren, as I do at this daye know, haue attained
    corrupte and foule pronuntiation'.

6. Bernard Shaw recalled, 'When I came to London in 1876, the Sam
    Weller dialect had passed away so completely that I should have given it

up as a literary fiction if I had not discovered it surviving in a Middlesex village, and heard of it from an Essex one' (Notes to *Captain Brassbound's Conversion* 1900). As late as 1891 the popular guide *Enquire Within About Everything* stigmatised the confusion as being typical of London and Essex (56ff). See also Weekley (1930, 138–61), 'Mrs Gamp and the King's English'.

7. The linguistic implications of this passage are discussed by Desmond Hawkins, 'Knowing one's onions' (*Thomas Hardy Journal* VI, 1,) further note by Raymond Chapman (ibid. VI, 2).

8. Vicunus (1974) gives a detailed account of this and other popular expressions of regional dialect. She notes that 'working-class dialect writers were unusually numerous and came from a wide variety of occupations' (192).

9. A critical examination of this character's idiolect is made by Christopher Dean, 'Joseph's speech in *Wuthering Heights*' (*Notes and Queries* NS 7.2 (February 1960). The conclusion is that 'Emily Brontë uses dialect in *Wuthering Heights* to serve a literary purpose. By it she achieves a local atmosphere . . . If in doing this she fails to give a thoroughly consistent exposition of the dialect in a scientific manner, this is no reflection upon her, for such is not her intention. The suggestion of dialect is there, and absolute fidelity is not demanded' (76). This well summarises one of the contentions of the present chapter.

10. '[Dickens] asserts that he sees integrity but reveals the belief which underpins the idea of non-standard speech as the usage of social inferiors – that those who use it are morally and intellectually impoverished' (Patricia Ingham, 'Dialect as realism: *Hard Times* and the industrial novel', *Review of English Studies* NS 37, (1986)).

11. Robert Laing commented on the rustic characters in *The Mill on the Floss* being 'like a voice of a Greek chorus, full of traditional warning and stern common sense, but speaking in the dialect of English rusticity', *Quarterly Review* 134 (April 1873). This is typical of the romantic view of peasant dialect which Oscar Wilde disliked: 'The amount of pleasure one gets out of dialect is entirely a matter of temperament. To say "mither" instead of "mother" seems to many the acme of romance. There are others who are not quite so ready to believe in the pathos of provincialisms' (Richard Ellmann, *Oscar Wilde*, Hamish Hamilton, London 1987, 278n).

CHAPTER 4
Register

The pattern of speech is not uniform, even for a single speaker with a limited range of language. We change our selection from the available lexis and syntax, according to the situation within which we are speaking, the relationship to the other people in the conversation or the degree of emotion which is being verbalised. The changes thus occasioned are switches of *register*. Useful definitions of register include, 'variation in the selection of linguistic items for various purposes'; 'a set of contextual features bringing about a characteristic use of formal features'; 'a variety of the use of language as used by a particular writer or speaker in a particular context'.[1]

Register is easier to identify in some languages than in others. The use of the second person singular, *tu*, *du*, etc. in many European languages can show intimacy, but also contempt or condescension; the same was true of English until the early seventeenth century. Japanese has a distinct morphological structure for the 'honorific' code of address. Register in modern English is harder to define, though native speakers accept it naturally. Intimacy can be shown by slang or informal usage, more laconic utterances, by stress and intonation, and by extra-linguistic factors such as facial expression and body language.

A novelist who purports to show any relationship to real life must convey the implied as well as the surface meaning of what characters are saying to each other. If dialogue is not designedly neutral – to convey information or ideas objectively, as may happen in life – the writer needs to work signals into the written code which give a connotative sense to the words used. Lexical and syntactic features are readily chosen in this way; others require graphological ingenuity or authorial comment. By whatever means, successful dialogue in fiction contains more than a semantic message and tells the reader something about such things as the permanent or changing relationships between characters, and the emotive level of the situation.

In terms of register, as in other aspects of language, the speech community develops what is needed by the social ethos. Register pointers have not disappeared in present-day English but they are in many ways different from those of the nineteenth century. Victorian authors and readers were familiar with a code which was more elaborate and which reflected a more formal and structured society. Qualities such as intonation are tantalisingly elusive and difficult to assess, but the verbal elements of spoken language as presented in writing can reveal much.

While the conventions of speech were not unchanged through the century, and were certainly challenged from time to time by groups and individuals, it may safely be said that the Victorians were acutely conscious of social class, with fine gradations especially within the middle class, and that a sense of respect was generally felt towards those of a higher class and shown in speech. Similar respectful pointers were used in more temporary relationships, such as those of tradesman and customer.

Firm conventions in conversation were not found only as between social classes and groups, but also within them. The degree of familiarity allowed was governed by rules which were accepted tacitly until they were broken. While the system was more elaborate and more rigidly adhered to among the upper and middle classes, there is evidence that people in all walks of life knew and respected the spoken signs of relationship. Elaborate linguistic codes can exist without a great range of vocabulary and syntax, and without corresponding sophistication in other aspects of speech. Peoples who would popularly be considered 'primitive' are found by anthropologists to have extremely complex linguistic conventions which are handed on orally and managed with ease. The rules governing the use of titles and names in the nineteenth century were not excessively complex or maintained with superstitious awe, but they had implications which the modern reader can often miss. Our almost universal use of Christian names after a short acquaintance is a very recent phenomenon and has brought with it an erosion of the combinations of titles, surnames and honorific words which not very long ago were socially accepted. When Thackeray characterised 'Bohemia' he added to it such features as 'much tobacco . . . tin-dish covers from taverns and frothing porter' that it was 'a land where men call each other by their Christian names' (*The Adventures of Philip* 1862, 5).

To break the conventions of spoken address could be a solecism bringing embarrassment to the perpetrator, or a deliberate trespass at which offence could be taken. It might also, of course, be reciprocated as a signal of a development in the relationship of the parties, tending either to greater intimacy or to estrangement, or to a temporary cooling or warming. Present-day readers may regard such conventions as artificial, as putting constraint on natural conversation and creating barriers. Artificial they were, like all conventions which exist as much in a permissive as in a hierarchical society. If their negative result was constraint, the positive side was a sense of security and shared understanding. Games played according to rules are more satisfying to the participants than a conflict of strength without agreement on its parameters. Relationships and feelings can be indicated by formal rather than referential linguistic means if there is enough shared agreement.

Use of names

For the novelists, Victorian register conventions provided opportunities which were freely used. Dramatic situations, tense, comic or potentially tragic, are signalled through register pointers in dialogue. Developing or regressing intimacy can emerge by what characters say to each other, whether or not reinforced by the comments of the narrator. A few examples with the use and misuse of Christian names will serve as introduction; these are episodes where the novelists makes the situation clear even to a reader unacquainted with the convention of the time.

When the Yorkshire characters in *Nicholas Nickleby* come together in London, Fanny Squeers responds vigorously to John Browdie's addressing her as 'Fanny', and distances him with title and surname: 'Thanking you for your advice, which was not required, Mr Browdie,' returned Miss Squeers with laborious politeness, 'have the goodness not to presume to meddle with my Christian name' (42).

The possibility of offence was not confined to the early Victorian period but lasted through the century. Nearly twenty years later the unctuous Mr Slope tries to advance his proposal with repetition of, 'Ah! Eleanor' which brings the authorial comment 'it seemed to be his idea that as he had once found courage to pronounce her Christian name, he could not utter it often enough' and the woman's reply, 'My name, Mr Slope, is Mrs Bold'. Previously the Signora has been more encouragingly coy with her response, 'Well, my name is Madeline ... but none except my own family usually call me so'

(*Barchester Towers* 27, 40). Philip Wakem anticipates affront: 'But it is not right, Maggie – don't you be angry with me, I am so used to call you Maggie in my thoughts' (*The Mill on the Floss* Book 5, 1). Later still Mr Pooter, arbiter of lower middle-class behaviour, records his views on the decorum of Christian names:

> The familiar way in which Mrs Posh and Lupin addressed each other is reprehensible. Anybody would think they had been children together. I should certainly object to a six months' acquaintance calling my wife 'Carrie'   (*The Diary of a Nobody* 23)

John Eames would have agreed with Mr Pooter. He warns his friend Cradell that the husband of Mrs Lupex – not so respectable a woman as Mrs Pooter – might make trouble over use of her Christian name: 'If you go on calling her Maria you'll find that he'll have a pull on you. Men don't call other men's wives names for nothing' (*The Small House at Allington* 41). The offence is not always caused by informality between the sexes. Mark Robartes is not softened by Sowerby's 'Mark, my dear fellow' when the latter has brought him into debt, and when the familiarity is repeated says angrily, 'Call me by my name, sir, and drop that affectation of regard' (*Framley Parsonage* 33).

A passage in *The Prime Minister* reveals both character and relationship by the use of names. A 'black cloud' comes on the face of Lopez when the vulgar Sexty Parker, with whom he is involved financially, calls him 'Ferdinand', but he says nothing. His wife Emily is affronted but imitates his silence:

> 'Upon my honour, Sexty, you are very familiar,' said Mrs Parker.
> 'It's a way we have in the city,' said Sexty. Sexty knew what he was about. His partner called him Sexty, and why shouldn't he call his partner Ferdinand?
> 'He'll call you Emily before very long,' said Lopez.
> 'When you call my wife Jane I shall, – and I've no objection in life. I don't see why people ain't to call each other by their Christian names. Take a glass of champagne, Mrs Lopez.' (46)

A whole social situation unfolds, strange and remote to the modern reader but vivid at the time. The barrier of class is crossed by business dependence; the 'inferior' speaker presses his advantage but retains verbal respect for Mrs Lopez, a barrister's daughter.

In happier circumstances, Christian names can bring hope of a deeper relationship. Argemone quickly corrects herself when she fears that Lancelot is in danger – 'Lancelot! Mr Smith!' cried Argemone. 'You shall not go!' But Lancelot reflects joyfully, 'She had called him Lancelot!' (*Yeast* 3). George Somerset has a similarly hopeful conversation with Paula Power:

> 'May I call you Paula?' asked he.
> There was no answer.
> 'May I?' he repeated.
> 'Yes, occasionally,' she murmured.
> 'Dear Paula! – may I call you that?'
> 'O no – not yet.' (*A Laodicean* Book 1, 15)

Similarly, Roger Hamley is overcome when Cynthia responds to his plea to be called 'Roger': he 'would have granted anything when she asked him by that name and in that tone' (*Wives and Daughters* 34). J.H. Shorthouse tells how the noble Percival 'mustered courage' to call Constance by her Christian name (*Sir Percival* 1886, 3), and Eliot's Felix Holt at last becomes bold with ' "Miss Lyon – Esther!" and her hand was in his grasp' (45). One feels that in some respects life must have been more exciting in those days. Lady Staveley finds it hard not to call her daughter's fiancé 'Mr Graham' and replies resignedly to, 'You must call him Felix, mamma', with 'Very well, my dear, I will' (*Trollope, Orley Farm* 1862, 80).

There is significant linguistic and psychological indication in such encounters. The given name, which at the level of utility distinguishes the individual from those who share the surname, assumes a function beyond that of identification. Defying the fact that words are not things but signifiers, it becomes an entity in its own right, a negotiable token in the development of a relationship. The sequence of phonemes which issues as 'Paula' or 'Lancelot' acquires qualitative force. The reader, colluding with the character's rising emotion, is drawn more intimately into the situation which the novelist has created. Our apprehension of Victorian fiction is greatly enhanced by knowledge and acceptance of a convention which has almost entirely disappeared from current usage.

The surname preceded by the appropriate title was the norm for both address and reference. It is used in so many relationships that it may almost be said that any other usage is a marked form and suggests something more than the acquaintance of equals. A woman speaks of her husband in this way to a stranger, as Dorothea refers to 'Mr Casaubon' when Ladislaw calls (*Middlemarch* 30). Before her marriage, she and her sister discuss him with the same title (2). A male colleague of long standing enquires formally about his friend's wife as 'Mrs Phillotson' (*Jude the Obscure* Part 4, 6). The wife herself speaks of a common acquaintance, her husband's former pupil, as 'Mr Fawley' (ibid. 3). Men not on intimate terms address each other with titles, as 'Mr Noggs' and 'Mr Crowl' (*Nicholas Nickleby* 14). A young woman's suitors punctiliously refer to each other as 'Mr Lydgate' and 'Mr Plymdale' (*Middlemarch* 27). A young man calls his girl friend's employer 'Mr Featherstone' when speaking to her (ibid. 25).

The same formality is often used within a family. It can be the address of a wife to her husband, especially when there is an underlying sense of protest: 'Well, Mr Tulliver, you know best; *I've* no objections' (*The Mill on the Floss* Book 1, 2). Lady Arabella addresses her husband as 'Mister Gresham' when she is opposing her stepson's marriage to Mary Thorne (*Doctor Thorne* 27). Elsewhere Trollope suggests that even titles of nobility may be used in such circumstances: 'Lord Kinsbury,' said the offended lady, 'I have always done my duty by the children of my first marriage as a mother should do' (*Marion Fay* 1882, 11). Mrs Tulliver uses the polite form in speaking to her sister-in-law, 'It's your brother's way, Mrs Moss; I'd never anything o' that sort before I was married' (Book 2, 2). A spouse sometimes uses the formal title with the initial of the surname, as Glegg calls his wife 'Mrs G' when he speaks with 'angry sarcasm' about her strictures on his family; her response to him is as 'Mr Glegg' (*The Mill on the Floss* Book 1, 12). A shopkeeper's wife, jealous for status, whose 'manners were lofty', objects to her husband calling her 'Mother' (*Esther Waters* 20).

The plain surname without addition is generally a prerogative of men, though Mrs Vincy addresses her husband affectionately enough, simply as 'Vincy' (*Middlemarch* 26, 36). 'Nothing is more objectionable than to hear ladies speak of gentlemen by their surnames only,' declares one arbiter of etiquette (Campbell 1898, 39), a censure which falls on Alice who at dinner 'laughed rather too loud, it might be, and was too much given to addressing her husband as "Willis" ' (*Demos* 22). When Sir Raffle Buffle is talking to Lily Dale about John Eames he continually refers to him as 'Eames' and Lily as consistently says 'Mr Eames' (*The Last Chronicle of Barset* 52). The style shows more than distant acquaintance and can be used even between close friends. David Copperfield and his former schoolmates continue to address each other as 'Copperfield', 'Steerforth' and 'Traddles', when Steerforth is not using the nickname 'Daisy' which causes such a quizzical response from Rosa Dartle. Professional colleagues use this mode; a fellow-member of the cathedral chapter addresses the Archdeacon as 'Grantly' (*Barchester Towers* 31), and when the Middlemarch doctors are dining together they exchange surnames, 'Toller', 'Hackbutt', 'Wrench' (45). So do those who consider themselves social equals, though their professions and even official standing may differ; in the same novel, Brooke is free with 'Casaubon' and 'Chettam' though the latter is a baronet, and causes no offence (2, 4). Meagles ventures to say, 'We are delighted to see you, Clennam (if you'll allow me, I shall drop the Mister)' (*Little Dorrit* Book 1, 16).[2] The mere initial without any title perhaps suggests a little more intimacy in the domestic scene as when Mrs Quiverful exhorts, 'Now, Q, don't be soft' and on receiving good news says simply, 'Oh, Q!' (*Barchester Towers* 25, 43).

The surname is also used to social inferiors and juniors. Even a favoured chaplain is called 'Slope' by his Bishop (ibid. 32) and Ralph Nickleby calls his clerk 'Noggs' (2). A lawyer feels free to speak 'in a haughtier tone than usual' and call an impoverished miller 'Tulliver' (*The Mill on the Floss* Book 5, 7). Another lawyer is similarly distancing: 'The attorney assuming an air of patronising condescension, always called the other Grimes; whereas Mr Scruby was treated with considerable deference by the publican and was always called Mr Scruby' (*Can You Forgive Her?* 1864, 13). Offence can be caused by its use when one of the parties regards himself as of higher rank or more distant acquaintance. Mr Edmonstone sees that Guy Morville has been affronted when Gordon 'rode up with his "Hollo, Morville!" The Morvilles have a touch of pride of their own' (*Yonge, The Heir of Redclyffe* 1853, 5). Although women seldom use this form, there are occasional examples. Rosamond, a woman conscious of her position as a doctor's wife, refers to an auctioneer as 'Trumbull', although she addresses him as 'Mr Trumbull'; he speaks to her respectfully as 'ma'am' (*Middlemarch* 64). Reporters of actual events bear out such usage. Ritchie describes a police court case in which the magistrate calls on the plaintiff, a publican, with, 'Well, Bird', and addresses a police sergeant as 'Brown' (Ritchie 1869, 208ff). Women servants are often called by their plain surnames, even by other women. Mrs

Transom reiterates the surname 'Denner' in speaking to her personal maid of long standing (*Felix Holt* 34). Esther Waters is commonly 'Waters' when she is in service but when she is on more relaxed terms with her employers they call her 'Esther'. As a married woman and the landlady of a public house, she is 'Mrs Latch' to the customers. There is social condecension bordering on insult when Rachel Verinder addresses a poor female relation simply as 'Clack' (*The Moonstone* Second Period, 1).

Specific areas and ways of life have their own hierarchy. Country people often address each other according to their callings. Hardy is particularly aware of such rural niceties as 'Shepherd Oak', 'Dairyman Crick', 'Farmer Derriman', 'Miller Loveday' or titles of proximity, 'Neighbour Loveday' or state of life, 'Widow Garland'. That this is not a trick of his imagination is borne out by an interesting passage in Munby, travelling into London in 1869 through what was then open country, from Stanmore through Edgware. 'Ours is no vulgar London omnibus; we take up Farmer This and Landlord That . . . Saunders the driver is addressed by every one as Mr Saunders' (Hudson 1972, 274f). When Richard Feverel moves from anger to supplication, he changes his formal 'Mr Blaize' to simple 'Farmer!' (24).

Although Christian names did not have the almost universal currency that they have today, they were generally used in close personal relationships. They are a matter of course between siblings and from parents to children, although members of the aristocracy were more formal. There is a revealing passage in Trollope which suggests that the situation was beginning to change later in the century. The Duke of Omnium enquires for the first name of his future son-in-law, a commoner whose suit he has accepted very grudgingly:

> 'What do they call you at home?'
> 'Frank', whispered Mary, who was with them.
> 'Then I will call you Frank, if you will allow me. The use of Christian names is, I think, pleasant and hardly common enough among us. I almost forget my own boy's name because the practice has grown up of calling him by his title.'   (*The Duke's Children* 1880, 79)

The Christian name is commonly used between married couples even though the more formal mode already illustrated is sometimes preferred. The Garths and the Cadwalladers in *Middlemarch* certainly address each other in the familiar way. A husband speaks to an old friend about his estranged wife as 'Susanna' and thus addresses her when she returns to him (*Jude the Obscure* Part 6, 4, 5). A young man may venture to use the Christian name to a girl he is courting if they have known each other for a long time, even without the tentative approach of Somerset to Paula Power quoted above. Thus Fred Vincy calls Mary Garth, known from childhood, 'Mary' without offence (*Middlemarch* 14).

Close friends, especially young people, use Christian names freely, though the usage seems more common between women than between men. In *Bleak House* it is 'Esther', 'Richard' and 'Ada' among the young people. Women of the working class, brought up from infancy in close physical proximity, use Christian names with little regard for comparative age (*Mary Barton*, passim). Married women of long acquaintance remain 'Harriet' and 'Selina' even when there is tension between them (*Middlemarch* 31). A group of men of equal social status, united by a common interest – in this case gambling – use Christian names freely (*Esther Waters* 30).

Servants are often both called and referred to by their Christian names, except the 'upper servants' who are addressed by their surnames like 'Tantripp' and 'Pratt' at Lowick in *Middlemarch*, and 'Grover' the governess in *Esther Waters*, or even have the dignity of a title like the housekeeper 'Mrs Dean' in *Wuthering Heights*. Osborne Hamley calls the butler 'Robinson' and in the same speech refers to a lower servant as 'Thomas' (*Wives and Daughters* 22). They in turn may use the title and Christian name to children of the family and the form may last into adult life. Bob Jakin calls Tom Tulliver 'Mister Tom' long after he has grown up. Richard Feverel is 'Mr Richard' and 'sir' in the same utterance by one of his father's servants (23). In *Esther Waters* both the mother and her confidential servant speak of the son as 'Mr Arthur' after many years of adult life. Even below stairs the servants refer to 'Mr Arthur' and 'Miss Mary'. Thus Robinson the butler addresses one son and refers to another: 'His lordship was very sorry not to see you, Mr Roger, and his lordship left a note for you. Mr Osborne took it, I think, when he passed through' (27). Another butler is moved by emotion to use two modes of address together: 'Mr Ralph, you must go to bed; – you must indeed, sir' (*Ralph the Heir* 1871, 34). This was considered to be distinctively a servant's usage: 'Don't say "Miss Mary", "Miss Susan". This strictly is permissible with servants only' ('Censor' 1880, 63).

Victorian formality, however, was not always as rigid as some usages may suggest. Diminutives and pet names were much used in families; 'Maggie' Tulliver, itself a diminutive, is 'Magsie' to her brother. The Brooke sisters in *Middlemarch* transmute 'Dorothea' and 'Celia' into 'Dodo' and 'Kitty'. Even Archdeacon Grantly permits himself to call his wife 'Sue' in a mood of euphoria: 'he did not call his wife Sue above twice or thrice in a year, and these occasions were great high days' (*Barchester Towers* 50). Phillotson uses the same diminutive to his wife, rendered as 'Soo' and drawing the comment 'this being the way in which he pronounced her name' (*Jude the Obscure* Part 4, 3). Jude has already allowed himself a cousin's liberty in so addressing her and in the first months of marriage calls his wife Arabella 'Abby' or 'Bella'. Lydgate affectionately calls Rosamond 'Rosy' and even the formal Charles Reding calls his young sister Caroline 'Carry' (*Loss and Gain* Part 2, 11). Familiarity may take many years of marriage. When Esther says, 'We can't see her go to prison, can we, Bill, without raising a finger to save her?' the authorial comment is 'She had never called him Bill before, and the familiar abbreviation touched him' (*Esther Waters* 37).

However, such intimacy is censured when thought to be misplaced. In Charlotte Yonge's *Hopes and Fears* (1860) there is a revealing dialogue between a girl and her male cousin which tells us much about Victorian tensions between freedom and formality, and the importance attached to use of names:

'Humfrey, I wish you would not object to the children giving me pet names.'

'I did not know that I had shown any objection.'

'As if you did not impressively say Miss Charlecote on every occasion when you mention me to them.'

'Well, and is it not more respectful?'

'That's not what I want. Where the natural tie is wanting, one should do everything to make up for it.'

'And you hope to do so by letting yourself be called Honeypots!'

'More likely than by sitting up distant and awful to be *Miss Charlecoted*!'

'Whatever else you might be called must become an endearment,' said Humfrey, uttering unawares one of the highest compliments she had ever received, 'and I own I do not like to hear those little chits make so free with your name.' (2)

The fictional cousin Humfrey was not alone in his disquiet. Alford was among those who disliked diminutives and endearments even between close relatives. He deprecates, 'the practice of using, in general society, unmeaning and ridiculous familiar nicknames or terms of endearment'. He recalls talking after dinner with 'an agreeable and sensible man'; as guests begin to leave:

> A shrill voice from the other end of the room calls out, 'Sammy, love!' All is out. He has a wife who does not know better, and he has never taught her better ... It is easy for husband and wife, it is easy for brothers and sisters, to talk to one another as none else could talk, without a word of this minced-up English. One soft tone, from lips on which dwells wisdom, is worth all the 'loveys' and 'deareys' which become the unmeaning expletives of the vulgar.   (Alford 1864, 241f)

Terms of endearment are used in families and between lovers, but not very freely. Sue calls Jude 'dear' and then 'dearest', when he is anxious over a letter from Arabella (*Jude the Obscure* Part 5, 3) and he goes farther in a burst of affection for her – 'If you, my dear darling, hadn't come to my rescue, I should have gone to the dogs with despair!' Vincy calls Rosamond 'dear' and later says it 'with the lingering utterance which affection gives to the word' (*Middlemarch* 58). Amy Reardon in *New Grub Street* calls her husband 'dear' and Lord Cumnor in *Wives and Daughters* says 'my dear' to his wife. Richard Feverel and Lucy are bolder when they are alone:

> 'Will he have seen me? Will he have known me?' whispered Lucy tremulously.
> 'And if he does, love?' said Richard.
> 'Oh! if he does, dearest – I don't know, but I feel such a presentiment.' (21)

Mrs Glegg regards her husband's use of 'sweetheart' as vulgar – 'it was never heared in my family' (*The Mill on the Floss* Book 6, 12). Tom Brown makes a conscious effort to reach the register of a village lad when he says, 'I've scarcely heard of – of – well, of my *sweetheart* – there, you'll understand that – for this year and more' (*Tom Brown at Oxford* 40). 'Beau', acceptable to an earlier generation, and until much later in the United States, has become a servants' word. When her maid talks of having had 'a beau', Mrs Greenon replies, 'But you don't suppose that I want beaux, as you call them?' (*Can You Forgive Her?* 47).

Young people who are neither children nor members of the family may be called by their Christian names, but never use them to their elders. Fred Vincy is greeted by Mrs Garth with, 'You, Fred, so early in the day?' and replies, 'I want to speak to Mr Garth' (*Middlemarch* 24). If a member of the company is a friend to another and a slight acquaintance to a third, the different relationships are clearly marked. Stephen Guest calls Maggie 'Miss Tulliver' while Lucy on the same occasion calls her 'Maggie' (*The Mill on the Floss* Book 6, 7). Grantly, trying to do his best 'to be gracious to his sister-in-law', calls her 'Eleanor' but she replies, whether from respect or annoyance, with 'Dr Grantly'; both refer formally to 'Mr Arabin' and 'Mr Slope' (*Barchester Towers* 29).

People uncertain of their standing with one another can test the water without asking an overt question. Pendennis ventures, 'You have the most beautiful figure and the slimmest waist in the world, Blanche – Miss Amory I mean. I beg your pardon'. Meeting no rebuff, he continues to use 'Blanche' freely (45). The uncertainty is often social rather than personal, though the two may be combined. Johnny Nunsuch completely loses himself in the mysteries of address. His 'Miss Eustacia' is accepted but the unadorned 'Eustacia' gets a stern rebuke, 'Miss Vye, sir' and he flounders into 'Miss Vy – stacia' (*The Return of the Native* Book 1, 6). People do not hesitate to show offence if social protocol is broken. Bulstrode tells Raffles, 'Any service you desire of me will be the more readily rendered if you will avoid a tone of familiarity which did not lie in our former intercourse, and can hardly be warranted by more than twenty years of separation'. Raffles understands the grounds of objection: 'You don't like being called Nick? Why, I always called you Nick in my heart', and emboldened by his possession of Bulstrode's guilty secret rubs in the familiarity. 'Why, if a man has got any heart, doesn't he want to see an old friend, Nick? – I must call you Nick – we always did call you young Nick when we knew you meant to marry the old widow' (*Middlemarch* 53).

Women may get the respect of title even when their husbands are called by the plain surname as social inferiors. Brooke makes his complaint known to his tenant as 'Dagley' but greets the wife with 'How do you do, Mrs Dagley' (ibid. 39).

Changes within a conversational situation may show growing

warmth and affection, as when John Bretton moves from 'Miss Snowe' to 'Lucy', without comment by either party (*Villette* 17). When Sir Guy Morville becomes plain 'Guy' his acceptance by the Edmonstones is plainly marked. Priggish Philip observes, 'So I perceive you have dropped the title already' and Mrs Edmonstone confirms, 'we were glad to do what we could to make him feel at home' (*The Heir of Redclyffe* 3). Even Casaubon changes his address when Dorothea has accepted him: 'My dear young lady – Miss Brooke – Dorothea' (*Middlemarch* 5).

Changes to a more formal register can show a cooling relationship or a temporary annoyance. Phillotson is greeted by his old friend as 'Dick' and responds with 'George' but a little later after some awkward talking about Sue and her subsequent departure, the friend's return elicits the polite but less intimate 'Gillingham' (*Jude the Obscure* Part 4, 4). The incompetent doctor Wrench becomes 'Wrench' to the irate Vincy, though Mrs Vincy still says 'Mr Wrench' (*Middlemarch* 26). Outside direct conversation, but using the same code, Casaubon writes in anger to his young cousin 'Dear Mr Ladislaw' and the author comments 'he had always before addressed him as Will' (ibid. 37).

Titles and forms of address

If names can convey a great deal, so can polite forms of address without a name. The uses of the little word *sir* are complex and reveal the subtleties of Victorian social relationships. It would be illuminating to have auditory record of vocal intonation as the title is used respectfully, formally or ironically. We have to depend on the written record, following the clues of situation and context.

The most common use is to a man regarded as superior in age, rank or immediate relationship. Servants regularly use it to the master of the house. William Latch calls the son of his former employer 'sir' after an absence of many years but himself receives the title from his child's foster-mother by virtue of his smart appearance; the initial 'I'm sure we're very glad to see you' is repeated as 'I'm sure, sir, we're very glad to see you' when she notices 'the fine gold chain which hung across his waistcoat, the cut of his clothes, and the air of money which his whole being seemed to represent' (*Esther Waters* 30, 26). A higher servant is honoured by a lower one: a groom says 'sir' to the stud-groom who is head of his household department (*Ravenshoe* 3). The sense of class is so strong that a poacher in a vigorous fight with

gamekeepers says, 'You're my man, if you please, sir', when he
challenges a 'gentleman' (*Yeast* 9). Even a female companion of
yeoman rank uses the title, as Mary Garth does to Featherstone. A
man who seems to be smart and therefore moderately wealthy is
addressed thus by those of more lowly status. Munby records without
apparent surprise how an 'old gentleman' said to his servant-wife
Hannah on a bus, 'I suppose you are very low?' and she answered 'Yes
sir, I am a maid of all work'. The unsolicited comment 'I can see by
your profile that you have good blood in you' would hardly serve by
modern standards to make amends, but nobody seems to have felt at
all affronted (Hudson 1972, 55). Dickens parodies the excessive use of
the word when subservient Job Trotter uses it in every 'turn' of his
conversation with Mr Pickwick (16). With no apparent humorous
intent, Kingsley makes Tregarva, a radical and superior gamekeeper,
use 'sir' in almost every sentence when he first speaks to Lancelot
Smith. This would be seen by the arbiters of etiquette as a solecism:
'We should not constantly repeat the name of anyone with whom we
may be talking, nor should we make excessive use of titles when
conversing with people of rank' (Campbell 1898, 37). Munby shows a
subtle class feeling towards 'trade' when he notes that Alexander
Macmillan has become an 'eminent Publisher . . . with obsequious
gentlemanly clerks who call him Sir' (Hudson 1972, 208).

Professional men, clergy, doctors and lawyers, are called 'sir' by the
poor with whom they come in contact. Even when Mary Barton is
indignant at a doctor's comment on Jem Wilson, she uses 'sir' twice in
her remonstrance: 'You say "*who murdered*", sir!' said Mary
indignantly. 'He is only taken up on suspicion, and many have no
doubt of his innocence – those who know him, sir' (24). Mrs Parker
continually calls Wharton 'sir' when she comes to receive money from
him, despite her husband's attempt to get on Christian name terms
with his son-in-law, quoted above (*The Prime Minister* 69). The
manual worker who comes to take English lessons from the
desperately poor Biffen says 'sir' to him and Biffen later remarks to
Reardon, 'You noticed how respectfully he spoke to me? It doesn't
make any difference to him that I live in a garret like this; I'm a man
of education, and he can separate this fact from my surroundings'
(*New Grub Street* 16). The comment makes overt a social system
which more often is silently implied in the words of dialogue. It was
not automatic; when Greenwood questioned a boy just released from

prison he was answered with 'mister', not 'sir', a response which he records without comment (Greenwood 1881, 243ff).

Men of the upper and middle class who are not known to each other regularly exchange 'sir' on an introduction or when entering into conversation. Carson calls the police superintendent who has called at his house 'sir' in a formal rather than respectful way when apologising for keeping him waiting (*Mary Barton* 18). When Pendennis sits down by another student at dinner in the hall of his lawyers' Inn, Lowson 'made acquaintance with him at the mess by opening the conversation: 'This is boiled beef day, I believe, sir', said Lowson to Pen. 'Upon my word, sir, I'm not aware,' said Pen . . . 'I'm a stranger; this is my first term' (29). The usage of fiction largely bears out what is said by Lady Colin Campbell's opinion, that by the last quarter of the century usage the polite terms were not used among acquaintances but only to superiors or strangers:

> Gentlemen and gentlewomen of the last century invariably addressed one another as Madam and Sir; the terms are now obsolete in ordinary conversation. An occasional interpolation of the name of the person with whom we are conversing is what is required, and more especially if we should happen to dissent in any degree, to contradict or to affirm.
>
> (Campbell 1898, 38)

The polite title can be used in impatience or anger, and here intonation as well as expression and stance must have been indicative. It may be used to a social inferior when the intention is anything but friendly: 'Here, you, sir' begins Squire Lavington's furious dismissal of Tregarva (*Yeast* 11). Squire Hamley drops his usual familiarity with the country doctor Gibson when he becomes angry: 'You know nothing about it, sir' (*Wives and Daughters* 52). The reiteration of the word, especially where it would not normally be given, is a sign of emotion. Tom Tulliver takes a haughty line with Philip Wakem over Maggie – 'Don't talk high-flown nonsense to me, sir!' (*The Mill on the Floss* Book 5, 5). Young Foker is insolent rather than respectful to the schoolmaster Wapshot when the latter intervenes angrily about Pendennis's challenge to Hobnell: 'and so he sent *you* with the answer – did he, sir? . . . Uncommon kind of you, sir, I'm sure . . . He prefers being flogged to fighting, sir, I dare say'. To which Wapshot replies in kind: 'My name is Wapshot, sir, and I am master of the Grammar School of this town, sir . . . and I want no refreshment, sir, I thank you, and have no desire to make your acquaintance, sir' (*Pendennis* 15).

The difference in age makes the use of the title here clearly ironic. Sometimes boys and very young men are so addressed by their elders in the same tone; the word becomes an equivalent of 'young puppy'. 'Pendennis, sir,' thunders the headmaster of Charterhouse, 'your idleness is incorrigible and your stupidity beyond example . . . A boy, sir, who does not learn his Greek play cheats the parent who spends money for his education' (ibid. 2). 'Go on, sir!' Philip Wakem's father shouts angrily at him (*The Mill on the Floss* Book 6, 8). There is evidence of the same usage outside the novel: a *Punch* cartoon of 1855 has the Head of a college accusing an undergraduate, 'Pray Sir, may I ask why you have not been attending Chapel?'. The delinquent replies with a more respectful 'sir' when he explains that he has 'become a Dissenter' (Vol. 28, 230). On the other hand, class is generally honoured irrespective of age. A bailiff in possession greets the young son of the house: ' "How do you do, sir?" said the man, taking his pipe out of his mouth, with rough, embarrassed civility' (*The Mill on the Floss* Book 3, 2).

Older male members of the family expect and receive the title. Tom's 'sir' to Mr Glegg would be usual from a nephew, especially to a rich uncle, but Glegg's wealth brings respect even from his distressed sister-in-law – 'Oh, sir, you don't know what bad luck my husband's had with his stock' (ibid. Book 3, 4). Trollope's young men generally address their fathers as 'sir' and the address is sometimes made by daughters. Stanhope, not a model father, gets 'Well, sir, give him another chance' from Charlotte (*Barchester Towers* 15). In the same family the word indicates a delicate balance between youthful impertinence and the anger of an older man to a younger:

'Well, sir?' said the doctor.

'And how did you get home, sir, with your fair companion?' said Bertie.

. . .

'Would it suit you, sir,' said the father, 'to give me some idea as to what your present intentions are?'

. . .

'I'll do anything you can suggest, sir' replied Bertie.   (Ibid. 45)

An improvident nephew gets the same ironic title from his rich uncle: 'So, sir, you've been paying ten per cent for money which you've promised to pay off by mortgaging my land when I'm dead and gone, eh?' and is answered, ' "I have contradicted it, sir," Fred said with a touch of impatience' (*Middlemarch* 12). Joe Willett receives a reiterated, 'Silence, Sir!' when he tries to discover how he has offended his father (*Barnaby Rudge* 1).

The nobility have their internal protocol, as Disraeli, keen observer of the 'silver fork' life, notes when the Earl of Marney takes silent exception to the use of his name without title:

'And how do you find the people about you, Marney?' said Lord de Mowbray, seating himself on a sofa by his guest.

'All very well, my lord, replied the earl, who ever treated Lord de Mowbray with a certain degree of ceremony, especially when the descendant of the Crusaders affected familiarity.

Disraeli comments that 'the old nobility of Spain delighted to address each other only by their names, when in the presence of a spic-and-span grandee . . . and then turning round with the most distinguished consideration, and appealing to the Most Noble Marquis of Esmeralda' (*Sybil* Book 2, 12).

The polite 'madam', later relegated to commercial use and now almost obsolete, was widely used. Women do not use it among themselves to the extent that men use 'sir' but it is the common address of respect from social 'inferiors'. It is the expected title from a servant: 'The horses are ready, madam, whenever you like to start', says a footman to Dorothea (*Middlemarch* 62). Esther Waters constantly uses it to her employers, though an unmarried member of the household may be 'Miss'. So too a hotel maid waiting on a customer calls her 'ma'am' (*Jude the Obscure* Part 4, 5). Jude, a civil working man, replies to his landlady's 'Mr Fawley' with 'ma'am' (ibid. Part 3, 4). Anne Brontë makes a servant say 'ma'am' to a governess who is treated with little respect by the family (*Agnes Grey* 1847, 7). Mr Slope allows himself a touch more familiarity when he defends himself against Mrs Proudie's stricture on his friendship with the Countess – 'Good gracious, my dear madam . . . Why, she is a married woman' (*Barchester Towers* 17). Sir Austin is consciously gallant when he replies to Mrs Grandison's wish to introduce her daughters that she 'knew well, madam, how to gratify me most' (*The Ordeal of Richard Feverel* 19).

Munby as usual bears out the novelists' usage. His Hannah is overwhelmed at being called 'ma'am' by a chambermaid at a hotel, 'for no one ever called her Ma'am before' (Hudson 1972, 240). Hannah was even more overwhelmed when a woman of whom she enquired the way called her 'my lady'. This was in 1874, three years after the publication of *Middlemarch*, in which Dorothea's enquiry whether Rosamond is at home receives the reply:

'I'm not sure, my lady: I'll see, if you'll please walk in', said Martha, a little confused on the score of her kitchen apron, but collected enough to be sure that 'mum' was not the right title for this queenly young widow with a carriage and pair. (77)

'Mum' or 'Mem' seems to have been a less respectful mode of address. The charwoman Mrs Blockson calls Mrs Knag 'Mem' at a point when she is losing her temper (*Nicholas Nickleby* 18). The syncopic form 'ma'am' is often written by novelists and it is difficult to discern any difference between this and the full 'madam'. It may be nothing more than a greater concession made by some writers to what was actually heard in speech. There are times, however, when the word fully pronounced seems to suggest the hostility and contempt that sometimes appears in the use of 'sir'.

'I – I wrote to you yesterday, if you please, ma'am,' Fanny said, trembling in every limb as she spoke.
    'Did you, madam?' Mrs Pendennis said. 'I suppose I may now relieve you from nursing my son.'   (*Pendennis* 52)

There is no doubt of the contempt in Mr Slope's reiterated use of the word when he has fallen from favour. 'May God forgive you, madam, for the manner in which you have treated me . . . and remember this, madam, that you yourself may still have a fall' (*Barchester Towers* 51).

Children too young to receive adult titles are known as 'master' or 'miss'. Mr Pontifex 'always put the prefix "master" or "miss" before the names of his grandchildren, except in the case of Alethea, who was his favourite' (*The Way of All Flesh* 3). Agnes Grey, as a governess, uses the title reluctantly to her pupils since 'it seemed to me a chilling and unnatural piece of punctilio between the children of a family and their instructor and daily companion' (7). The use of 'Miss' can extend into early womanhood, less respectful than 'madam' and capable of conveying social contempt, as when a footman thus addresses Kate Nickleby, 'in a tone which rendered "Miss" something more offensive than "My dear" ' (17).

Parents in respectable families are 'Papa' and 'Mamma' from young children, and generally from older girls. Edith Wharton in *The Prime Minister* calls her father 'Papa' when she is of marriageable age and so does Madeline Staveley in *Orley Farm* when she discusses her engagement. Molly Gibson uses the same word, but cannot bear to call her stepmother 'mamma' (*Wives and Daughters* 15). Eleanor Bold, widowed and about to remarry, still calls her father 'dear papa' when she speaks to him (*Barchester Towers* 47). The devious and sophisticated Blanche Amory says 'mamma' to her mother (*Pendennis* 40). It will be recalled that Mrs General considered 'Papa is a preferable mode of address, Father is rather vulgar', although her reason was partly that the word 'gives a pretty form to the lips' (*Little Dorrit* Book 2, 5). However, Louisa Gradgrind says 'Father' in her tense conversation about marrying Bounderby (*Hard Times* Book 1, 15). In the more humble class of Esther Waters her little boy calls her 'Mummie' but his father is 'Father' (20, 26).

Adult sons call their fathers 'Sir' and their mothers 'Mother'. Everett Wharton receives his father's displeasure with, 'I am sorry for that sir'. 'Circumstances, mother, make people different' says Arthur Fletcher (*The Prime Minister* 4, 71). Ernest Pontifex, suppressed by parental control, takes longer to make the change. When his parents come to meet him on his release from prison: 'Mother' (it was the first time he had called her anything but 'Mamma'), 'we must part' (*The Way of All Flesh* 69). Lady Colin Campbell dismisses 'Pa' and 'Ma', 'after the manner of the Misses Pecksniff' as 'objectionable' and recommends, 'For "grown-up" children, the terms "Father" and "Mother" are more becoming than "Papa" or "Mamma" ' (Campbell 1898, 39). This suggestion of a change later in the century is borne out by Marian Yule's regular use of 'father' in *New Grub Street*.

Some modes of address were studiedly offensive. To apostrophise a woman of any class as 'woman' was to invite anger, as Benjamin Allen discovers when he tells Mrs Radstock that she is 'such an unreasonable woman'. ' "I beg your parding, young man," said Mrs Radstock in a louder and more imperative tone. "But who do you call a woman? Did you make that remark to me, Sir?" ' (*Pickwick Papers* 32). Such indignation suggests the outrage felt by Mrs Proudie when she has been bullying Mr Crawley:

'Peace, woman,' Mr Crawley said, addressing her at last. The bishop jumped out of his chair at hearing the wife of his bosom called a woman. But he jumped more in admiration than in anger.

'Woman!' said Mrs Proudie, rising to her feet as though she really intended some personal encounter.   (*The Last Chronicle of Barset* 18)

The use of 'woman' as reference rather than address was more acceptable. The anonymous author of *Society Small Talk* (1879) finds the correct choice of word to be difficult and concludes that a man could say, 'I met a rather agreeable woman the other night' rather than 'agreeable lady', but 'a lady, a friend of mine' rather than 'a woman' and certainly not 'which of the women did you take in to dinner?' In time, 'lady' came to be seen as something of a genteelism:

The constant use of the word 'lady' and the term 'lady friend' is also objectionable. It is to be presumed that all your female acquaintances are 'ladies'. A writer sarcastically observes, 'There is scarce one *woman* to be met with; the sex consists almost entirely of *ladies*'.

(Campbell 1898, 49)

Even greater umbrage is taken at 'female', despite Campbell's use of 'female acquaintances'. The wrath of Mrs Radstock, quoted above, is compounded when Knag says, 'Will you hold your tongue – female!'. The sharp if equivocal response is, 'and with regard to being a female, Sir, I should wish to know what you considered yourself?' followed by giving her notice. The word was offensive when applied to a human being; Moon takes Alford to task for daring to use it of Queen Victoria:

Why when speaking of women do you apply to them the most debasing of all slang expressions? You speak of the highest person in the land, and that person a lady, and your description of her is one that is equally applicable to a dog! – Her Majesty is – *a female*! I am sure that all who desire your welfare will join me in hoping that Her Majesty will not see your book.   (Moon 1865, 114f)

A popular manual of etiquette is equally condemnatory: 'Don't say *female* for *woman*. A sow is a female, a mare is a female. The female sex of the human kind is entitled to some distinctive term' ('Censor' 1880, 66).

Once again social comment is supported by fiction. Meredith has an amusing novella, *The Case of General Ople and Lady Camper*

(1898), about the courtship of an elderly couple, in which the General is often censured for his choice of words. When he hesitates about calling Lady Camper 'Angela' though agreeing that 'there is not a more beautiful female name', he draws the devastating reply, 'Spare me that word "female" as long as you live' (4). Later she finds more fault: 'I forbid you ever – to afflict my ears with that phrase "lady-friend"!' (5). Richard Feverel takes umbrage when Adrian picks up his account of how his wife 'pleaded and implored' with, 'Where's the lass that doesn't?' 'Call my wife by another name, if you please' (36). A neat distinction is made by the steward's daughter Penelope Betteredge when her mistress snubs a cousin of whom she disapproves: 'There's one woman in the world who can resist Mr Godfrey Ablewhite at any rate; and if I was a lady, I should be another' (*The Moonstone* 9).

However, 'man' and 'men' do not seem to cause offence. The bookmaker who says to successful punters, 'Now, my men, what is it?' is answered with a civil request (*Esther Waters* 9); Lancelot Smith's promise to a poacher, 'I won't tell, my man' is received with gratitude (*Yeast* 8). This is supported by Greenwood's description of a charitable tea for dustmen, where the lady in charge says, 'Come along in, men, we are nearly ready for you!' (Greenwood 1881, 121). 'Person' is condescending; Miss Knag believes that Mrs Nickleby may be 'a very respectable old person'. So too is 'fellow'; Fanny Squeers takes offence at a waiter's casual attitude to her father, 'as if he were a feller' (*Nicholas Nickleby* 39). Benjamin Allen angrily accuses Mr Pickwick of improperly using Sam Weller, 'your fellow', as an agent in abduction (48). On the other hand, Rokeby is affectionate rather than scornful when he says of Sloppy, 'he seems to be an amiable fellow' (*Our Mutual Friend* Book 1, 16), and the epicene Sally Brass is not offended when Dick Swiveller calls her 'old fellow' (*The Old Curiosity Shop* 1841, 36).

The word 'gentleman' appears continually in the dialogue of the time, usually without comment. However, objections are sometimes raised to it, and it seems to have been a matter of contention. In a chapter significantly headed 'Men and Gentlemen' Gaskell makes the industrialist Thornton eloquent in reply to Margaret Hale's question about another character 'He cannot be a gentleman – is he?'. Thornton will not 'decide on another's gentlemanliness' but prefers to say that Morison 'is no true man'. In the discussion that follows, he declares himself 'rather weary of this word "gentlemanly" . . . I am induced to class it with the cant of the day' (*North and South* 1855, 20). This is the voice of the new man, whose confidence comes from money and power, not lineage; it is the voice of Dickens's Rouncewell. Yet the unease is uttered also in the Barsetshire parsonage: Grace Crawley fears that 'Gentleman is such a frightful word to have to use to a gentleman; but I did not know what else to say' (*The Last Chronicle of Barset* 41). Mrs Swancourt rebukes Elfride for noticing 'several ladies and gentlemen looking at me' with, 'My dear, you mustn't say "gentlemen" nowadays ... We have handed over "gentlemen" to the lower middle class' (*A Pair of Blue Eyes* 14). Probably the ex-governess Hyacinth Kirkpatrick betrays herself when she follows a long list of her views on etiquette with a reference to 'a gentleman – he was a lieutenant in the 53rd' (*Wives and Daughters* 11). The more respectful peasant community is less frightened by a fine gradation. Speaking of a prosperous tradesman, Hardy's Joseph Poorgrass corrects himself. 'Levi Everdene – that was the man's name, sure. "Man", saith I in my hurry, but he were of a higher circle of life than that – 'a was a gentleman-tailor really, worth scores of pounds' (*Far from the Madding Crowd* 8). Victorian unease about 'lady' and 'gentleman', which prepared for their virtual banishment from middle-class speech in the next century, is discussed further in Phillipps (1984), 4ff.

Some of the most revealing passages are those which show confusion of register in uncertain relationships. Nowhere, perhaps, does the otherness of the nineteenth century seem more apparent. The speaker may be aware of the difficulty, as when a father exaggerates the status of a son returned from work in London: 'Owing to your coming a day sooner than we first expected,' said John, 'you'll find us in a turk of a mess, sir – "sir," says I to my own son! but ye've gone up so, Stephen' (*A Pair of Blue Eyes* 23). Dickens, always ready to draw out and elaborate a point, treats a similar situation more fully and with greater poignancy in *Great Expectations* (1861):

'Us two being now alone, Sir' – began Joe.

'Joe,' I interrupted, pettishly, 'how can you call me Sir?'

Joe looked at me for a single instant with something faintly like reproach. Utterly preposterous as his cravat was, and as his collars were, I was conscious of a sort of dignity in the look.

. . .

'Well, Sir,' pursued Joe, 'this is how it were. I were at the Bargemen t'other night, Pip;' whenever he subsided into affection he called me Pip, and whenever he relapsed into politeness he called me Sir. (27)

The uncertainty shown here leads towards the fine passage when Joe nurses Pip through a severe illness and as he recovers speaks familiarly – 'dear old Pip old chap'. Then, when Pip is well enough to resume his life as a 'gentleman', the distance starts to return, 'Dear old Pip, old chap, you're almost come round, sir' and soon afterwards Joe steals away quietly, leaving a note, 'not wishful to intrude' (57). The sensitivity breaks through even to a generation alien to the niceties of formal address. But deliberate switch of register can be insulting and can reveal a change in comparative status. When Morgan is triumphant with Lightfoot he moves through 'sir', 'Mr Lightfoot', 'Lightfoot' and 'Frederic Lightfoot' in the course of a few sentences (*Pendennis* 60).

Another use of the respectful 'sir' perhaps even less comprehensible to a modern reader, is from a working girl to a man of higher social rank who is, or is trying to be, her lover. A whole chapter of social history is written in the flirtation of Pendennis with Fanny, where the barrier of rank is accepted by both:

'How beautiful they are, sir!' she cried.

'Don't call me sir, Fanny,' Arthur said.

A quick blush rose up in the girl's face. 'What shall I call you?' she said in a low voice, sweet and tremulous. 'What would you wish me to call you, sir?'

'Again, Fanny! Well, I forgot; it is best so, my dear,' Pendennis said, very kindly and gently. 'I may call you Fanny?'

'O yes!' she said, and the little hand pressed his arm once more very eagerly, and the girl clung to him so that he could feel her heart beating on his shoulder.

'I may call you Fanny, because you are a young girl, and a good girl, Fanny, and I am an old gentleman. But you mustn't call me anything but sir, or Mr Pendennis, if you like, for we live in very different stations, Fanny.' (46)

Respect in words may continue after things have gone farther: Tess says 'Very well, sir' and 'No, sir' to Alec after he has kissed her. When Mary Barton is trying to extricate herself from Carson, she keeps a conversational distance even though his arm is around her waist:

'Have I done anything to offend you?' added he, earnestly.

'No, sir,' she answered gently, but yet firmly. 'I cannot tell you exactly why I have changed my mind; but I shall not alter it again; and as I said before, I beg your pardon if I've done wrong by you. And now, sir, if you please, good night.' (11)

Here again, the novelists are not being fanciful. Munby records how working girls with whom he joined in a boisterous game at the Crystal Palace called him 'sir' and retails the conversation of a shopgirl who, if a male customer 'wanted to joke me' would say, 'one of the young men'll attend to you, sir' (Hudson 1972, 103, 98). In a different world, and without such liberties being taken, Lucy Robartes continues to call her suitor 'Lord Lufton', until she checks his ardour with 'You must not call me Lucy any longer, Lord Lufton; I was madly foolish when I first allowed it' (*Framley Parsonage* 16).

Notes

1. Bennett (1948), 50; Fowler (1970), 14; Darbyshire (1967), 23.

2. This is a Victorian courtesy which endured long into the twentieth century. In the 1960s the present writer was invited by a senior colleague to 'drop the Mr on both sides' when exchanging letters.

CHAPTER 5
Religious speech

There have been many misapprehensions about the place of religion in the nineteenth century. Conversation did not consist exclusively of pious observations heavily supported by biblical texts. Nor did it consist of anguished debate about the certainty of faith in the face of new challenges. The Victorian Sunday did not find every member of the population in church two or three times. The survey of church attendance carried out in connection with the 1851 census was unscientific and inconsistent, but it showed that probably less than half the population went to any place of worship on Sunday (Chadwick 1966, 363–9). These correctives are necessary because of the modern tendency either to lament the passing of a great age of faith or to blame the faults of the era on the strength of its religion. Nevertheless, there is no doubt that life in the nineteenth century was lived against a background of Christian belief, ignored by many but actively questioned by few. Churchgoing and personal prayer may not have been universal but they were certainly far more common than they are today.

The class which produced most of the writers and readers of novels had a higher proportion of believers, mostly members of the Church of England, than the population as a whole. There was certainly strong faith and devout practice also among many of the poor, catered for particularly by the dissenting sects, and later by the Anglo-Catholic wing. The sects developed their own distinctive idioms, but they shared the religious style which had developed in the English language. Based on the Authorised Version of the Bible, and for Anglicans and 'Church Methodists' also on the Book of Common Prayer, it preserved such otherwise archaic forms as the second person singular, the *-eth* ending of the present tense and a plethora of scriptural phraseology which spilled over into hymns, sermons and conversation. It does not seem out of keeping for the poor clergyman Crawley, who lives in a world of his own, to receive the news that he has been cleared of a charge of theft with, 'it seemeth to me that you are a messenger of glad tidings, whose feet are beautiful upon the mountains' (*The Last Chronicle of Barset* 74).

When fictional characters not distinguished for special piety use scriptural and theological language, their idiom can be accepted as part of the realism which was increasingly characteristic of the novel. People said these things because they grew up with continual exposure to sermons and Bible reading. It does not seem forced in context when Yonge's worthy Dr May says to his daughter, 'the rugged path and dark valley will come in His own fit time. Depend upon it, the good Shepherd is giving you what is best for you in the green meadow' (*The Daisy Chain* 1856, 26). A nurse says of a peaceful death, 'The Lord be praised for all his mercies' (*Barchester Towers* 1). Less devoutly, but with equal naturalness, a landowner hearing of the Irish Land Bill says, 'God in his mercy forbid that a landlord in England should ever be robbed after that fashion' (*The Prime Minister* 70). Pecksniff exhorts Martin Chuzzlewit, 'You will be jovial, my dear Martin, and will kill the fatted calf if you please!', and Dickens draws attention to the inappropriate idiom by remarking that 'no such animal chanced at that time to be grazing on Mr Pecksniff's estate' (6). In her short-lived period of piety Arabella says, 'I am not the woman to find fault with what the Lord has ordained' (*Jude the Obscure* Part 5, 7). Sue Bridehead, overwhelmed by the death of her children and believing that people are talking about her, exclaims, 'We are made a spectacle to men and to angels'. Jude makes the ironic reply, 'No, they are not talking of us. They are two clergymen of different views arguing about the eastward position.' He adds another biblical phrase, 'Good God – the eastward position and all creation groaning' (*Jude the Obscure* Part 6, 2).

Not all speakers are so apt or so accurate in their references. Confusion and misunderstanding were common when Bible passages were exposed to unsophisticated minds, and the results could be a source of humour for the novelists. There must have been many like the little girl in *The Heir of Redclyffe* who 'had hardly ever been at church; and though she had read one or two Bible stories, it seemed to have been from their being used as lessons at school' (18). Disraeli has a working girl with a 'vacant face' who testifies that her young man 'believes now in our Lord and Saviour Pontius Pilate, who was crucified to save our sins; and in Moses, Goliath, and the rest of the Apostles' (*Sybil* Book 3, 4). If this seems an outrageous exaggeration, it can be compared with the conversation which Munby heard in 1860 from 'three dirty little street boys' who were looking at a picture in a shop window of an old priest blessing little children, which the biggest insisted was, 'Jesus Christ to be sure, a blessing of the little children, which they brought 'em to Him, and "of such is the Kingdom of Heaven", that's what he said'. So far so good, but when another of the boys persisted, 'But what did He do to them?' the reply was '*I* don't know, but I know *He burns them when they're wicked!*' (Hudson 1972, 53). Not all the Manchester workers are as accurate as John Barton, quoted above; Mrs Wilson asserts that her son Jem is 'as steady as Lucifer, and he were an angel, you know' (*Mary Barton* 19). An itinerant tinker relates his experience at sea to the Bible, but with some confusion about apostolic status – 'We were as nigh wrecked as the prophet Paul' (*The Ordeal of Richard Feverel* 3). Dickens particularly rejoices in the comic possibilities of misunderstanding. Miggs in *Barnaby Rudge* has a confused mixture of scriptural words and phrases, as when she speaks of 'the meekness and forgiveness of her blessed dispositions' (80). Mrs Gamp is supreme in this field, with her wish to see the Antwerp packet 'in Jonadge's belly' (*Martin Chuzzlewit* 40).

Sermons play little direct part in fiction. They were often published, and indeed formed a major part of Victorian book production. A realistic sermon would have seemed out of place in even the more didactic type of novel, and a parody would have been distasteful to the majority. Trollope observes primly, 'It would not be becoming were I to travestie a sermon, or even to repeat the language of it in the pages of a novel' (*Barchester Towers* 41). When he gives the final words of Crawley's parting sermon, the idiolect is the old-fashioned clerical English which the character has throughout used in conversation: 'I have always known my own unfitness, by reason of the worldly cares with which I have been laden. Poverty makes the spirit poor, and the hands weak, and the heart sore – and too often makes the conscience dull. May the latter never be the case with any of you' (*The Last Chronicle of Barset* 69). The effusions of characters like Stiggins and Chadband, not being formal church sermons or assigned to a particular denomination, were acceptable. Novelists who wished to use fiction as a direct medium for religious teaching might give a whole sermon, as Shorthouse does in *Sir Percival* and *Blanche, Lady Falaise* (1891). The less devout and more mischievous might venture on parody, like the disguised Evangelical sermon given by Hankey in *Erewhon Revisited* and the Broad Church one in Mallock's *The New Republic*.

While the content of sermons was discussed in pious families, hearers sensitive to language could be more critical of their style and delivery. Kingston-Oliphant, finding the best English in the Authorised Version of the Bible and the Book of Common Prayer with their 'old Teutonic words, with a dash of French terms mostly naturalised in the thirteenth century', goes on to observe:

> The pulpit, on the other hand, too often deals in an odd jargon of Romance, worked up into long-winded sentences, which shoot high above the heads of the listeners. I have myself heard a curate turn Addison's *government of the world* into *cosmic regime* . . . A preacher has been known to translate 'we cannot always stand upright' into 'we cannot always maintain an erect position'.
>
> (Kingston-Oliphant 1873, II, 227)

This, he laments is the product of the schools and universities, for 'much care is there bestowed on Latin and Greek but none on English'.

This is the complaint that Newman puts into the mouth of Sheffield, who hears pretentious Latinate diction delivered in an affected manner in university sermons:

> I go into St Mary's, and I hear men spouting out commonplaces in a deep or a shrill voice, or with slow, clear, quiet emphasis and significant eyes – as that Bampton preacher not long ago, who assured us, apropos of the resurrection of the body, that 'all attempts to resuscitate the inanimate corpse by natural methods had hitherto been experimentally abortive'.   (*Loss and Gain* 4)

George Eliot finds similar faults in a less distinguished preacher:

> Some passages of Massillon and Bourdaloue, which he knew by heart, were really very effective when rolled out in Mr Stelling's deepest tones; but as comparatively feeble appeals of his own were delivered in the same loud and impressive manner, they were often thought quite as striking by his hearers.   (*The Mill on the Floss* Book 1, 4)

This is close to the criticism made by Dean Hole that some preachers 'rely too much upon a loud resonant tone, which sets the echoes flying, and which without modifications soon becomes as irksome and monotonous to their hearers as the sermons in a lower key' (Hole 1901, 195f). The Baptist Charles Spurgeon, one of the most popular of all Victorian preachers, was praised because, 'There is no cant or whining about him; he is natural as the day; and were it not for time and place, few would suppose from look, tone or style, that they listened to a sermon' (*The British and Foreign Evangelical Review*, 1866, cit. Jay 1986, 89). Spurgeon was presumably not the only preacher to speak naturally in the pulpit, but the novelist's ear was alert for the more comic effect of mannered diction. Trollope issues a diatribe against some preachers: 'I yawn over your imperfect sentences, your repeated phrases, your false pathos, your drawlings and denouncings, your humming and hawing, your oh-ing and ah-ing, your black gloves and your white handkerchief' (*Barchester Towers* 6).

Casual allusions in conversation show how religion permeated the Victorian consciousness and critical comments on sermons tell their own story about the special style often affected by preachers. More significant in the art of the novel is the use of religious style to develop character and show relationships. The shared style based on Bible language could take many variations in different classes and churches. The religious census of 1851 revealed thirty-five Christian sects; it is unlikely that even an acute observer could have identified each one by the speech of its members, but there seem to have been certain shared characteristics within the major groupings.

The clerical voice was often affected and mannered, not in the pulpit alone. Newman's Charles Reding objects to clergymen with a high lifestyle 'waving their hands and mincing their words, as if they were the cream of the earth' (*Loss and Gain* 12). One word, more often associated with Uriah Heep, seems to have been something of a shibboleth for the clergy. Alford complains that: 'We still sometimes, even in good society, hear "*ospital*," "*erb*," and "*umble*," – all of them very offensive, but the last of them by far the worst, especially when heard from an officiating clergyman' (Alford 1864, 39).

The charge was disputed by a critic who found the aspirate an affectation rather than a mark of breeding:

> It was formerly almost as common to say *umble* as it is to say *onour* and
> (h)*our* . . . We believe that the reason why the Clergy have so
> commonly adopted the practice of sounding the 'h' in *humble* is because
> educated persons cannot endure the idea of its being said of them that

they drop their 'h's'; directly, therefore, the custom became prevalent of aspirating *humble*, the Clergy at once took it up.

(*The English Churchman* 28 January 1864, 150 f)

However, Gaskell has no doubt about the undesirable quality of the 'strange curate' who took temporary duty – 'a man who dropped his h's and hurried through the service' (*My Lady Ludlow* 1858, 11).

Evangelical speech

Of all the Christian groups, the most often parodied were the Evangelicals. By the time of the great Victorian novelists, the term had become wide and somewhat vague. The movement began about the middle of the eighteenth century with the aspirations of a number of Anglican clergymen for a purer, more personal and more fervent expression of the Gospel at a time when 'enthusiasm' was in general something to be condemned. It grew to strong influence, exemplified early in the nineteenth century by men like William Wilberforce and others of the 'Clapham Sect'. It had lost much of its momentum by the middle of the century, but had some power in the decade from 1850 when Palmerston was Prime Minister and Sumner Archbishop of Canterbury. Without trying to over-simplify a profound and often noble religious position, it may be said that the Evangelicals were characterised by insistence on conviction of sin and man's fallen state as the beginning of salvation, individual conversion to an acceptance of personal redemption and theological emphasis on the centrality of the Atonement to Christian faith. It had remained a significant though never dominant element in the Church of England and had become general among the nonconformist churches, proving capable of accommodating both Calvinist and Arminian views of election and inspiring both educated and simple believers.

What brought the Evangelicals into observation, and often into ridicule, was their belief in preaching the Gospel at all opportunities. It was their open and constant preaching of Atonement faith which led them into controversy with the Tractarians after the appearance of the Tracts on *Reserve in Communicating Religious Knowledge* written by Isaac Williams in 1837 and 1840. While preaching from the pulpit might be welcomed or at least tolerated, a sudden irruption of the 'message' in social gatherings, usually accompanied by the handing out of tracts, was acceptable only to a few. It offended against the native reticence in matters of religion. The Evangelicals were also unpopular for their restrictive attitude to many worldly pleasures, including the theatre and for a long time the novel, which the *Evangelical Magazine* in 1800 had placed on a 'Spiritual Barometer' as equal with scepticism and lower than adultery (Quinlan 1941, 114). There was also the feeling that the most fervent Evangelicals were often ill-bred and not quite gentlemanly. Butler's description of the Simeonites at Cambridge in *The Way of All Flesh* is typical; Trollope's Mr Slope was a sizar at Cambridge and is described even by the charitable Mr Harding as 'not gentleman-like in his manners' (*Barchester Towers* 13).

Evangelical idiolects frequently aroused the amusement or contempt of many of the novelists. Dickens and Trollope were particularly severe on Evangelicals. They tended to fasten on the more demotic manifestations; there was a great deal of difference between the speech of Melchiszedek Howler or Stiggins, and that of well-informed Evangelicals like the reforming Lord Shaftesbury, or Edward Bickersteth who founded the Evangelical Alliance in 1841. In portraying the less restrained Evangelical outbursts, were the novelists guilty of exaggeration or unrealistic invention?

In fact criticism came from some of the Evangelicals themselves, including indictments of features found in later fiction. John Foster was a Baptist minister who found much that was distasteful in the popular expression of the Evangelical faith which he shared. His criticisms were written early in the nineteenth century but their continued reprinting down to 1876 suggests that they were not outmoded. Some of his remarks support the veracity of the major novelists.[1] The irruption of Stiggins or Chadband into a domestic assembly was not wild imagining:

> You have sometimes observed, when a person has introduced religious topics, in the course of perhaps a tolerably rational conversation on other interesting subjects, that, owing to the cast of expression, fully as much as to the difference of the subject, it was done by an entire change of the whole tenour and bearing of the discourse, and with a formal an announcement as the bell ringing to church. (234)

Foster found the language of some of his co-religionists as distressing as did the unsympathetic novelists.

> Another cause which I think has tended to render evangelical religion less acceptable to persons of taste is the *peculiarity of language* adopted

in the discourses and books of its teachers, as well as in the religious conversation and correspondence of the majority of its adherents. (218f)

Was this 'peculiarity of language' faithfully reflected in fiction?

In this matter, as in many others, Dickens took full and exuberant advantage of the potential for humour. He was too much a wooer of the public to attack any specific church or sect; his comic Evangelicals, like many of his other eccentrics, are isolated from a recognisable group; the readers can comfortably assume that they are 'one of them, not one of us'. Stiggins is an early and not fully developed example. He interpolates biblical phrases such as 'man of wrath' and is pleased to be called a 'shepherd'. Slope woos Eleanor Bold with the hope of making 'to myself friends in this fold to which it has pleased God to call me as one of the humblest of his shepherds' (*Barchester Towers* 16). Stiggins addresses his hearer as 'my young friend' and uses inflated language in inappropriate contexts, as when his frustrated desire for rum makes him exclaim, 'Oh, the hardness of heart of these inveterate men! Oh, the accursed cruelty of these inhuman persecutors!' (*Pickwick Papers* 45). Chadband is a much more developed and subtle character, in whom some of the Stiggins idiolect is retained and elaborated. One of his most famous effusions is worth quoting at length, without the interpolated exclamations of other characters and authorial comment:

> I say this brother, present here among us, is devoid of parents, devoid of relations, devoid of flocks and herds, devoid of gold, of silver, and of precious stones, because he is devoid of the light which shines in upon some of us. What is that light? What is it? I ask you what is that light? It is the ray of rays, the sun of suns, the moon of moons, the star of stars. It is the light of Terewth. Of Terewth. Say not to me that it is *not* the lamp of lamps. I say to you, it is. I say to you, a million times over, it is. I say to you that I will proclaim it to you, whether you like it or not; nay, that the less you like it, the more I will proclaim it to you. With a speaking-trumpet! I say to you that if you rear yourself against it, you shall be bruised, you shall be battered, you shall be flawed, you shall be smashed.   (*Bleak House* 25)

This is the kind of speech which could make a cultivated Evangelical like Foster complain of 'A peculiar phraseology [which] gives to what is already by its own nature eminently distinguished from common subjects an *artificial* strangeness, which makes it difficult for discourse to slide into it, and revert to it and from it, without a formal and uncouth transition' (234). Chadband uses the rhetorical question which published as well as spoken record shows to have been a favourite trick of Evangelical speakers. He uses the address, 'My young friends' which, with or without the 'young', was common in sermon and informal discourse. Butler particularly noticed and disliked it. Mr Hawkes who comes as a visiting speaker to the Cambridge Simeonites begins his discourse, 'My young friends, I am persuaded that there is not one of you here who doubts the existence of a Personal God' (*The Way of All Flesh* 49). Even in the country of Erewhon, Professor Hankey has adopted the Evangelical style and begins his sermon, 'My friends, let there be no mistake' (*Erewhon Revisited* 1901, 16).

There is also in Chadband's speech the inappropriate use of biblical words and phrases, with concrete imagery adding to the association: 'devoid of flocks and herds, devoid of gold and silver', and the reiteration of a construction drawn from biblical phraseology: 'the ray of rays, the sun of suns, the moon of moons, the star of stars'. The latter imitates the 'Lord of lords and King of kings' of *Revelation* (17.24), a book very popular with the more extreme and vociferous Evangelicals. Direct imperatives and repetitive phrases make what could be effective hyperbole collapse into the grotesque. One of the strengths of the serious Evangelicals was their intimate knowledge of the Authorised Version of the Bible, which could become a snare for those who read ignorantly and without discrimination. It is not surprising that Foster protested:

I suppose it will be instantly allowed, that the mode of expression of the greater number of evangelical divines, and of those taught by them, is widely different from the standard of general language, not only by the necessary adoption of some peculiar terms, but by a continued and systematic use of phraseology; insomuch that in reading or hearing five or six sentences of an evangelical discourse, you ascertain the school by the mere turn of expression, independently of any attention to the quality of the ideas. (221)

The misuse of biblical language is even more comically shown in the words of the Little Bethel preacher who tries to stop Kit from leaving with his infant brother:

'Stay, Satan, stay!' roared the preacher again. 'Tempt not the woman
that doth incline her ear to thee, but hearken to the voice of him that
calleth. He hath a lamb from the fold ... He beareth off a lamb, a
precious lamb! He goeth about like a wolf in the night season, and
inveigleth the tender lambs!'   (*The Old Curiosity Shop* 41)

It was of such analogies that Foster remarked sadly, 'In the
conversation of illiterate christians the supposed man of taste has
perhaps frequently heard the most unfortunate metaphors and similes,
employed to explain or enforce evangelical sentiments' (207).

Trollope creates a minor Chadband in Mr Prong, who also uses
scriptural style and reference, with the familiar apostrophe 'my friend';
he shares Chadband's greedy eating, as he pontificates, 'with the
debris of a large dish of shrimps' in front of him, to Mrs Prime who
has been shocked by the activities of some of her new acquaintance:

> You cannot return to them now, if you are to countenance by your
> presence dancings and love-makings in the open air, and loud
> revellings, and the absence of all good works, and rebellion against the
> Spirit. No, my friend, no. It must not be so. They must be rescued from
> the burning, but not so, – not so.   (*Rachel Ray* 1863, 9)

His mother had presented an Evangelical clergyman, Mr Cartwright,
as a leading character in *The Vicar of Wrexhill* (1838). Frances
Trollope lacks the vigour and the compelling exaggeration of Dickens
but she sustains through speech the creature of her imagination.[2]
Described specifically as a Calvinist, and depicted as grasping and
hypocritical, Cartwright speaks in pious terms about his plan to marry
a rich widow:

> There have already been some singular and remarkable manifestations
> of the Lord's will in this matter; and it is the perceiving of this, which
> has led me to believe, and indeed full certain, that my duty calls upon
> me so to act, that this wealthy relict of a man too much addicted to the
> things of this world, may finally, by becoming part and parcel of myself,
> lose not the things eternal. (2, 7)

Claims to special revelation, inclination made into duty, and the
eschewing of 'worldliness' were constantly attributed to Evangelicals,
and indeed sometimes became the abuses of their true and laudable
piety. The last phrase, from a collect in the book of Common Prayer,

reminds us that Evangelicalism was by no means confined to nonconformists but was at that time influential in the Church of England.

Did anyone really talk like that? The frequency and the shared features of the speech of such characters in fiction suggests that what the novelists presented was caricature but not wild imagination. Nearly ten years after *Bleak House*, Munby heard 'a specimen of the fastfailing school of "Evangelical" clergymen' and noted both his faults as a preacher and his power over his hearers: 'It was curious to observe the emotion which his speech, rambling and pointless, even vulgar and ungrammatical, aroused even amongst those of his audience whom I knew to be most refined and most sensitive to the ludicrous' (Hudson 1972, 27 April 1864). Such observations make credible the ascendancy of a Stiggins or a Chadband over the company in which their ministry is accepted.

The language of these speakers is presented as a mark of hypocrisy, as a cover for their greed and avarice. In the Preface to the 1847 edition of *Pickwick Papers*, Dickens was careful to explain that he was attacking only 'that coarse familiarity with sacred things which is busy on the lip, and idle in the heart'. The comment of Foster's words are a perfect gloss on Chadband:

> The usual language of hypocrisy, at least of vulgar hypocrisy, is cant; and religious cant is often an affected use of the phrases which have been heard employed as appropriate to evangelical truth; with which phrases the hypocrite has connected no distinct ideas, so that he would be confounded if an intelligent examiner were to require an accurate explanation of them; while yet nothing is more easy to be sung or said. (236)

Extreme Evangelical diction may characterise hypocrisy of another kind, like the sadism of Brocklehurst, who draws freely on biblical idiom to cover repressed sexuality when he speaks at Lowood School:

> I have a master to serve whose kingdom is not of this world; my mission is to mortify in these girls the lusts of the flesh: to teach them to clothe themselves with shamefacedness and sobriety, not with braided hair and costly apparel; and each of the young persons before us has a string of hair twisted in a plait which vanity itself might have woven: these, I repeat, must be cut off. (*Jane Eyre* 1847, 7)

Eliot presents Tryan, who has become an Evangelical clergyman after a profligate youth, more sympathetically and gives him speech which reflects his genuine repentance. 'I asked for nothing through the rest of my life but that I might be devoted to God's work, without swerving in search of pleasure either to the right hand or the left' (*Janet's Repentance* 1857, 18). Trollope too is not always hard on Evangelicals and gives a sympathetic treatment to Saul in *The Claverings* (1867).

More moderate Evangelical language is used by speakers who are drawn in more depth and whose religious persuasion is an element in their character rather than its principal feature. Bulstrode is pious but also practical in his advice to Vincy about Fred's future:

> I cannot regard wealth as a blessing to those who use it simply as a harvest for this world. You do not like to hear these things, Vincy, but on this occasion I feel called upon to tell you that I have no motive for furthering such a disposition of property as that which you refer to. I do not shrink from saying that it will not tend to your son's eternal welfare or to the glory of God.   (*Middlemarch* 13)

When he hears of the danger of a cholera epidemic he says, without giving an impression of affectation, 'we may well beseech the Mercy-seat for our protection' (67). Collins's Miss Clack is closer to parody, but perhaps not far removed from the outbursts of the pious for whom the moment of opportunity diminished tact. ' "Oh, Rachel, Rachel!" I burst out. "Haven't you seen yet, that my heart yearns to make a Christian of you? Has no inner voice told you that I am trying to do for you, what I was trying to do for your dear mother when death snatched her out of my hands?" ' (*The Moonstone* Second Period, 7).

Charlotte Brontë is merciless in depicting the cruel hypocrisy of Brocklehurst; she is penetrating but more sympathetic about St John Rivers in the same novel. He is intelligent and genuinely devout but struggling still against a dominating and passionate nature: 'a cold, hard man' as he says of himself. His reply when Jane suggests, 'You would describe yourself as a mere pagan philosopher' is brilliantly conceived. In every sentence his inner tension is felt through the formal, measured language. The phraseology is typically Evangelical, with its metaphors of agriculture, militaristic tone of missionary effort and final Pauline quotation:

No. There is this difference between me and deistic philosophers: I believe, and I believe the gospel. You missed your epithet. I am not a pagan but a Christian philosopher – a follower of the sect of Jesus. As His disciple I adopt His pure, His merciful, His benignant doctrines. I advocate them: I am sworn to spread them. Won in youth to religion, she has cultivated my original qualities thus: – From the minute germ, natural affection, she has developed the overshadowing tree, philanthropy. From the wild, stringy root of human uprightness, she has reared a due sense of the Divine justice. Of the ambition to win power and renown for my wretched self she has formed the ambition to spread my Master's kingdom; to achieve victories for the standard of the cross. So much has religion done for me; turning the original materials to the best account; pruning and training nature. But she could not eradicate nature: nor will it be eradicated 'till this mortal shall put on immortality'.   (*Jane Eyre* 32)

The sermons and discourses of Evangelicals were a rich source of humour for the novelists. More subtle in depiction of character is the use of similar language carried over into ordinary conversation. Butler takes the idiom to an improbable but entertaining extreme in the words of Dr Skinner, whose rhetorical questions and self-answers echo the style of Chadband: ' "And what shall it be to drink?" he exclaimed persuasively. "Shall it be brandy and water? No. It shall be gin and water. Gin is the more wholesome liquor." ' (*The Way of All Flesh* 27). Butler knew his Evangelicals as thoroughly as he disliked them. Theobald Pontifex has recourse to biblical stereotypes, moving from *Revelation* to *Isaiah* in a manner singularly inappropriate for the sick old woman to whom he is speaking: 'You must please to take my word that at the Day of Judgment your sins will be all washed white in the blood of the Lamb, Mrs Thompson. Yea', he exclaimed frantically, 'though they be as scarlet, yet shall they be as white as wool' (15).

Newman also came from an Evangelical background and knew how scriptural reference was used in serious conversation. Freeborn, like Pontifex, draws on both Testaments for his imagery: 'Faith is as poor as Job in the ashes; it is like Job stripped of all pride and pomp and good works: it is covered with filthy rags: it is without anything good; it is, I repeat, a mere apprehension' (*Loss and Gain* Part 1, 16). The more aggressive Dr Kitchen, who calls on Charles Reding just before his secession, combines the stock idiom with the Evangelical custom of giving out tracts. 'You are at present under the influence of the old Adam, and indeed in a melancholy way. I was not unprepared for it;

and I have put into my pocket a little tract which I shall press upon you with all the Christian solicitude which brother can show towards brother' (Part 3, 8).

Simpler and less professional Evangelicals can also reveal themselves by their idiolect. Mrs Clennam is of the company which has heard many sermons. 'The world has narrowed to these dimensions, Arthur ... It is well for me that I never set my heart upon its hollow vanities ... The Lord has been pleased to put me beyond all that' (*Little Dorrit* Book 1, 3). Catherine Earnshaw incurs the wrath of Joseph, whose broad dialect makes his pious invective the more intimidating:

> 'T' maister nobbut just buried, and Sabbath no o'ered, und t' sound o' t' gospel still i' your lugs, and ye darr be laiking! Shame on ye! sit ye down, ill childer! There's good books enough if ye'll read 'em! Sit ye down, and think of yer sowls!'   (*Wuthering Heights* 3)

'Sabbath' for 'Sunday' was a frequent Evangelical word; its use by Slope and the Proudies was disliked by the more traditional Barchester clergy. ' "Sabbath-day schools!" repeated the archdeacon with an affectation of surprise. "Upon my word, I can't tell; it depends mainly on the parson's wife and daughters" ' (*Barchester Towers* 5). Joseph's diatribe might have seemed 'above his station' in a more conventional household than that of Wuthering Heights. However, servants sometimes took advantage of the apparent intimacy of family prayers and the equality of persons which Evangelicals usually honoured more in theory than in practice:

> After the chapter, my father read one of 'Thornton's Family Prayers', and, indeed, the use of that book was a distinctive sign of true Evangelicalism. Some friends of ours tried extempore prayers, and one worthy baronet went so far as to invite contributions from the servants. As long as only the butler and housekeeper voiced the aspirations of their fellows, all was decorous; but one fine day an insubordinate kitchen-maid took up her parable, saying, 'And we pray for Sir Thomas and her Ladyship too. Oh, may they have new hearts given to them!' The bare idea that there was room for such renovation caused a prompt return to the lively oracles of Henry Thornton.[3]

If Dickens had depicted that scene in his own idiolect and had given the words to a servant such as Miggs, some critics would have accused him of exaggerated fancy. The Victorian age had no lack of living material to feed the imagination.

Denominational speech

The name and style of Evangelicalism were often used loosely to identify any individual or group in whom the religious dimension seemed to the observer fervent or obtrusive beyond the expectations of society. The novelists did not generally differentiate minutely among the various Christian groups, though there are many characters whose religious affiliation is precisely stated. The Methodists had divided, and there was a considerable difference socially and in doctrine between the respectable Wesleyans and the more enthusiastic Primitives. The most developed Methodist character in Victorian fiction is Eliot's Dinah Morris in *Adam Bede*, drawn from a period earlier than that of writing and considered simply as plain 'Methodist'. Dinah's diction has been criticised as unrealistic.[4] Comparison with the known speech of Methodists, such as George Eliot's aunt Mrs Evans, shows her to be broadly Evangelical rather than specifically Methodist. Dinah speaks with simplicity and sincerity far removed from the unction of Chadband, and without those features which cultivated Evangelicals like Foster found distasteful. Yet she has something of the Evangelical style, including the direct apostrophe of 'friends' and the use of rhetorical questions:

> Ah! dear friends, we are in sad want of good news about God; and what does other good news signify if we haven't that? For everything else comes to an end, and when we die we leave it all. But God lasts when everything else is gone. What shall we do if he is not our friend? (2)

This is the tone of public preaching; in personal exhortation, Dinah has fewer Evangelical features and her lexis is drawn from her present encounter rather than from convention:

> Hetty, you are shutting up your soul against him by trying to hide the truth. God's love and mercy can overcome all things – our ignorance and weakness, and all the burden of our past wickedness – all things but the wilful sin; sin that we cling to and will not give up. (45)

A less sympathetic account of Methodist diction is given by Eliot's Mr Brooke, who has sat as a magistrate when a Methodist preacher was accused of poaching. The social contempt for nonconformity is as strong as the dislike of its idiom, when he recalls 'Flavell in his shabby black gaiters, pleading that he thought the Lord had sent him and his wife a good dinner, and he had a right to knock it down, though not a mighty hunter before the Lord, as Nimrod was' (*Middlemarch* 39). Kingsley's Tregarva is a Wesleyan Methodist, whose speech again is Evangelical rather than specifically denominational, liberally sprinkled with texts and sincere in its simplicity:

> I believe, sir, that the judge of all the earth will do right – and what's right can't be wrong, nor cruel either, else it would not be like him who loved us to the death. That's all I know; and that's enough for me. To whom little is given, of him is little required. He that didn't know his master's will, will be beaten with few stripes, and he that did know it, as I do, will be beaten with many, if he neglects it – and that latter, not the former, is my concern.
>
> (*Yeast* 8)

The accuracy of such dialogue is supported by Dean Hole's sympathetic recollection of a Methodist explaining why he had ceased to attend the parish church.

> We wanted to feel our hearts glow within us, like the two disciples with whom he went to Emmaus on the Resurrection Day, and spoke to them of the things belonging to their peace. We have found that which we sought and we know that which we prayed that we might know.
>
> (Hole 1901, 296f)

W.H. White, brought up as an Independent and intended for the ministry, moved in a more urban and narrower dissenting circle. His fiction is notably lacking in direct speech but his reported diction catches the characteristic use of exaggerated biblical language out of context which Foster disliked. Thus a lay preacher 'never prayed without telling all of us that there was no health in him, and that his soul was a mass of putrefying sores' (*Autobiography of Mark Rutherford* 1881, 1). A fellow-student at the theological college would 'describe for twenty minutes, in a kind of watery rhetoric, the passage of the soul to bliss through death, and its meeting in the next world with those who had gone before' (2). In direct conversation, he suggests the affected gentility rather than the doctrinal position of the denomination, as when objection is taken to reading aloud from *The Vicar of Wakefield*, ' "Because, you know, Mr. Rutherford," he said with his smirk, "the company is mixed; there are young leedies present, and *perhaps*, Mr. Rutherford, a book with a more requisite tone might be more suitable on such an occasion" ' (3); this is the speech of Podsnap rather than Chadband.

The Quakers, for long considered the most extreme and most often persecuted example of 'peculiarity', had by this time won social respect and had changed many of their distinctive speech habits. Trollope is very unsympathetic to the traditional diction, describing an old Quaker as ' "thee-ing" and "thou-ing" all those whom he addressed', but who permitted his daughter to use normal speech, so that she 'escaped that touch of hypocrisy which seems to permeate the now antiquated speech of Quakers' (*Marion Fay* 15).

The Plymouth Brethren, founded in 1830 by an Irish clergyman, J.N. Darby, were similar to the Quakers in eschewing any kind of ordained ministry, but were more sacramental and specifically Evangelical in their worship. They were strict against any activities that could be considered 'worldly' and tended to keep company only with their own circle. *Esther Waters* is brought up among them and George Moore gives their distinctive language to the elders who rebuke her father for his trade in second-hand goods: 'Of course, this is between you and the Lord, but these things' (pointing to the old glass and jewellery) 'often are but snares for the feet, and lead weaker brethren into temptation. Of course, it is between you and the Lord' (3). Esther's employer Mrs Barfield is a member of the sect and her more educated speech is indistinguishable from general Evangelical discourse: 'Say no more, Esther. I hope the Lord may give you strength to bear your cross. Now go and pack up your box. But, Esther, do you feel your sin? Can you truly say honestly before God that you repent?' (12). A man of the lower middle class is more fervent and more precise in his judgement: 'Those who transgress the moral law may not kneel at the table for a time, until they have repented; but those who believe in the sacrifice of the Cross are acquitted, and I believe you do that' (23). His old mother is equally gentle and calls the Bible to her aid: 'You were led into sin, but you've repented. We was all born into temptation, and we must trust to the Lord to lead us out lest we should dash our foot against a stone' (24). Esther herself, with no formal education, knows the tenets of her faith when infant baptism is mentioned:

'Baptise them?' Esther repeated. 'That's not the way with the Lord's people;' and to escape from a too-overpowering reality she continued to repeat the half-forgotten patter of the Brethren. 'You must wait until it is a symbol of living faith in the Lord!' (19)

Of the new sects, the most successful for a time were the Irvingites, followers of the Scottish minister Edward Irving who believed that he was charged with founding the Catholic Apostolic Church in preparation for an imminent Parousia. His chapel in London attracted many adherents. When Newman brings one of this sect to try to convert Reding in *Loss and Gain*, the speech is characterised by its content, explaining the odd hierarchy, rather than the style:

We follow wherever the Spirit leads us; we have given up Tongue. But I ought to introduce you to my friend, who is more than an Angel . . . who has more than the tongue of men and angels, being nothing short of an Apostle, sir.   (Part 3, 7)

The Church of England formed the largest denomination and its members naturally figure most frequently in fiction. Apart from the treatment of Evangelicals, Anglican clergy do not generally show distinct forms of speech outside the pulpit. Trollope's novels abound in clergymen, but there is little specific in their language except a high incidence of lexical items connected with their calling. They show a certain formal dignity, shared with others of their class and professional standing rather than peculiar to their profession. The same is true of Eliot's Casaubon, who speaks pedantically rather than clerically on everyday matters. Dickens gives a cathedral Dean an idiolect which reads like the parody of a stage clergyman, with liturgical phraseology, bumbling repetition, moral exhortation and the continuance of the elevated style into mundane affairs: 'I hope Mr. Jasper's heart may not be too much set upon his nephew. Our affections, however laudable, in this transitory world, should never master us; we should guide them, guide them. I find I am not disagreeably reminded of my dinner, by hearing the dinner-bell' (*Edwin Drood* 1870, 2). This is veritable Dickens rather than realism; it reads like a collection of spoken features, any of which might have been heard from a clergyman but which were unlikely to be united in a short speech.

While the Evangelical clergy of all denominations were often satirised in the earlier period, it was the heirs of the Tractarians, known as Anglo-Catholics by themselves and as Ritualists by their opponents, who were most criticised after the middle of the century. One of their critics, after animadverting on the distinctive dress of Anglo-Catholic priests, continues:

> Who does not know that the wearer of this costume will talk of 'the Holy Altar' and 'the Blessed Virgin', of 'Saint Ignatius Loyola', and 'Saint Alphonso de Liguori' . . . Who has not heard him intoning the prayers, and preaching in his surplice on the 'holy obedience' due from laity to priesthood?[5]

The objection was to the referents of the words rather than to the language itself, the implications of high sacerdotalism and leanings to Rome, abhorred of true Englishmen. In a sympathetic portrait of a clergyman of the new school George Eliot incorporates some of these features into his speech. Dr Kenn is advising Maggie after the disgrace of her escapade with Stephen Guest:

> Your prompting to go to your nearest friends – to remain where all the ties of your life have been formed – is a true prompting, to which the Church in its original constitution and discipline responds – opening its arms to the penitent – watching over its children to the last – never abandoning them until they are hopelessly reprobate. And the Church ought to represent the feeling of the community, so that every parish should be a family knit together by Christian brotherhood under a spiritual father.   (*The Mill on the Floss* Book 7, 2)

Much of this could have come from an Evangelical – 'opening its arms to the penitent', 'the hopelessly reprobate'. The difference lies in the insistence on the power of the Church and the 'spiritual father'. Butler treats his High Church curate Pryer similarly, but with less sympathy, and it is what he says rather than how he says it that is parodied:

> You know, my dear Pontifex, it is all very well to quarrel with Rome, but Rome has reduced the treatment of the human soul to a science, while our own Church, though so much purer in many respects, has no organised system either of diagnosis or of pathology – I mean, of course, spiritual diagnosis and spiritual pathology . . . we are spiritually mere horse doctors as compared with the Roman priesthood, nor can we hope to make much headway against the sin and misery that surround us, till we return in some respects to the practice of our forefathers and of the greater part of Christendom.   (*The Way of All Flesh* 52)

Newman makes an Anglican priest object to Reding saying that 'God calls me' – 'God *calls* you! what does that mean? I don't like it; it's dissenting language', and he is not mollified by the reply, 'You know it is Scripture language' (*Loss and Gain* Part 3, 5). Shorthouse creates a Puseyite curate, Damerle, who comes to a bad end; his diction is distinguished for its fervour rather than its specific idiom: 'they give us the cold shoulder, then they call us Enthusiasts, Socialists, Romanists, Ultramontanes. Therefore we turn to the poor. The Lord was poor' (*Blanche, Lady Falaise* 4).

Earnest lay followers of the Oxford Movement acquired some features of the clerical style. A scrupulous girl like Charlotte Yonge's Emma Brandon can rival any Evangelical in scriptural echo – 'you ought to abstain from all appearance of evil' – but a few speeches later she voices in Anglo-Catholic phrase her guilt about inheriting the land of a former priory – 'Think, think if I should die in the guilt of sacrilege' (*Heartsease* 1854, 14) Kingsley, who took a very different view of Tractarian influence, is satirical rather than approving in the speech of Argemone Lavington when she censures Lancelot Smith for his Wordsworthian statement 'might not that very admiration of nature have been an act of worship?' ' "Ah", sighed the lady, "why trust to these self-willed methods, and neglect the noble and exquisite forms which the Church has prepared for us as embodiments for every feeling of our hearts? . . . Oh, that you would but try the Church system!" ' (*Yeast* 3). Constance, the narrator of *Sir Percival*, is shocked by Percival's casual reference to the Holy Grail as 'the cup of the Sacrament or something of that sort', and corrects him with, 'It was the Holy Vessel of the Sacrament, that was used by our blessed Lord Himself' (3). Even those who turn away from Anglo-Catholic worship retain the precision of its language, as Yonge's Angela says, 'It is the whole principle of auricular confession, to which nothing shall ever bring me back' (*The Pillars of the House* 1873, 43).

Roman Catholic priests have few roles in Victorian fiction, and those mostly minor. They were still little known to the majority of people, and regarded with traditional distrust which was extended to the Ritualists. The priest whom Lucy Snowe meets is of course a foreigner, but his speech as rendered in English suggests an extrapolation of words read or reported rather than heard:

I, daughter, am Père Silas; that unworthy son of Holy Church whom you once honoured with a noble and touching confidence, showing me the core of a heart and the inner shrine of a mind whereof, in solemn truth, I coveted the direction in behalf of the only true faith . . . Passed under the discipline of Rome, moulded by her high training, inoculated with her salutary doctrines, inspired by the zeal she alone gives – I realise what might be your spiritual rank, your practical value; and I envy Heresy her prey.   (*Villette* 34)

Kingsley is not a great deal more convincing when he sends Lancelot to see a priest, 'a certain remarkable man' who receives him 'with the most winning courtesy and sweetness' and is probably based on reports of Newman after his secession; the quarrel which led to the *Apologia* was still some years ahead:

'You may make what efforts you will for his re-conversion. The Catholic Church', continued he, with one of his arch, deep-meaning smiles, 'is not, like popular Protestantism, driven into shrieking terror at the approach of a foe. She has too much faith in herself, and in Him who gives to her the power of truth, to expect every gay meadow to allure away the lambs from her fold.'   (*Yeast* 14)

This, with its bold statement of confidence in possession of the truth and its commonplace religious metaphor, has little sense of actuality and suggests a character put up to make a point for the author, through his hero, to confute. Kingsley's brother Henry has several Roman Catholic priests in *Ravenshoe*, who have few specific speech features except the occasional greeting *Benedicite* or such improbable remarks as, 'your mother is wearing out the stones of the oratory with her knees, praying for her first-born' (1). Father Mackworth, cast as a villain, is made to speak as a stage impression of a sinister Jesuit rather than a credible priest: 'As for you, you poor little moth, when the time comes I will crush you with my thumb against the wall' (16). Lay Catholics in the same novel reveal themselves only by sometimes exclaiming, 'Holy Mother of God' or, 'the Virgin be praised'. The presentation of Roman Catholics in general suggests a literary tradition passed from one writer to another rather than personal acquaintance. It is in contrast to the richness of Evangelical diction, based on speech that no Victorian could go far without hearing.

The line between specifically 'religious' speech, whether in public or private discourse, and ordinary serious conversation is not always easily drawn. The Victorians certainly spoke of their faith and discussed its problems far more readily than their descendants. It is reasonable to make a pious character like Guy Morville say after escape from a storm, 'It was most merciful. That little boat felt like a toy at the will of the winds and waves, till one recollected who held the storm in His hand' (*The Heir of Redclyffe* 23).

Human responses were varied then as now and much depends on the circle in which the author chooses to place his characters. Trollope was no doubt right in suggesting that even in clerical families the pious voice might sometimes be put down. When Vesey Stanhope asserts that 'as sure as God rules in heaven' he will not maintain his son any longer, 'Oh, ruling in heaven!' said Charlotte. 'It is no use talking about that. You must rule him here on earth; and the question is, how you can do it' (*Barchester Towers* 45).

Notes

1. John Foster, *Essays in a Series of Letters to a Friend*; first published in 1805 but frequently reprinted, and revised by Foster down to 1830. All quotations and page references from the 17th edition: Bohn, London, 1843.

2. It was widely supposed that Cartwright was based on Cunningham, the vicar of Harrow, where the Trollope family had lived. Mrs Trollope specifically denied this in a letter to her eldest son (Glendinning 1992, 77).

3. G.W.E. Russell (1902), 241. I have been told orally of a story handed down in a family where on a similar occasion a servant ventured to use the master's Christian name in the petition, 'O Lord, bless 'Erbert, and keep him 'umble'.

4. 'Doubtless the idiom is a faithful record of the speech of [Eliot's] Aunt Samuel and other Methodists, but it none the less a self-conscious and irritating mode of speech' (Bennett 1948, 108). However, the authenticity of Dinah's speech as a Methodist is questioned by Watson (1971).

5. W.J. Conybeare, 'Church Parties', *Edinburgh Review* **98**, 1853, 315; reprinted in his *Essays Ecclesiastical and Social* 1856. Conybeare attacked the Anglo-Catholics in his novel *Perversion* 1856.

CHAPTER 6
Oaths and euphemisms

The claim of the Victorian novelists to reproduce true life in their pages was not honoured in every respect. The reticence of the period about sexual and other bodily matters has come to be regarded as the essence of all that is 'Victorian' in a pejorative sense. Any lingering belief that the Victorians were unaware or unconcerned about sexuality has been dispelled by the work of researchers like Marcus (1969), Pearsall (1969), Gay (1984, 1986) and Federico (1991). Nevertheless, there were taboo areas for public discourse, and the words referring to them, or even to clothing and other articles associated with them, were regarded as unsuitable for speech or print. Yet it was an era when illicit sexuality flourished, when pornography was readily available to the initiated, and when entertainments in the poorer areas of the cities were frequently scurrilous and obscene. If men were reticent before women and children, they often talked more freely among themselves and used words which they would have been loudly shocked to meet in a novel or a newspaper.

The tension is often taken as evidence of Victorian hypocrisy. The historian of the period does not make it a ground for judgement, but rather for investigation and record, perhaps wisely reflecting that no age is free from tensions and hangups and that neither individuals nor societies are ever wholly consistent. Literary critics may indeed regard the reticence forced upon authors as partially an artistic benefit and a source of imagery and stylistic subtlety. In terms of literary dialogue, we have to engage with an artificial code, generally approved and accepted by contemporary readers, which reflects the canon of public morality and depends on a shared agreement about what underlies it.

Control grows more rigid as the reign moves from the freedom inherited from the Regency, though the early years of the nineteenth century saw the beginning of the change.

There were signs at the end of the eighteenth century that people were becoming slightly prudish in their choice of language. This tendency increased as other forms of social conservatism flourished. There was probably no single reason for the development of various verbal taboos, though the middle-class emphasis upon rather artificial rules of propriety had more to do with it, perhaps, than the religious revival or the reaction to the French Revolution.   (Quinlan 1941, 231)

Restraint was probably most strict in the 1860s, relaxing slightly over the last fifteen years of the century; 'Podsnappery in all its fullness is a phenomenon of the sixties, and is probably related to the rise of the shilling magazines which expanded the family reading of fiction still further' (Tillotson 1954, 55). In 1841 Dickens defended himself in a preface to the third edition of *Oliver Twist* by reminding his readers that 'some of the characters in these pages are chosen from the most criminal and degraded of London's population; that Sikes is a thief, and Fagin a receiver of stolen goods; that the boys are pickpockets and the girl is a prostitute'. In the preface to the 1867 edition, the last phrase was omitted.

Swearing

Oaths and blasphemy in conversation were a problem for the novelists. Their full graphological realisation was frowned on and printers who set work for the pornographic underground press ran the risk of prosecution, a risk incurred also by printers of more serious literature until well into the twentieth century. The novelists made the best they could of this imposed restraint and circumvented the prejudice against 'strong language'. Those readers who could penetrate the fairly transparent code would understand the relevance of what was said to character and situation, without damage to their professed abhorrence; the others might be supposed to remain unenlightened and unshocked. It was in fact a benevolent conspiracy to share the representation of 'token speech', usefully defined as 'the use of conventional and generally accepted substitutes for items in dialogue which would, in their "straight" form, be regarded as unacceptable at a given time' (Page 1973, 105).

The oaths thus represented were usually of the milder sort; 'damn', 'hell' and 'devil' are the only ones allowed for most of the century, and may often be taken to stand for stronger words. Readers whose personal speech was not confined to these items would be able silently

to make the probable adjustment. How 'strong' was the language of
the ordinary person in uninhibited company? Greenwood gives a
sample of young people's conversation overheard at the rather
disreputable 'Johnson's Retreat' in Hornsey, north London. The
youths were:

> Handing about the brown jug, and ejaculating 'Damn', and 'So help
> me' this, and 'Strike me' t'other, with an earnestness and frequency
> calculated to impress the two young ladies that though young they are
> lads of mettle and knowing cards, up to the snuff of every degree of
> strength and variety of flavour and possessing a knowledge of the time
> of day to the fraction of a tick.   (Greenwood 1881, 139)

This is the kind of record which tantalises and frustrates the
researcher into Victorian speech. Did the lads confine themselves to
such mild expressions in deference to mixed company, or did
Greenwood bowdlerise in deference to a mixed readership? What
exactly is concealed behind 'this' and 't'other'? It may be assumed that
factual observers and writers of fiction shared the same code, the one
to convey as much as they dared of heard conversation and the others
to create an acceptable approximation to what would fit the
characters they conceived. Munby, writing for his own eyes only,
seems credible when, in 1872, he records how he 'made a
demonstration of disgust' to a man who had indecently 'chaffed' some
waitresses and who left the restaurant 'with an audible "Damn" '
(Hudson 1972, 308).

The novelists represent spoken oaths in various ways. The code
which they shared with their readers was not tidily consistent and the
same writer will use different forms of evasion within the same novel.
The milder oaths are quite often printed in full throughout the period.
'Damn' seems to have been a favourite among men of all classes and
not to have greatly offended readers. 'Damn that 'ere bag' says the
coach guard when it is delayed (Oliver Twist 48) and Sir Mulberry
Hawk in his illness exclaims 'Damn!' (Nicholas Nickleby 38). It is
common currency at Wuthering Heights, used by the boy Hareton
(11), and by Hindley (8), who also swears 'Damn the hellish villain!'
(17). It flourishes at every level of Middlemarch society, used by
Hawley the town clerk (18) and by Mr Vincy (36). Hawley, 'whose
bad language was notorious in that part of the county', also says 'a
devilish deal better than too much' (18) and Lydgate wishes that his

cousins 'may go to the devil' (45). Jude tells Sue that he is 'Glad I had
nothing to do with Divinity – damn glad' (Part 6, 3) and admits to
Arabella that he feels 'damn bad' (ibid. 7). Stronger words are seldom
used in full; George Moore reflects a slightly greater freedom in the
1890s by making a drunken man shout, 'You'll bring in no bloody
policeman' and another say, 'papers all so much bloody rot' (*Esther
Waters* 34, 37).

More often, the offending word is indicated by its initial letter and
a dash, but there seems no reason for one choice above another. The
guard in *Oliver Twist* and Mulberry Hawk are given their oaths in full,
but in the same novels respectively the widowed man, to whose house
Oliver goes with Sowerberry, says 'D—n you, keep back' (5) and
Walter Bray exclaims 'D— n you' (46). Disraeli gives 'D— him' to Sir
Vavasour Firebrace (*Sybil* Book 2, 3). In *Pendennis* Garbett says 'D— if
I carry challenges' (12). Strong has 'd— him, serve him right too, –
the d– impudent foreign scoundrel' (27) and Francis Clavering
describes himself as 'the d—est miserable dog in all England' (60). 'If
only I knew who the b— was' says William, wondering who has
informed on him for illegal betting (*Esther Waters* 40). Jude declares
he would 'marry the W— of Babylon rather than do anything
dishonourable' (*Jude the Obscure* Part 6, 7), unexpected coyness for a
biblical phrase in a novel castigated for its crudity. Sometimes the
unadorned dash leaves what is said entirely to the reader's
imagination. 'I wish you were at the –' screams Heathcliff (3), whom
young Hareton reports to have said that 'the curate should have
his—teeth dashed down his—throat, if he stepped over the threshold'
(11). Collins mocks the reticence forced on novelists when he makes
Drusilla Clack report the angry exclamation of the lawyer Bruff: 'Miss
Jane Anne Stamper be —!' 'It is impossible for me to write the awful
word which is here represented by a blank' (*The Moonstone* Second
Period, 1).

The author may refuse to be committed to anything and merely
make reference to swearing; the innocent reader is not offended and
the sophisticated can fully indulge his (or possibly her) knowledge of
profane speech. Just before the guard says 'damn', Sikes 'with a
hideous imprecation overthrew the table' (48). More flippantly in the
same novel, the dash is reinforced by comment which helps to
establish the speech habits of the character. Fang the Bow Street
magistrate says, 'If you stand there, refusing to give evidence, I'll
punish you for disrespect to the bench; I will by —'. Dickens adds:

By what or by whom, nobody knows, for the clerk and jailer coughed
very loud, just at the right moment; and the former dropped a heavy
book upon the floor, this preventing the word from being heard –
accidentally, of course. (11)

Mulberry Hawk presumably goes further than the words already
quoted when he 'confirmed the muttered threat with a tremendous
oath' (38). Mary Barton is exposed to vigorous male language in her
pursuit of Jem's ship; the boatmen shout her message 'interlarding it
with sailor's oaths' and when the captain replies, 'alas they heard his
words. He swore a dreadful oath; he called Mary a disgraceful name'
(28). Charlotte Yonge even more primly records how Charles
Edmonstone is abashed by the presence of Guy:

> 'I only know if I was not condemned to this – this life' (had it not been
> for a sort of involuntary respect to the gentle compassion of the
> softened hazel eyes regarding him so kindly, he would have used the
> violent expletive that trembled on his lip). (*The Heir of Redclyffe* 6)

In another high-minded novel Shorthouse makes a nobleman check
himself in time when reporting another's words in the presence of
women, 'I am in luck, he is a – something – good fellow' (*Sir Percival*
11). Another nobleman, Lord Jocelyn, is evasive when he warns
Harry Goslett about the consequences of taking up an artisan's
position: 'You will find yourself in a workshop full of disagreeable
people, who pick out unpleasant adjectives to tack them on to
everything' (Besant, *All Sorts and Conditions of Men* 1882, 17). Henry
Kingsley's well-born Densil Ravenshoe is reticent, perhaps constrained
by the presence of a priest, when he says of a supposed witch, 'She
must have made such a deuced hard bargain that I shouldn't like to
cheat her out of any of the small space left her between this and –
thingammy' (*Ravenshoe* 13). Even a publisher, lower in social esteem,
remembers his manners: ' "Your historical novel, Lady Carbury, isn't
worth a—", Mr Loiter stopping himself suddenly and remembering
that he was addressing himself to a lady, satisfied his energy at last by
the word "straw" ' (*The Way We Live Now* 1875, 89).

Trollope is equally coy about how Archdeacon Grantly actually
spoke of Mrs Proudie. 'The archdeacon hereupon forgot himself. I will
not follow his example, nor shock my readers by transcribing the term
in which he expressed his feeling as to the lady who had been named'
(*Barchester Towers* 6). Hindley 'entered vociferating oaths dreadful to

hear' and at another time says to Nellie Dean 'you — , Addressing me by some elegant term that I don't care to repeat' (9, 17). Kingsley, ever robust, finds humour in the language of Squire Lavington who, when his carriage had an accident, 'thrust his head out of the window, and discharged a broadside of at least ten pounds' worth of oaths (Bow Street valuation) at the servants', and who later abuses Tregarva and 'rounded off his oration by a torrent of oaths' (Yeast 7, 11).[1] Imagination can reinforce the social comment of the experience of Esther Waters and her companion at Epsom races: 'a young aristocrat cursed them from the box-seat' (33). Dickens gives a coy evasion to the narrator of 'the Baron of Grogzwig': 'cursing the other all round [he] bade them go to – but never mind where. I don't know the German for it, or I would put it delicately that way' (Nicholas Nickleby 6). Ginevra Fanshawe feels the same about foreign languages: 'I . . . send lessons au diable (one daren't say that in English, you know, but it sounds quite right in French)' (Villette 6). Alford deplores such evasions:

> Persons whose reverence for the Deity is properly shown in their English conversation by a becoming unwillingness to make a light use of His holy name, have no hesitation in exclaiming Mon Dieu! in frivolous conversation. The English name for the Father of Evil is not considered to be a very respectable noun, but its French synonym is to be heard 'in the best society'.   (Alford 1864, 251)

A reviewer, possibly G.H. Lewes, defends Dickens for the propriety of his dialogue and deplores the 'affected, mincing girls . . . who utter all their indelicate words in French [and] say they cannot read "Boz", he is so low!' (National Magazine and Monthly Critic December 1837). Once again the remarks of characters in fiction are borne out by other evidence. A French resident in England notes that 'Englishwomen, who are much more easily shocked by the name of a thing than by the thing itself, have been very happy in avoiding the English names of certain more or less unmentionable parts of their dress' (O'Rell 153f).

The evidence of both novelists and observers is clear. Men swore a good deal but their language was not socially acceptable. The novelists, caught between the desire for realism and the need not to upset their readers or the circulating libraries, protected themselves by various devices without attempting consistency. Trollope uses 'd—d 'odd' and 'D— it' in the same novel, with no apparent reason for the different transcriptions (*The Prime Minister* 1, 43). On a single page, Thackeray uses the abbreviated oath, the plain dash and the paraphrase for the same speaker. Lord Steyne, in two successive speeches, has 'Why, d— it , Wenham, he's your age . . . Wenham, you affect me', said the great man, with one of his usual oaths. 'By — you do' (*Pendennis* 14).

The last phrase presumably conceals the word 'God', which is treated with the same caution and inconsistency as profane oaths. Catherine Linton exclaims, 'My God!' (*Wuthering Heights* 11) and Hindley swears, 'I've formed my resolution, and by God I'll execute it!' (16). Mary Barton cries, 'Oh God!' when Job is unwilling to prove Jem's innocence (22). Stephen Guest says in anger, 'Good God! . . . what a miserable thing a woman's love is to a man!' (*The Mill on the Floss* 14). In *Middlemarch* the lawyer Standish calls Dorothea 'an uncommonly fine woman, by God!'; Will Ladislaw says, 'Good God! what do you mean?' (10, 59). Forster records as a matter of fact how Macready cried out 'My God! there's Wainwright' when he saw the notorious poisoner in Newgate (Forster 1874, I, 160). Sir Mulberry Hawk, loaded with many oaths, is represented as saying 'by G—' (50). Jem urges young Carson to tell him the truth about his relations with Mary 'and, by G—, I will know' (*Mary Barton* 15).

In all this there is a tacit collusion between author and reader which extended to reports of speech which were, or claimed to be, factual. Here again, as in transcriptions of dialect and deviant speech, we meet a convention shared by imaginative and referenial writers within the public expectation. Kirwan tells us that a man disturbed in a cheap lodging-house asks indignantly, 'Who the d—l send you at this time o' night?' and that a vagrant shouts 'Will you shut up, d—n you?' (Kirwan 1870, 27, 69). Greenwood is less explicit and thus suggestive of worse language when a prostitute is recorded as saying to a sailor who offers to give her his jacket to sell, 'I'd sell your — life if I had the chance'. A man who takes a cab when Greenwood is riding with the driver asks 'What the — does that fellow want on the box with you?' (Greenwood 1881, 8, 110). Dickens tells of himself in Italy replying to a man who said he could not understand what was said, 'Yes I do, d— you!' (Forster 1874, II, 158).

Concealed oaths

The evidence for the use of predictable expletives by men of all
classes is clear enough, but some other questions remain. It was
accepted that strong language was not to be used in mixed company,
but did women in fact use such words themselves? There is no doubt
that among the criminal and most depressed classes the language of
both sexes was lurid; the episode recorded by Kirwan quoted above is
an example. But how far up through the social layers did the freedom
extend? The novelists seldom allow such words on the lips of women,
and they probably reflect reality as well as honouring convention. In
Agnes Grey the hoydenish Matilda Murray at the age of fourteen 'from
her father's example had learned to swear like a trooper'. She shouts,
No, damn it, no! . . . you'll be such a damned long time over it' and
her language is considered by her governess to be a 'shocking habit'
(9). Matilda is a rare case, but 'Dammy', variously spelled, seems to
have been a form which women sometimes favoured. Arabella says to
Jude, 'Dammy, one would think you were a young bachelor, with
nobody to look after but yourself!' (Part 5, 6). It was not solely female;
the frequently profane Sikes mutters, 'Damme, I'll risk it' (48),
Clavering exclaims 'dammy' and Major Pendennis 'daymy' (*Pendennis*
5, 56).

It is difficult to tell whether the use of 'minced oaths' reflects
actual usage or is another concession to the bowdlerising convention.
Evasion of the offensive word by a vowel change or other distortion is
shown in literary dialogue from the sixteenth century, notably in
Restoration drama. It reflects a prevailing human tendency to
euphemism, which allowed the novelists to avoid writing taboo words
without departing from realism. Instead of Ginevra Fanshawe's
evasion in French, 'devil' is often changed into 'deuce'. 'Please the
deuce!' exclaims Mr Vincy, and Caleb Garth's 'Deuce take the bill' is
said to have 'comprised his whole store of maledictory expression'
(*Middlemarch* 36, 24). In the real world of London, Ritchie hears 'a
few clerks and warehousemen' at the music hall say that one of the
performers is 'a doosed fine gal' (Ritchie 1869, 231), an affected
pronunciation that is echoed by Clavering's 'why can't Lady C live
abroad, or at Tunbridge, or at the doose?' (*Pendennis* 62), and also by
the vulgar Sexty Parker, 'Now I call Dovercourt a dooced nice little
place' (*The Prime Minister* 46). A farm labourer is unexpectedly
temperate in his language, calling his loss of employment 'a darn'd

bad case' and later exclaiming, 'Dash'd if I can help it, sir!' (*The Ordeal of Richard Feverel* 3, 26). The initial favoured by novelists and others in print is sometimes spoken. 'I'll be dee'd if I'll leather my boy to please you' says Dagley to Brooke (*Middlemarch* 39). A robust man like Henchard could take exception to such modesty; Victorian euphemism subverts itself when Stubberd relates his arrest of the furmity woman:

> 'Says she, "Dost hear, old turmit-head? Put away that dee lantern. I have floored fellows a dee sight finer-looking than a dee fool like thee, you son of a bee, dee me if I haint," she says.' . . .
> Henchard broke out impatiently, 'Come – we don't want to hear any more of them cust dees and bees! Say the words out like a man, and don't be so modest, Stubberd; or else leave it alone!'
>
> (*The Mayor of Casterbridge* 28)

It will be recalled that Captain Corcoran in *HMS Pinafore* 'Never swears a big, big D . . . well, hardly ever'. 'If I was yer sister I'd see yer further before I'd give yer my money' is a female comment on an overheard plea (*Esther Waters* 17); to see someone further is a common euphemism for 'go to hell'. A more delicate habit is shown by Meredith's farm girl who on a surprise meeting 'invoked her Good Gracious, the generic maid's familiar' (*The Ordeal of Richard Feverel* 21).

'God' is often spoken with a change of vowel.[2] 'By Gad!' is the exclamation of Francis Claverton (*Pendennis* 5), and plain 'Gad!' of Sir Hugo (*Daniel Deronda* 1876, 35). Mr Slum, who affects a military style, says, 'By Gad, it's quite Minervian!' when he admires Mrs Jarley's waxworks (*The Old Curiosity Shop* 28). A more genuine military man, Major Pendennis, also favours 'Good Ged' and 'by Ged' (7, 54). What was at first an upper-class survival declined into popular euphemism: Munby heard people in the street exclaiming 'Good Gad' when the end of the Abyssinian war was announced in 1868 (Hudson 1972, 252).

Women often use an indirect form of 'Lord'. Ellen exclaims, 'Lor'! Mister Ernest' when she hears of his prison sentence (*The Way of All Flesh* 71) and 'Lor', what a lot of people' is a girl's reaction to Epsom on Derby Day. Esther's sister greets her unexpected appearance with 'Lorks, ain't she grand?'. A nurse dressing a patient cries, 'Lord, what a job!' (*Esther Waters* 32, 13, 17). Mrs Roby says, 'Laws, Mr Wharton;

how uncivil you are!'. It is not a solely female choice; in the same novel the virtuous Arthur Fletcher says, 'Oh Lord! That's a blow' (*The Prime Minister* 32, 15). Forster tells of a charwomen exclaiming, 'Lawk, ma'am' when she finds herself cleaning in the house where Dickens's son is living (Forster 1874, II, 308). The innocent boy Ripton exclaims, 'Lord' in argument with his friend (*The Ordeal of Richard Feverel* 2).

Social attitudes to swearing

The strength of feeling in some quarters against swearing can be gauged from a passage of dialogue in *Eric or Little by Little* (1858) by the Evangelical F.W. Farrar. Here, as so often, minor fiction which is weak in structure and conception can tell us something about the attitudes of at least a section of contemporary readers. Eric is annoyed when a master does not acknowledge him:

> 'What a surly devil that is,' said Eric, when he had passed; 'did you see how he purposely cut me?'
> 'A surly . . . ? Oh, Eric that's the first time I ever heard you swear.'

Eric blushes and replies

> 'Pooh, Edwin, you don't call that swearing, do you? You're so strict, so religious, you know. I love you for it, but then, there are none like you. Nobody thinks anything of swearing here.'

When Edwin will not be drawn he persists:

> 'And after all, I didn't swear; I only called the fellow a surly devil.'
> 'Oh hush! Eric, hush!' said Russell sadly. 'You wouldn't have said so half a year ago.'

Silently, Eric realises that 'all his moral consciousness was fast vanishing, and leaving him a bad and reckless boy' (8). All of which, from other evidence, does not give a totally realistic picture of the Victorian public school but does remind us of how careful the serious novelists had to be and how much courage they sometimes showed.

Their cautious evasions did not always make the result acceptable. Throughout the period critics censured the use of improper language in fictional dialogue. The Brontë sisters came under attack more than once. A reviewer of *Wuthering Heights* observed that:

> It may be well to be sparing of certain oaths and phrases which do not materially contribute to any character and are by no means to be reckoned among the evidences of the writer's genius.
>
> (*Examiner* 8 January 1848)

The critic in the *Christian Remembrancer* (June 1849) discounted the possibility of female authorship, since 'throughout there is masculine power, breadth and shrewdness, combined with masculine hardness, coarseness, and freedom of expression'. Another reviewer deplored the presence in *Wuthering Heights* of 'low and brutal creatures, who wrangle with each other in language too disgusting for the eye or the ear to tolerate' (*North British Review* August 1849). A generally favourable review of *The Tenant of Wildfell Hall* regretted the 'profane expressions, inconceivably coarse language, and revolting scenes and descriptions' (*Sharpe's London Magazine* August 1848).

However, the tension between realism and restraint could be creative. When a character uses bad language and another objects to it, we sense a living situation, while the author has satisfied both realism and convention. Hareton is given moderate freedom of expression – his 'witch' may be taken as a euphemism for 'bitch' – and is then put down by Nelly to the satisfaction of genteel readers:

> 'I'll see thee damned before I be *thy* servant!' growled the lad.
> 'You'll see me *what?*' asked Catherine in surprise.
> 'Damned – thou saucy witch!' he replied
> 'There, Miss Cathy, you see you have got into pretty company', I interposed. 'Nice words to be used to a young lady!' (18)

Thackeray gets the credit of both evasion and comment when Pendennis has attacked Hobnell:

> 'The — coward insulted me, sir,' he said; and the Doctor passed over the oath, and respected the emotion of the honest suffering young heart. (15)

Trollope makes a whole social situation out of the accepted abbreviation when Lord Kingsbury gives his opinion of his chaplain in his wife's presence. The conventions of polite society and the novelist's wry comment on the code of restraint imposed on him are combined in one episode:

> 'D— Mr Greenwood!' said the Marquis. He certainly did say the word at full length, as far as it can be said to have length, and with all the emphasis of which it was capable. He certainly did say it, though when the circumstances were afterwards not infrequently thrown in his teeth, he would forget it and deny it. Her ladyship heard the word very plainly, and at once stalked out of the room, thereby showing that her feminine feelings had received a wrench which made it impossible for her any longer to endure the presence of a foul-mouthed monster.
>
> (*Marion Fay* 18)

Emily Wharton is less controlled when her husband says, 'you'd see me d—d before you would open your mouth for me to the old man', for 'he had never sworn at her before, and now she burst out into a flood of tears'. Later his 'I don't care a d—' 'absolutely quelled her . . . She had been altogether so unused to such language that she could not get on with her matter in hand, letting the word pass by her as an unmeaning expletive' (*The Prime Minister* 44, 47). Thus Trollope assures his male readership that swearing is not very serious, while honouring the outrage of his female ones. Perhaps most wives accepted the male habit; when Grandcourt says, 'I wondered how long you meant to stay in that damned place' the authorial comment is, 'one of the freedoms he had assumed as a husband being the use of his strongest epithets' (*Daniel Deronda* 35).

Swearing was not taboo only in mixed society. The parish clerk objects to 'damn', with a nice distinction of person and office. 'I am afraid I cannot allow bad words to be spoke in this sacred pile . . . As far as my personal self goes, I should have no objection to your cussing as much as you like, but as an official of the church my conscience won't allow it to be done' (*The Hand of Ethelberta* 45). Objectors could confuse profane swearing and blasphemy; when Charley Tudor exclaims, 'That's d— nonsense', he is rebuked, 'Oh! don't swear,' said M'Ruen – 'pray don't take God's name in vain. I don't like it.' The response is brief: 'I shall swear, and to some purpose too, if that's your game' (*The Three Clerks* 19). This sounds a convincing piece of dialogue. Kingsley was over-optimistic when he wrote in the preface to the 1851 edition of *Yeast*, 'one finds, more and more, swearing banished from the hunting-field, foul songs from the universities, drunkenness and gambling from the barracks'.

Sexual euphemisms

Discussion of any aspect of sexual activity raises the same questions. Does fictional dialogue reflect accurately the reticence of common speech or are the novelists compelled to tone down what would really be said in the kind of situation depicted? The answer, as for swearing, is probably that those from whom their readers were principally drawn spoke in the guarded terms given to fictional characters, that men were freer among themselves and that the poorest of both sexes were a great deal more frank. The reports of social observers show that sexual activity and its consequences could not be ignored by anyone who passed along a public thoroughfare. But the majority did not want open discussion of these things in print and the novelists accepted the constraint, with a degree of chafing which became more apparent as the century progressed.

In a sense it is true that 'the language, the diction, of Victorian fiction had no way of accommodating to itself the specialised and isolated diction of sex' (Marcus 1969, 234). Nevertheless, the novelists developed language which conveyed more than its surface meaning.

The reluctance of a lower middle-class family to speak openly of sexual matters is delightfully conveyed by Dickens in the discussion of whether little Morleena Kenwigs should go on the stage:

'Kenwigs is afraid', said Mrs K.

'What of?' inquired Miss Petowker, 'not of her failing?' 'Oh, no,' replied Mrs Kenwigs, 'but if she grew up what she is now – only think of the young dukes and marquises.'

'Very right,' said the collector.

'Still,' submitted Miss Petowker, 'if she has a proper pride in herself, you know —'

'There's a great deal in that,' observed Mrs Kenwigs, looking at her husband.

'I only know —' faltered Miss Petowker, – 'it may be no rule to be sure – but I have never found any inconvenience or unpleasantness of that sort.'   (*Nicholas Nickleby* 14)

'Inconvenience or unpleasantness' is a splendid euphemism for the trials which, in turn, Elizabeth Gaskell, Trollope, Moore and Hardy among others were to be censured for depicting. By the end of the century, Hardy could write of seduction and illegitimacy but his characters still speak obliquely about sex. Sue Bridehead confides in her cousin Jude: 'it is said that what a woman shrinks from – in the early days of her marriage – she shakes down to with comfortable indifference in half-a-dozen years' (Part 4, 2). Even when she has left her husband for Jude she can only hint at the physical: 'My liking for you is not as some women's perhaps. But it is a delight in being with you of a supremely delicate kind, and I don't want to go further and risk it by – an attempt to justify it.' She pleads, 'You do care for me very much, don't you, in spite of my not – you know?' (Part 4, 5). It may be said that Sue is an extreme case of sexual frigidity; but she is an 'emancipated' woman who speaks freely and explicitly about her scepticism and disregard for convention but is unable to articulate her physical fear. A male barrister is equally embarrassed about the consummation of marriage when he is asked whether a minor's wedding can be annulled:

> 'A-hm! well!' pursued Brandon. 'Perhaps if you could arrest and divide them before nightfall, and make affidavit of certain facts . . .'
> 'Yes?' the eager woman hastened his lagging mouth.
> 'Well . . . hm! a . . . in that case . . . a . . . Or if lunatic, you could prove him to have been of unsound mind.'
>
> (*The Ordeal of Richard Feverel* 33)

When the virtuous Fred Parsons is being nice to Esther Waters about her state as an unmarried mother, both of them avoid speaking directly of the sexual act:

> 'It may not be a woman's fault if she falls, but it is always a man's. He can always fly from temptation.'
> 'Yet there isn't a man who that can say he hasn't gone wrong.'
> 'No, not all, Esther.'
> Esther looked him full in the face.
> 'I understand what you mean, Esther, but I can honestly say that I never have.' (*Esther Waters* 23)

Esther is no more at ease with a sympathetic spinster employer to whom she begins her confession but breaks off with 'my story is not one that can be told to a lady such as you'. Miss Rice perhaps speaks for many contemporary readers when she answers, 'I think I am old enough to listen to your story' (22). This is not the view of a spinster to her younger sister who has heard about a wild young man 'many things; some that I don't think you ought to hear, Phoebe' (*Wives and Daughters* 40).

Even a mature man speaks obliquely about his son's preparation for life:

> 'Let him, then,' continued the baronet, 'see vice in its nakedness. While he has yet some innocence, nauseate him! Vice, taken little by little, usurps gradually the whole creature. My counsel to you, Thompson, would be, to drag him through the sinks of town.'
>
> (*The Ordeal of Richard Feverel* 17)

Sometimes the novelists make their tacit protest against restriction by the use of oblique and symbolic language. When Gradgrind is trying to persuade his daughter Louisa to marry Bounderby, their conversation anticipates the Freudian theory of the unconscious, lets the perceptive reader into the girl's fears and repugnance, and allows Dickens to make his point without offending against the taboo on explicit language:

> She sat so long looking silently towards the town, that he said, at length: 'Are you consulting the chimneys of the Coketown works, Louisa?'
>
> 'There seems to be nothing there but languid and monotonous smoke. Yet when the night comes, Fire bursts out, father!' she answered, turning quickly.
>
> 'Of course I know that, Louisa. I do not see the application of that remark.' To do him justice, he did not, at all. (*Hard Times* Book 1, 15)

In reality men could be a great deal more explicit in their addresses to women. 'Walter' records hearing a working man call to two girls, 'I should like to tickle up both of your legs a bit', receiving the reply, 'Tickle us up then'. By his own account he then accosts one of them and begins a series of adventures; after a few meetings he is saying to her, 'I'll give you a sovereign if you'll let me put my prick between your legs' (Marcus 1969, 141, 144). 'Walter' was an extreme, though surely not a unique case. Other men made their approaches more delicately, like the young man who followed Munby's Hannah calling, 'Oh you naughty girl' and 'Would you like a glass of ale?' (Hudson 1972, 337). Such catchphrases could well have been put into the mouth of a fictional character; the novelists avoided the overt coarseness which was often to be heard in the streets but did not depart totally from reality.

Sometimes indeed they resort to report and paraphrase, as when Nicholas Nickleby overhears Mulberry Hawk discussing Kate with other men:

> He heard his sister's sufferings derided, and her virtuous conduct jeered at and brutally misconstrued; he heard her name bandied from mouth to mouth, and herself made the subject of coarse and insolent wagers, free speech and licentious jesting. (31)

Words like 'coarse' and 'licentious' are employed also by social observers, equally unable to be explicit about what they have heard. Cheap public entertainments, from the lower type of music hall to the 'penny gaff' in a public house, were generally bawdy. Ritchie describes a 'Cave of Harmony' where a singer known in other circles as a respectable entertainer 'sang, with accompanying action, some dozen verses of doggerel, remarkable for obscenity and imbecility', and a music hall where 'some of the songs are outrageously obscene and indecent, meant to be so by the singer, and accepted as such by the occupants, male and female, of the crowded benches' (Ritchie 1869, 231, 235). A popular amusement was a 'Judge and Jury' when a mock trial was held with salacious 'evidence'. Greenwood saw one at the notorious 'Coal Hole' in the Strand with 'a disgusting wretch in woman's attire, and who was supposed to be a native of Germany, importing filthy blunders into his broken English' (Greenwood 1869, 104). 'Walter' recounts an evening at a public house in the London dock area where 'we asked the women to bet which of us had the biggest prick, and the girls felt us outside quite openly'. He adds the remarkable comment, 'There was, however, nothing likely to shock people there. Of lewd talk there was plenty, though no grave indecency was practised' and says that customers were turned out if they went too far. Marcus shrewdly relates this account to the Six Jolly Fellowship Porters in *Our Mutual Friend* (Marcus 1969, 107).[3] It also gives reality to the beer tent which Lancelot and Tregarva enter at a country fair, where the girls 'defend themselves from the coarse overtures of their swains' and where after a poaching song, 'one of the lowest flash London school – filth and all – was roared in chorus in the presence of the women'. Tregarva explains that the 'field-work' causes the country women to 'get accustomed from childhood to hear words whose very meanings they shouldn't know' (*Yeast* 13).

This is the truth which is implicit in the later *Tess of the D'Urbervilles*. 'Walter' brings a hard light of reality to the rape or seduction of Tess. After he has assaulted a field girl he presses a sovereign on her, promising 'I'll give you more another day; it will help to keep you a while – hold your tongue and no one will know' and the overseer backs him up – 'the squire won't harm you; I think you be in luck if he loikes you; – say you nought – that be my advice' (Marcus 1969, 138f). This is not far from Tess's mother:

> 'And yet th'st not got him to marry 'ee! . . . I did hope for something to come out o' this! See what he has give us – all, as we thought, because we were his kin. But if he's not, it must have been because of his love for 'ee. And yet you've not got him to marry!
>
> (*Tess of the D'Urbervilles* 12)

Other euphemisms

Pregnancy and childbirth were almost as taboo in speech as sexual intercourse. Two women discuss the matter indirectly, the only overt comment being that when the husband is told, 'thinks he – losin' breath – "I'm a father!" ' (*The Ordeal of Richard Feverel* 40). In the last decade of the century, George Moore shocked some readers by his description of a maternity hospital, although the dialogue runs mainly on such harmless lines as 'It is a boy; and he will be given to you when we get you out of the labour ward' and 'Hasn't she been confined yet?' (*Esther Waters* 16). Dickens uses Micawber's idiolect to satirise euphemism: 'The twins no longer derive their nourishment from Nature's founts – in short, they are weaned' (*David Copperfield* 17).

Euphemism could extend to absurd lengths, so much so that we sometimes wonder if the novelist is merely satirising social trends. Yet a comic evasion like that of Giles in *Oliver Twist* would not have possessed even satirical value unless the readers could recognise the possibility of something like it:

> I tossed off the clothes . . . got softly out of bed; drew on a pair of —'
> 'Ladies present, Mr Giles,' murmured the tinker.

'Of *shoes*, Sir,' turning upon him and laying great emphasis on the
word.   (*Oliver Twist* 28)

The genteel poor are almost as coy about drink and money as
about sex. 'There's a little – a little something else in it' says Mrs
Corney, offering Bumble a drink of 'peppermint' (*Oliver Twist* 26). A
respectable spinster rebukes her sister for saying 'drunkard' with, 'don't
let me hear such coarse words' (*Wives and Daughters* 40). Sexty
Parker's wife is indirect about his drinking habits: 'he comes home a
little flustered, and then takes more than his regular allowance' (*The
Prime Minister* 45). References to intoxication are examples of the
difference between language used to those of higher rank and to
equals or inferiors. An undergraduate with a hangover is told by his
college servant, 'you ain't used to being pleasant, sir' but one of his
friends explains that he was 'as drunk as a besom' and 'screwed'
('Cuthbert Bede', *The Adventures of Mr Verdant Green* 1857, 8). An
alcoholic woman is told by her sympathetic landlady that she wants
'something to pick you up', but a friend of her husband's mistakes her
for 'a drunken chorus lady' when she is drunk in the street (*A
Mummer's Wife* 1885, 24, 26). Mr Pickwick mistaken for a vagrant is
briefly described by Captain Boldwig, 'He's drunk; he's a drunken
plebeian' (19).
    Poverty also is not to be named by those clinging to respectability:
' "You see in what a painful position we are placed," continued the
euphemistic lady' (*New Grub Street* 20). Dorrit's evasions in asking for
money – 'some little Testimonial' – are given credibility by the
anonymous author of *The Habits of Good Society* (1859), just two years
after the last monthly number of *Little Dorrit*:

> The small genteel, you will observe, never speak of rich and poor, but
> of 'those of large and those of small means'. Another piece of flummery
> is the expression. 'If anything should happen to me', which everyone
> knows you mean for 'If I should die'.   (cit. Phillipps 1984, 53)

Euphemisms for death are associated with the twentieth rather than
the nineteenth century; some at least of the population were already
speaking evasively. ' "If anything did – go wrong, you know," said
Cynthia, using a euphuism (*sic*) for death, as most people do (it is an
ugly word to speak plain out in the midst of life)' (*Wives and Daughters*
37). Miss Flite, in an area where reticence outlived the Victorian age,
says of Krook, 'he is a little – you know – M—!' (*Bleak House* 5).

Prostitution

Prostitution was widespread in Victorian England. Estimates varied; for London alone, 'figures ranging anywhere from 6,000 to 80,000 and above were offered' (Marcus 1969). Social observers agree at least that no one could walk through parts of the cities of Britain without being aware of it. People knew that it existed but they did not know how to speak of it except by allusion and indirection. Prostitution was a fate always leering at the woman who became destitute. Arabella pleads with Jude:

> If you can't take me and help me, Jude, I must go to the workhouse or to something worse. Only just now two undergraduates winked at me as I came along. 'Tis hard for a woman to keep virtuous where there's so many young men! *(Jude the Obscure* Part 6, 6)

A prostitute was, in euphemistic terms, a woman who had gone 'on the streets'. A girl whose family is near to starvation will be good 'if I gets the chance' and then protests, 'I didn't mean that I was a-going on the streets right away this very evening, only that a girl left alone in London may go wrong, if luck's against her'. Another 'had to go out on the streets' in Belgium to keep her lover – 'He couldn't starve, could he?' (*Esther Waters* 17, 34). She could also be described as 'ruined' or, even more remotely, as 'gay', an adjective which had no homosexual connotation until much later.[4] Collins, however, uses its antonym to introduce two women 'members of the sad sisterhood' (*The Fallen Leaves* 1879, Book 6, 1). A girl asked for her occupation when seeking hospital treatment replies, 'I'm unfortunate, sir' (*New Grub Street* 27). The taboo extended to social observers; Greenwood heads his section on the subject 'Fallen Women', and uses the word 'prostitute' very sparingly in his text (Greenwood 1869).

When Carry Brattle is being cross-examined in a murder trial the euphemistic words which Trollope gives to the defending barrister ring true and accord with other evidence. After asking her if she has been 'indiscreet', he continues:

> It is my duty to prove to the jury on their [the accused] behalf that the life of this young woman has been such as to invalidate her testimony against them; – and that duty I shall do, fearless of the remarks of any one. Now I ask you again, Caroline, whether you are not one of the unfortunates? . . . Your silence tells me all that I wish the jury to know.
> (*The Vicar of Bullhampton* 1870, 69)

The significant point here, apart from the evasion of the word 'prostitute', is the agreement that such a woman's testimony will inevitably be unreliable. Even in the last decade of the century a novelist of the 'naturalist' school allows a male character to make the same assumption. Waymark 'was well acquainted with the characteristics of girls of this class; he knew how all but impossible it was for them to tell the truth, the whole truth, and nothing but the truth' (Gissing, *The Unclassed* 1884, 17). The common assumption which the novelists share is challenged by a social reformer. William Booth writes with compassion of the 'fallen woman': 'her word becomes unbelievable, her life an ignominy, and she is swept downward, ever downward, into the bottomless perdition of prostitution' (Booth 1890, 13).

The full-time prostitutes had competition from the 'dollymops', young working women who supplemented their low wages by occasional sex. They resented being regarded as prostitutes, and 'Walter' records a revealing conversation with one of them:

> 'How long have you been gay?' 'I ain't gay,' said she, astonished. 'Yes you are.' 'No I ain't.' 'You let men fuck you, don't you?' 'Yes, but I ain't gay.' 'What do you call gay?' 'Why the gals who come out regular of a night, dressed up, and gets their livings by it.'   (Marcus 1969, 106)

Prostitutes feature in Victorian fiction more often than the general reticence about sex might lead us to expect, a fact which itself points to the extent of their presence. They are seldom called by that name; the magistrate who sentences Ernest Pontifex blames him for lacking 'the common sense to be able to distinguish between a respectable girl and a prostitute' (*The Way of All Flesh* 62) but in more private conversation evasion is generally practised. Alford deplores the evasive use of French, but the point is not that he desires the plain word but finds any such reference in polite society distasteful:

> Things are said under the flimsy veil of foreign diction which could not very well be said in plain English. To talk in the presence of ladies about disreputable women by the plain English names which belong to them is not considered to display a very delicate mind, but anybody may talk about the *demi-monde* without fearing either a blush or a frown.   (Alford 1864, 250)

Novelists who introduced prostitutes into their books often felt the need to defend themselves in a preface.[5]

Prostitutes who appear as characters are generally highly articulate, and eager to accommodate their remarks to what respectable society expects of them. They declare themselves repentant, unfit to consort with the respectable, especially other women, and unable ever to think of release from their condition. Nancy meeting Brownlow and Rose is a prime example. Certainly she gains little encouragement from Brownlow's offer of escape, prefixed by his remark that:

> The past has been a most dreary waste with you, of youthful energies mis-spent, and such priceless treasures lavished, as the Creator bestows but once, and never grants again, but, for the future, you may hope.

One cannot help feeling that we are in a melodrama and that she takes her proper cue when she says:

> Look before you, lady. Look at that dark water. How many times do you read of such as I who spring into the tide, and leave no living thing to care for, or bewail them. It may be years hence, or it may be only months, but I shall come to that at last . . . It will never reach your ears, dear lady, and God forbid such horrors should! (*Oliver Twist* 46)

The Thames was only too often the most convenient form of suicide for the despairing and the image of cleansing by that much polluted river was a gift to the novelists who wanted to combine the realistic and the symbolic. 'I should have been in the river long ago,' says Martha Endell, who then speaks of Em'ly:

> 'How can I go on as I am, a solitary curse to everyone I come near!' Suddenly she turned to my companion [Mr Peggotty] 'Stamp upon me, kill me! When she was your pride, you would have thought I had done her harm if I had brushed against her in the street. You can't believe – why should you? – a syllable that comes out of my lips. It would be a burning shame upon you, even now, if she and I exchanged a word.'
> (*David Copperfield* 47)

The phrase 'a syllable that comes out of my lips' scarcely rings true for this speaker; but the assumption that prostitutes have taken leave of all truth and honour is generally accepted in the novels, even by the fictional prostitutes themselves. Thus Esther, fearing that Mary Barton too will 'fall':

> How can I keep her from being such a one as I am; such a wretched, loathsome creature! She was listening just as I listened, and loving just as I loved, and the end will be just like my end. How shall I save her? She won't hearken to warning, or heed it more than I did; and who loves her well enough to watch over her as she should be watched? God keep her from harm! And yet I won't pray for her; sinner that I am! Can my prayers be heard? No! they'll only do harm.   (*Mary Barton* 10)

Collins's Mercy is equally pious, more resigned and even less credible in telling of how she was affected by a sermon:

> What happier women might have thought of his sermon, I cannot say; there was not a dry eye among us at the Refuge. As for me, he touched my heart as no man has touched it before or since. The hard despair melted in me at the sound of his voice; the weary round of my life showed its nobler side again while he spoke. From that time I have accepted my hard lot. I have been a patient woman.
>
> (*The New Magdalen* 1873, Book 1, 2)

Collins is in his melodramatic rather than his realist vein here; clichés like 'not a dry eye', 'touched my heart', 'the weary round of my life' are aimed more at the satisfaction of the reader than at the representation of heard speech.

The moral theology of the prostitute in fiction depends upon the sympathy of her role. If, like Nancy, Martha and Esther, she can do good to one of the virtuous characters, she is allowed repentance and even some piety. Those who are vindictive and destructive speak accordingly:

> There was a criminal called Alice Marwood – a girl still, but deserted and an outcast. And she was tried, and she was sentenced. And Lord, how the gentlemen in the court talked about it! And how grave the judge was on her duty, and on her having perverted the gifts of nature – as if he didn't know better than anybody there, that they had been made curses to her!   (*Dombey and Son* 34)

Trollope, ever mindful of his readership but striving with his own bluff honesty, makes his Carry Brattle suitably abject; 'I never had a husband, nor never shall, I suppose, what man would take the likes of me?' (*The Vicar of Bullhampton* 24).

Records which purport to be factual suggest that the Victorian prostitute was likely to be neither lachrymosely penitent nor savage in her speech. When Munby declines a prostitute's solicitation because it is Sunday, she says, 'What, are you so *froom* as all that? (Hudson 1972, 30).[6] Another, whom he formerly knew as a servant, is 'arrayed in gorgeous apparel' when he meets her in Regent Street. 'She had got tired of service, wanted to see life and be independent; & so she had become a prostitute, of her own accord & without being seduced . . . her manners were improved – she was no longer vulgar: her dress was handsome and good' (ibid. 41). This is precisely the situation of Hardy's 'Ruined Maid' who tells her friend from the country of her new fortune; allowing for the constraints of verse form, the dialogue is probably truer to life that much of the sentimentalising in prose fiction.

The uninhibited 'Walter' reports more baldly that a prostitute told him, 'I spend when I want fucking . . . and if I like the man, though he be a stranger, I ask him to fuck again if he pleases me; why shouldn't we?' (Marcus 1969, 120). This of course is not the language of the novel, nor even of the social observer whose work is published under a respectable imprint. Greenwood says that the common reply from a prostitute offered an opportunity to change her life would be, 'I don't care. It's a life good enough for me. A pretty image I should appear in well-bred company, shouldn't I? It's no use your preaching to me. I've made my bed and I must lie on it' (Greenwood 1869, 325). Mayhew reports a similar response:

> They do say I'm a bit cracky, but that's all my eye. I'm a drunken old b— if you like, but nothing worse than that. I was once the swellest woman about town, but I'm come down awful. And yet it ain't awful. I sometimes tries to think it is, but I can't make it so. If I did think it awful I shouldn't be here now; I couldn't stand it. But the fact is life's sweet, and I don't care how you live. It's as sweet to the w— , as it is to the hempress, and mebbe it's as sweet to me as it is to you.
>
> (Mayhew 1862, 100)

The word 'whore' is too much for Mayhew to write, as Hardy seems to have thought it to be for Jude to utter, but the report has the ring of truth. Allowing for probable bowdlerisation of oaths, there is credibility also in Kirwan's report:

> Tired of my life? You may believe it that I am; but what of that. No
> one would take me by the hand after leaving this life. I am not such a
> fool as to jump from the frying pan into the fire. I get tight about twice
> a week, and then I come here and talk and drink more, and that serves
> to pass the time.   (Kirwan 1870, 142)

If Kirwan is, as he seems to be, a fairly honest reporter, what are we to
make of the words of the lower class of prostitute whom he meets
under London Bridge and who turns on her male companion:

> 'If I am bad, Jem', burst out the girl, raging with passion and her eyes
> filled with tears, 'who made me so? Who kept chiming into my ears
> that I had a pretty face and that I ought to sell it? Who was it,'
> continued the girl, 'struck me last Christmas night, come two years, and
> pitched me out of the hole that we lived in on Saffron Hill? And then I
> had to seek a livin' in the streets, and when I was hungry I took money
> and sold myself to perdition; and then I had a father who used to steal
> it from me when I'd come home to sleep, and he'd take the few
> shillings that I earned by my shame, to go and drink it, and none of ye
> were ashamed to live on the money that lost my poor soul.'   (Ibid. 68)

We turn back to Nancy with a new perspective; was Dickens here
again justified in saying that he did not depart far from what he knew
to be true, if a prostitute of the lowest type actually said that she 'sold
herself to perdition'?

This was certainly an area of dialogue which the novelists found
difficult to handle. The speech of prostitutes in fiction becomes more
realistic as the century passes. Collins makes Sally, like many of his
other characters, sound melodramatic but there is a sense of truth in
her words and the repetition of 'the streets' both calls up the grim
reality and comments on the common use of the phrase as an evasion
of that reality:

> I don't like to make you sorry; and you did look sorry – you did – when
> I talked about it before. The streets, the streets, the streets, little girl or
> big girl, it's only the streets; and always being hungry or cold; and cruel
> men when it isn't cruel boys. I want to be happy, I want to enjoy my
> new clothes!   (*The Fallen Leaves* Book 6, 3)

This was Collins's second attempt at depicting a prostitute. The
speech of Mercy in *The New Magdalen* a few years earlier is even more
artificial and theatrical; yet much of what she says conveys a bitter

reality. Thus she describes her first seduction after she had collapsed in the street and woke to find herself in bed in a strange room:

> Three or four women came in, whose faces betrayed even to my inexperienced eyes the shameful infamy of their lives. I started up in bed; I implored them to tell me where I was and what had happened – Spare me! I can say no more. Not long since, you heard Miss Roseberry call me an outcast from the streets. Now you know, as God is my judge I am speaking the truth! Now you know what made me an outcast, and in what measure I deserved my disgrace.
>
> (*The New Magdalen* Vol. 2, 207)

The language – 'the shameful infamy of their lives' – is that of Collins and the expectations of his readers, but the substance is a story constantly repeated. Mayhew records one of many such:

> I refused to touch any wine, so I asked for some coffee, which I drank. It made me feel very sleepy, so sleepy indeed that I begged to be allowed to sit down on the sofa. They accordingly placed me on the sofa, and advised me to rest a little while, promising, in order to allay my anxiety, to send a messenger to my aunt. Of course I was drugged, and so heavily I did not regain consciousness till the next morning. I was horrified to discover I had been ruined, and for some days I was inconsolable, and cried like a child to be killed or sent back to my aunt.   (Mayhew 1862, 84)

Here again the language – 'to allay my anxiety', 'horrified to discover I had been ruined' – is less convincing than the story. It seems not so much that the novelist has violently wrenched his dialogue into an artificial form but rather that for both novelist and observer the censor and the convention of written record combine against the accuracy of someone like 'Walter'.

By the 1890s a prostitute could be depicted in fiction as neither a drunken harridan nor an abject penitent. She is allowed to speak like a normal character and to be articulate without being rhetorical; this is perhaps one of the most significant changes in the development of dialogue. Ida Starr is perhaps excessively well-spoken and fluent, as if in Gissing's reaction against the evasions of previous decades. A new convention of speech replaces the old as she tells her story of seduction by the son of the family whose service she has left:

I had just turned a corner, when some one came up to me, and it was Mr. Bolter. He had followed me from the house. He laughed, said I had done quite right . . . I had not the least affection for him, but he had pleasant, gentlemanly ways, and it scarcely even occurred to me to refuse his offers. I was reckless; what happened to me mattered little, as long as I had not to face hard work. I needed rest. For one in my position there was, I saw, only one way of getting it. I took that way.

(The Unclassed 17)

The real words of these women were probably never fully caught in print. Both novelists and observers made concessions to verbal taboos and to the general tidying of speech into writing. Yet there are passages which bring us close to the reality of their mingled wretchedness and defiance.

Notes

1. The Squire's langauge must have been exceptionally lurid. Under a statute of George II (19 Geo II, v. 21) the fines for 'profanely cursing or swearing were fixed at one shilling for a labourer, soldier or sailor, two shillings for any 'other person under the degree of a gentleman' and five shillings for a 'gentleman or person of superior rank'. Dickens once insisted on the prosecution of a girl whom he heard swearing in the street. He invoked a more recent Police Act and had some difficulty in persuading the police and the magistrate to proceed ('The Ruffian' in *All the Year Round* 10 October 1868).

2. This, like much Victorian non-standard speech, is a survival of upper-class usage. Spellings like 'Gad' and 'stap' are common in Restoration comedy, and through most of the eighteenth century. It is heard in Sir Pitt Crawley's injunction to his son, 'Shut up your sarmons' (*Vanity Fair* 10). In the later period this previously affected pronunciation discreetly evaded the normal sound of the direct use of 'God'.

3. Marcus makes some other telling comparisons between the gross frankness of 'Walter' and the concealments of Dickens; a lecherous major is likened to Major Bagstock in *Dombey and Son* 110f.

4. In the 'Cleveland Street Scandal' of 1889 a male prostitute called his associates 'gay' but probably in allusion to their trade rather than their orientation. For further discussion of the development of the new meaning, see Hughes (1991), 232f.

5. For example, Trollope is defensive in his preface to *The Vicar of Bullhampton* about 'the character of a girl whom I will call, – for want of a truer word that shall not in its truth be offensive, – a castaway', feeling sure that good women 'can pity the sufferings of the vicious, and do something perhaps to mitigate and shorten them, without contamination from the vice'. Collins's preface to the 1879 edition of *The Fallen Leaves* is happy that 'the scrupulous delicacy of treatment, in certain parts of the story, has been as justly appreciated as I could wish'.

6. Partridge (1974) gives *froom* as a Jewish colloquialism for strongly orthodox in religion.

CHAPTER 7
Speech of women and children

While it is true that the Victorian ethos produced a restricted code for speaking and writing about sexual matters, it is equally true that there was acute awareness of sexual difference. Mixed company, 'the presence of ladies', modified speech and behaviour in other ways than the taboo on swearing and physical reference. Women were also to be on their guard in social gatherings; the author of *Enquire Within About Everything* (1891) warns:

> The woman who wishes her conversation to be agreeable will avoid conceit or affectation, and laughter which is not natural and spontaneous. Her language will be easy and unstudied, marked by a graceful carelessness, which, at the same time, never oversteps the limits of propriety. Her lips will readily yield to a pleasant smile; she will not love to hear herself talk; her tones will bear the impress of sincerity, and her eyes kindle with animation as she speaks. (78)

The sexes were segregated for much of the time, from schooldays to the withdrawal of women at an agreed point in a dinner party. Until late in the century, few professions were open to women. Married women had no rights over their property until 1882; divorce, difficult for a man to obtain, was almost impossible for a woman. There were few role models for women – wife and mother, devoted spinster daughter or aunt, governess or companion. For the working class there was the prospect before marriage of 'service' or manual labour, with the terror of 'the streets' as the final abyss.

Yet women were articulate and often influential, albeit generally through their relationship with the men who defined their social position and could put their ideas into practice. Only a minority campaigned for Parliamentary franchise, but their voice grew steadily louder and more determined as the century went on. They had also their male supporters, such as John Stuart Mill; and Disraeli surprised the House of Commons in 1866 by saying that in a country governed by a Queen, in which women had many legal rights, there was no logical reason why they should not be able tó vote. The professions were gradually opened to women, until the lot of the governess or 'companion' was no longer the only alternative to spinsterhood in the parental home. The majority of women had other things to say for themselves and the formal disability for public action sometimes sharpened private tongues. That this was nothing new is evidenced by literary figures like the Wife of Bath, Mistress Quickly, Lady Teazle and many more.

The novel was a gift of the period to women. To the leisured and frequently bored of the middle class it was a recreation and escape. For a few it became a source of activity, income and possibly fame. Writing was something that could be done at home, with little equipment and no set time. Some, like Frances Trollope and Mrs Henry Wood, wrote to help family finance and pay their husbands' debts. Trollope created a representative in Lady Carbury who was 'driven very hard for money' and, although distressed by bad reviews 'was disposed to think that her literary career might yet be a success' (*The Way We Live Now* 2, 11). The majority were less successful, never reaching print or achieving only a brief and modest place in the lists, while a handful were among the greatest of the century.

Women's idiom

Since women characters are prominent in all the novels, and dominant in some, it might be expected that the special qualities of their lives would be reflected in their speech. It cannot in fact be said that there is a distinctive woman's style which prevails throughout Victorian fiction, but there are indications of content and expression which relate to contemporary society.

Women are commonly presented as uninformed about public affairs, accepting their ignorance and receiving with docility the expressed views of men.[1] Brooke speaks for his sex when he says, 'Young ladies don't understand political economy, you know' (*Middlemarch* 2), an attitude echoed at a younger age by Tom Tulliver's assertion that girls can't learn Latin. Charles Reding's young sister Caroline who boasts that she has 'read Goldsmith, and a good deal of Rollin, besides Pope's Homer' is soon put down when questioned by her brother about Pelopidas and confesses that she

'never could learn the *memoria technica*' (*Loss and Gain* Part 2, 11).
Trollope remarks that a girl with a good ear for music would still not
detect an error in Latin verse while a boy who is 'familiar with the
metres of the poet, will at once discover the fault' (*Autobiography* 12).

Some women, drawn closer to the concerns of the male world,
acquit themselves better. Lady Marney combines political acumen
with the discursive idiolect which the novelists often associate with
women's speech:

> 'Oh! I have no doubt', said Lady Marney, 'that we shall have some
> monster of the middle class, some tinker or tailor, or candlestick-maker,
> with his long purse, preaching reform and practising corruption; exactly
> as the Liberals did under Walpole: bribery was unknown in the time of
> the Stuarts, but we have a capital registration, Mr Tadpole tells me.'
>
> (*Sybil* Book 1, 4)

By contrast, Lady Glencora takes the more personal and uninformed
view generally assigned to women when her husband seems likely to
become Prime Minister:

> Of course it must be a mixed kind of thing at first, and I don't care a
> straw whether it run to Radicalism or Toryism. The country goes on its
> own way, either for better or for worse, whichever of them are in. I
> don't think it makes any difference as to what sort of laws are passed.
> But among ourselves, in our set, it makes a deal of difference who gets
> the garters, and the counties, who are made barons and then earls, and
> whose name stands at the head of everything.   (*The Prime Minister* 6)

At times of crisis, a woman can become positive about her lack of
knowledge and use her gift of direct, commonsense penetration to
break through male obfuscation. Mrs Doria questions a barrister about
Richard's marriage:

> I know – I am firmly convinced that no law would ever allow a boy to
> disgrace his family and ruin himself like that, and nothing shall
> persuade me that it is so. Now tell me, Brandon, and pray do speak in
> answer to my questions, and please to forget you are dealing with a
> women. *Can* my nephew be rescued from the consequences of his folly?
> *Is* what he has done legitimate? *Is* he bound for life by what he has
> done while a boy?'   (*The Ordeal of Richard Feverel* 33)

Lack of forensic skill and technical idiom may be turned to advantage when sincerity is recognised, in public as well as private discourse. George Eliot is explicit on this when Esther Lyon comes to give evidence for Felix. 'When a woman feels surely and nobly, that ardour of hers which breaks through formulas too rigorously urged on men by daily practical needs, makes one of her most precious influences: she is the added impulse that shatters the stiffening crust of cautious experience.' Her evidence is gracious in its simplicity, in the plain statements and short sentences that might seem contrived without the preceding authorial comment on her sincerity:

> I am Esther Lyon, the daughter of Mr Lyon, the Independent minister at Treby, who has been one of the witnesses for the prisoner. I know Felix Holt well. On the day of the election at Treby, when I had been much alarmed by the noises that came from the main street, Felix Holt came to call upon me. He knew that my father was away, and he thought that I should be alarmed by the sounds of disturbance.
>
> (*Felix Holt* 46)

The point is made, and established by dialogue, but a doubt remains of how far George Eliot was depending on court reports rather than experience for Esther's words, which read suspiciously like a transcript.

When discourse is neither public nor emotional, women are often content to be an audience for men when the great world is being discussed. Newman gives a sense of reality when he creates the conversation of White, the advanced Anglo-Catholic, with the women of the Bolton family. White imagines a Catholic conversion of Oxford:

> 'Didn't you say the Pope confessed, Mr White?' asked Miss Bolton; 'it has always puzzled me whether the Pope was obliged to confess like another man.'
>
> 'Oh, certainly,' answered White, 'every one confesses.'
>
> 'Well,' said Charlotte, 'I can't fancy Mr Hurst of St Peter's, who comes here to sing glees, confessing, or some of the grave heads of houses, who bow so stiffly.'
>
> 'They will all have to confess,' said White.
>
> 'And what will the heads of houses be?' asked Miss Charlotte.
>
> 'Abbots or superiors,' answered White; 'they will bear crosses; and when they say Mass, there will be a lighted candle in addition.'
>
> (*Loss and Gain* Part 1, 8)

Newman's comparative lack of literary artifice makes the essence of the rather stilted dialogue more credible. The clergy seem to be particularly privileged in receiving passive feminine attention and taking full advantage of it. The social levels range from the largely female attendance on Stiggins and Chadband to Arabin who talked to women 'without putting out all his powers, and listened to them without any idea that what he should hear from them could either actuate his conduct or influence his opinion' (*Barchester Towers* 20).

Perhaps it is a result of masculine disregard for their opinions that women often speak obliquely and in hints. Dickens in particular portrays this type of discourse. His exemplars of this trait cover a range of women otherwise differentiated socially and individually. Mrs Wickham, a waiter's wife who is Paul Dombey's nurse, speaks in her own class dialect: 'I couldn't say how, nor I couldn't say when, nor I couldn't say whether the dear child knew it or not, but Betsy Jane has been watched by her mother' (*Dombey and Son* 1848, 8). Rosa Dartle is more genteel and more sinister in her obliquity; she is pleased to learn from Steerforth that common people 'are not easily wounded': 'Live and learn. I had my doubts, I confess, but now they're cleared up. I didn't know, and now I do know; and that shows the advantage of asking – don't it?' (*David Copperfield* 19). Hardy gives evasive speech in a rural setting to Aunt Edlin when she speaks of Phillotson: 'There be certain men here and there that no woman of any niceness can stomach. I should have said he was one. I don't say so *now*, since you must ha' known better than I, – but that's what I *should* have said' (*Jude the Obscure* Book 2, 9).

On matters which society regards as more properly their own, women speak with a directness that men may lack. In the absence of a professional medical man they are confident in matters of health; thus Lady Chettam: 'Ah! like this poor Mrs Renfrew – that is what I think. Dropsy! There is no swelling yet – it is inward. I should say she ought to take drying medicines, shouldn't you? – or a dry hot-air bath. Many things might be tried of a drying nature' (*Middlemarch* 10).

Despite the taboos on discussion of sexual matters, marriage and courtship are a staple of women's conversation, especially when no men are present. It is a topic that all social classes can share; Mary Barton and Sally Leadbitter talk of young Carson:

'Well, I shall tell Mr Carson tomorrow how you're fretting for him; it's no more than e's doing for you, I can tell you.'

'For him, indeed!' said Mary, with a toss of her pretty head.

'Ay, miss, for him! You've been sighing as if your heart would break now for several days, over your work; now aren't you a little goose not to go and see one who I am sure loves you as his life, and whom you love? "How much, Mary?" "This much," as the children say' (opening her arms very wide).

'Nonsense,' said Mary, pouting; 'I often think I don't love him at all.' (*Mary Barton* 8)

The sisters of Harry Carson, who is regarded as Mary's lover, discuss his flirtation with Jane Richardson, a girl of his own class. 'Though he is our own brother, I do think he is behaving very wrongly. The more I think of it, the more sure I am that she thinks he means something, and that he intends her to think so' (18). Rosamund Vincy and Mary Garth show both their shared femininity and their different temperaments in matrimonial discussion:

'It is very different with you, Mary. You may have an offer.'

'Has anyone told you he means to make me one?'

'Of course not. I mean, there is a gentleman who may fall in love with you, seeing you almost every day.'

A certain change in Mary's face was chiefly determined by the resolve not to show any change.

'Does that make people fall in love?' she answered, carelessly; 'it seems to me quite often a reason for detesting each other.'

'Not when they are interesting and agreeable. I hear that Mr Lydgate is both.' (*Middlemarch* 12)

Hardy comes closer to the more basic conversation of working girls, though even as late as the 1890s his work was considered obscene. Arabella talks with her friend after throwing the pig's penis at Jude. Her pretended indifference to Jude and his ambitions receive a reply that sounds more authentic than the delicacy of Mary Barton half a century earlier:

O, don't ye! You needn't try to deceive us! What did you stay talking to him for, if you didn't want un? Whether you do or whether you don't, he's as simple as a child. I could see it as you courted on the bridge, when he looked at 'ee as if he had never seen a woman before in his born days. Well, he's to be had by any woman who can get him to care for her a bit, if she likes to set herself to catch him the right way. (*Jude the Obscure* Part 1, 6)

In the presence of an eligible man the woman's speech may be less direct and more flirtatious. Dolly Varden and Estella are familiar examples of the 'flirt'. Badinage between the sexes, with whatever restrictions class and situation impose, ranges widely. Arabella as a barmaid has a different style for male customers:

> 'O, Mr Cockman, now! How can you tell such a tale to me in my innocence!' she cried gaily. 'Mr Cockman, what do you use to make your moustache curl so beautiful?' As the young man was clean shaven the retort provoked a laugh at his expense.   (Part 3, 8)

Blanche Amory has her own method of trying to outface Arthur Pendennis:

> You wicked, satirical creature, I can't abide you! You take the hearts of young things, play with them, and fling them away with scorn. You ask for love and trample on it. You – you make me cry, that you do, Arthur, and – and don't – and I *won't* be consoled in that way – and I think Fanny was quite right in leaving such a heartless creature.
> (*Pendennis* 64)

These conversations show the constraints and privileges of gender; but in more neutral contexts it is difficult to discern any consistent features in the lexis and syntax of women's speech. Simplicity is a mark of some characters, but seems to spring from their nature and position rather than their sex. Many of Dickens's heroines are simple and direct to the point of naivety, but similar discourse can be found in some of his male characters; the same is true of other novelists. Kate Nickleby is unaffected and unadorned in speech, but scarcely more so than her brother Nicholas. The archness of Blanche Amory contrasts with the directness of Laura in the same novel to reveal character differences between women:

> 'You know, mamma,' the young lady said, 'that I have been living with you for ten years, during which time you have never taken any of my money, and have been treating me just as if I was a charity girl. Now, this obligation has offended me very much, because I am proud and do not like to be beholden to people. And as, if I had gone to school, it would have cost me at least fifty pounds a year, it is clear that I owe you fifty times ten pounds, which I know you have put into the bank at Chatteris for me, and which doesn't belong to me a bit.' (21)

Outside the world of fiction, Bulwer-Lytton is censorious about the repetitive and limited vocabulary of women, when they discuss novels:

> The ladies usually resort to some pet phrases, that, after the manner of shorthand, express as much as possible in a word: 'What do you think of Lady –'s last novel?' 'Oh! they say 'tis not very natural. The characters, to be sure are a little overdrawn; and then the *style* – so – so – I don't know what – you understand me – but it's *a dear* book altogether! – Do you know Lady – ?' 'Oh dear, yes! *nice* creature she is.' 'Very *nice* person indeed.' *Nice* and *dear* are the great To Prepon and To Kalon of feminine conversational moralities.
>
> (Bulwer-Lytton 1833, 158f) [2]

Bulwer-Lytton reads like a man irritated by the affectations of a particular social group, whose observation is not borne out by the novelists' wider treatment of women's speech.

Short sentences tend to be a more common feature with women than with men. The well-formed and clearly punctuated sentences of written speech, which stand for the idea-groups and pauses of actual conversation, may suggest the hesitancy of shyness about social intercourse and lack of specialist knowledge as compared with men. Women do not use this feature consistently, but rather show it in excitement or emotion, like Catherine Linton:

> I cannot sit in the kitchen. Set two tables here, Ellen: one for your master and Miss Isabella; the other for Heathcliff and myself, being of the lower orders. Will that please you, dear? Or must I have a fire lighted elsewhere? If so, give directions. I'll run down and secure my guest. I'm afraid the joy is too great to be real!   (*Wuthering Heights* 10)

Women of the lighter-minded sort are characterised by inconsequential speech; such is Ginevra Fanshawe:

> I am going to school. Oh, the number of foreign schools I have been at in my life! And yet I am quite an ignoramus. I know nothing – nothing in the world – I assure you; except that I play and dance beautifully, and French and German of course I know, to speak; but I can't read or write them very well.   (*Villette* 6)

This kind of breathless, disorganised speech, marked by incomplete sentences and anacolutha, is often given to women in the novels. Does it derive from aural experience, or is it an example of male contempt for the female intellect? We have all heard women – and men too – who speak in this way but the high incidence of the style in Victorian fiction seems larger than life. Perhaps it reflects contemporary belief that women were incapable of organised thought; and their comparative lack of educational opportunity may have affected their way of talking. The style tends to become a literary fashion to present a certain type of woman. Dickens is its most familiar and most frequent creator. Readers will think of Mrs Gamp, Mrs Nickleby, Mrs Chivery and Mrs Skewton. The last is interesting in that she changes her inconsequential public tone when she talks privately with her daughter: in life the manner may have been a defence rather than an involuntary mode. Mrs Jupp in *The Way of All Flesh* is typical of the derivative character, drawn from women like Mrs Gamp, even though Butler decried Dickens as 'literary garbage'. Gissing, who thought better of Dickens, gives some of the same characteristics more moderately to Mrs Yule in *New Grub Street*.

Perhaps Dickens's most interesting exemplar of this type of speech is Flora Finching in *Little Dorrit*. When Arthur Clennam meets as a middle-aged widow the woman he had once loved, Dickens was partly reliving his own experiences with Maria Beadnell. Flora is much more than a middle-class version of Sarah Gamp; her inconsequential chatter barely masks her emotional insecurity, her fear of ageing and her sexual unrest. 'Flora, who had been spoiled and artless long ago, was determined to be spoiled and artless now':

> 'Oh Mr Clennam you insincerest of creatures', said Flora, 'I perceive already you have not lost your old way of paying compliments, your old way when you used to pretend to be so sentimentally struck you know – at least I don't mean that, I – oh I don't know what I mean! . . . No one could dispute, Arthur – Mr Clennam – that it is quite right you should be formally friendly to me under the altered circumstances and indeed you couldn't be anything else, at least I suppose not you ought to know, but I can't help recalling that there *was* a time when things were very different.'   (Book 1, 13)

Dickens is here showing the cruelty which was sometimes the bedrock of his humour, but he is probably also showing the dark side of the Victorian woman's life. Men were so often assumed to be superior in intellect and understanding that it became almost a warrant of femininity to affect mindlessness. The verbal flow could degenerate further into the hysteria and invalidism which struck some women, perhaps sometimes the most intelligent. Tentative and inconsequential speech could also conceal a savage temper: Rosa Dartle has been quoted as seemingly uncertain of herself in the male world, but she is vicious to Emily seen as her rival for love for Steerforth: 'Listen to what I say, and reserve your false arts for your dupes. Do you hope to move *me* by your tears? No more than you could charm me by your smiles, you purchased slave' (*David Copperfield* 50).

Lest the rambling idiolect be regarded as nothing more than unjust male fantasy, a fuller example can be given from a woman novelist. When Elizabeth Gaskell gives Lady Cumnor's monologue to Clare Gibson, she may be accepting the literary convention or she may be reproducing what she had heard. It is one of those points on which the individual reader has to make a judgement. The exclamation marks and the parenthetical order to a servant add to the effect:

> Well, Clare! I really am glad to see you. I once thought I should never get back to the Towers, but here I am! There was such a clever man at Bath – a Doctor Snape – he cured me at last – quite set me up. I really think if ever I am ill again I shall send for him: it is such a thing to find a really clever medical man. Oh, by the way, I always forget you've married Mr Gibson – of course he's very clever, and all that. (The carriage to the door in ten minutes, Brown, and desire Bradley to bring my things down.) What was I asking you? Oh! how do you get on with your stepdaughter? She seemed to me to be a young woman with a pretty stubborn will of her own. I put a letter down for the post somewhere, and I cannot think where; do help me look for it, there's a good woman. (*Wives and Daughters* 25)

Protest speech

Some of the most interesting women's speech is evoked by protest and indignation. Women are presented as more easily moved emotionally; the convention of the age was that men should suppress their feelings and not parade them in public. The evidence of fiction suggests that this was a convention often broken – one has only to think of Nicholas Nickleby defying Squeers or the rages of Michael Henchard. Nevertheless, there is significance in the verbal outbursts given to women, which often suggest release of anger that had no outlet in action. An emotive character like Catherine Linton gives rein to her feelings without inhibition, encouraged perhaps by the generally tempestuous nature of her environment:

'Ah! you are come, are you, Edgar Linton?' she said, with angry animation. 'You are one of those things that are ever found when least wanted, and when you are wanted, never! I suppose we shall have plenty of lamentations now – I see we shall – but they can't keep me from my narrow home out yonder: my resting-place, where I'm bound before spring is over! There it is: not among the Lintons, mind, under the chapel-roof, but in the open air, with a headstone; and you may please yourself, whether you go to them or come to me!'

(Wuthering Heights 12)

The pious and less passionate Argemone Lavington can voice a telling woman's protest when she says to Lancelot, 'You treat me like an equal; you will deign to argue with me. But men in general – oh, they hide their contempt for us, if not their own ignorance, under that mask of chivalrous defence' (*Yeast* 2).[3] Trollope's Lady Mabel makes the same case to Tregear:

'You, if you see a woman that you fancy, can pursue her, can win her and triumph, or lose her and gnaw your heart; – at any rate you can do something. You can tell her that you love her so again and again even though she should scorn you. You can set yourself about the business you have taken in hand and can work hard at it. What can a girl do?'

'Girls work hard too sometimes.'

'Of course they do; – but everybody feels that they are sinning against their sex. Of love, such as a man's is, a woman ought to know nothing. How can she love with passion when she should never give her love till it has been asked, and not then until her friends tell her that the thing is suitable?'   (*The Duke's Children*, 10)

Sue Bridehead, a very different woman in a different ambience, starts with cool rational arguments but turns to pleading when she appeals for release from the trap of her marriage situation:

Why can't we agree to free each other? We made the compact, and surely we can cancel it – not legally, of course; but we can morally, especially as no new interests, in the shape of children, have arisen to be looked after. Then we might be friends, and meet without pain to

either. O Richard, be my friend and have pity! We shall both be dead
in a few years, and then what will it matter to anybody that you
relieved me from constraint for a little while? I daresay you think me
eccentric, or super-sensitive, or something absurd. Well – why should I
suffer for what I was born to be, if it doesn't hurt other people?

(Jude the Obscure Part 4, 3)

Gissing's Amy Reardon urges the same case less passionately and with
a shrewder knowledge of current affairs. When her contention that
married people should be free to separate and remarry is met by
cautious Mrs Yule with 'I suppose it would lead to all sorts of troubles',
she replies like a true 'New Woman', though perhaps with her
author's voice:

> So people say about every new step in civilisation. What would have
> been thought twenty years ago of a proposal to make all married women
> independent of their husbands in money matters?[4] All sorts of absurd
> dangers were foreseen, no doubt. And it's the same now about divorce.
> In America people can get divorced if they don't suit each other – at all
> events in some of the States – and does any harm come of it? Just the
> opposite I should think.   (*New Grub Street* 26)

The angry or passionate woman is of course part of the literary
tradition, as well as a reality of life. The shrew, the wronged wife, the
betrayed girl are recurring characters who can become clichés of
drama and fiction or can be made credible characters. Novelists can
show concealed aggression, perhaps under apparent flippancy. The
disadvantage of women caught between unwished marriage or
drudgery elsewhere is told in a light tone that belies anxiety. Thus
Ginevra Fanshawe:

> By-and-by we are to marry – rather elderly gentlemen, I suppose, with
> cash: papa and mamma manage that. My sister Augusta is married now
> to a man much older-looking than papa. Augusta is very beautiful – not
> in my style – but dark; her husband, Mr Davies, had the yellow fever in
> India, and he is still the colour of a guinea; but then he is rich, and
> Augusta has her carriage and establishment, and we all think she has
> done perfectly well. Now this is better than 'earning a living', as you
> say.   (*Villette* 6)

The older married woman asserts herself in different ways as Lady
Blandish teases her husband about his accusation that women worship

strength and play with purity: 'I see,' she said archly, 'we are the lovelier vessels; you claim the more direct descent. Men are seedlings: Women – slips! Nay, you have said so' (*The Ordeal of Richard Feverel* 26). Mrs Transome, whose 'tongue could be a whip upon occasion', contains her resentment by studied politeness when her son returns home:

> I suppose you have been used to greater luxury; these rooms look miserable to you, but you can soon make any alteration you like ... There is the steward's room, it is not used, and might be turned into a bedroom. I can't offer you my room, for I sleep upstairs.
>
> (*Felix Holt* 1 27)

When other interests than their own are concerned, women often express their anger more directly, as does Nellie Dean to Hindley in *Wuthering Heights* when he nearly kills the child Hareton and asks if he is injured:

> 'Injured!' I cried angrily; 'if he is not killed, he'll be an idiot! Oh! I wonder his mother does not rise from her grave to see how you use him. You're worse than a heathen – treating your own flesh and blood in that manner!' (9)

Wives sometimes leave their husbands in no doubt about their feelings, as when Mrs Glegg speaks in tones that subvert her words of apparent humility and ignorance: 'Perhaps I'm wrong, and you can teach me better – but I've allays heard as it's the husband's place to stand by his wife, instead of rejoicing and triumphing when folks insult her' (*The Mill on the Floss* Book 1, 12). More overtly hostile language from wife to husband is a commonplace of Victorian fiction. The nagging tongue is heard from women far apart in the social scale and in spoken idiom. The fight for women's emancipation was expressed not only in the speeches of Barbara Bodichon; it is echoed by the redoubtable Mrs Proudie: 'My lord, am I to be vouchsafed an answer or am I not?' (*Barchester Towers* 26) and by the bedraggled Kate of Moore's *A Mummer's Wife*: 'I will drink! And not because I like it, but to spite you, because I hate you' (26).

Women can be very direct to each other; Eleanor Bold reacts angrily to her sister's insinuations about Slope and his letters:

How can I help his having written to me? But you are all so prejudiced against him to such an extent, that that which would be kind and generous in another man is odious and impudent in him. I hate a religion that teaches one to be so one-sided in one's charity.

(*Barchester Towers* 28)

Trollope portrays a more concealed and feline response in his short story 'The Journey to Panama' (1861). A married woman is discussing with an unmarried one the situation of a girl on board:

'The best way is to take things as they come', said Miss Viner – perhaps meaning that such things never did come in the way of Amelia. 'If a lady knows what she is about, she need not fear a gentleman's attentions.'

'That's just what I tell Amelia; but then, my dear, she has not had so much experience as you and I.'

The insinuation that Amelia is not attractive is checkmated by the married woman tacitly associating the unmarried one with her in 'experience'; the position of the Victorian spinster is encapsulated in a sentence.

There are fewer examples of overt complaint and indignation about the woman's position, but they are effective when they come. The activists for women's emancipation did not get massive support from their own sex, but they were building on a foundation of more private protest which was sometimes verbalised and was unknowingly working for a later generation. Mrs Transome drops polite pretence when Jermyn asks if her son is good to her: 'Oh, to be sure – good as men are disposed to be to women, giving them cushions and carriages, and recommending them to enjoy themselves, and then expecting them to be contented under contempt and neglect' (*Felix Holt* 9). George Eliot may be expressing some of her own anger, but male authors can be equally sensitive. Sue makes her point clearly, if rather stiltedly: 'An average woman is in this superior to an average man – that she never instigates, only responds' (*Jude the Obscure* Part 6, 3). Lady Blandish protests gently but scathingly when Sir Austin sympathises 'women have so much to bear':

'It is our lot,' she said. 'And we are allowed many amusements. If we fulfil our duty in producing children, that, like our virtue, is its own reward. Then, as a widow, I have wonderful privileges ... I have no trouble now in polishing and piecing that rag the world calls – a character. I can sit at your feet every day unquestioned. To be sure, others do the same, but they are female eccentrics, and have cast off the rag altogether: mind mends itself.' (*The Ordeal of Richard Feverel* 13)

Masculine women

The 'female eccentric' took many forms and was another portent of coming change. To depart from the stereotype of femininity was to pose a threat to the male establishment and also to the woman's own security; the successive steps of 'losing reputation' being 'ruined' and going 'on the streets' always loomed as threatening shadows when conduct or speech was stigmatised as 'unladylike'. As we have seen, women were not supposed to indulge even in the mildest oaths allowed to men. The taboo is sometimes kept, and feelings relieved, by expletives regarded as harmless: 'the delicate vituperations gentle ladies use instead of oaths', such as 'Fiddlededee' or 'Fiddle-faddle' (*The Ordeal of Richard Feverel* 33, 30, 40) or 'Hoity-toity' (*Jude the Obscure* Part 1, 6). Trollope, as often, both honours convention and protests mildly against it when he comments on Lady Aylmer's use of a word from normal lexis which echoes a masculine oath:

> 'If there were any doubt' she continued to say, – 'but there is no doubt. These are the damning proofs.' There are certain words normally confined to the vocabularies of men, which women such as Lady Aylmer delight to use on special occasions, when strong circumstances demand strong language.   (*The Belton Estate* 1866, 17)

'Strong language' is only a symptom of a strain of masculinity that upsets the stereotype. The virago in the true sense is not simply an angry woman but one who takes the characteristics of aggression and hard speaking traditionally associated with men. What is said of Dickens's dialogue is true for Victorian fiction as a whole. 'When a woman talks like a woman, no one is conscious of special characteristics, but when she uses expressions that are more often used by men, the reader realises that these are not expressions that a woman would normally use' (Brook 1970, 60). The deviation may be only a more direct and practical turn of speech than was usually associated with women, like Lady Rosina recommending her local shoemaker:

He's very good, and very cheap too. Those London tradesmen never think they can charge you enough. I find I can wear Sprout's boots the whole winter through and then have them resoled. I don't suppose you ever think of such things? . . . I have to calculate exactly what they cost. (*The Prime Minister* 27)

The more aggressive variety of the type roused ambivalent feelings in the Victorian male. Dickens shows the negative side in Sally Brass who is so epicene that

if it had consorted with [her] maiden modesty and gentle womanhood to have assumed her brother's clothes in a frolic and sat down beside him, it would have been difficult for the oldest friend of the family to determine which was Sampson and which was Sally, especially as the lady carried upon her upper lip certain reddish demonstrations which, if the imagination had been assisted by her attire, might have been mistaken for a beard. (*The Old Curiosity Shop* 33)

Sally is addressed as 'chap' and fellow' by her brother and her own speech is masculine in its directness and refusal of the hints and evasions generally shown by women in the novels who want to carry a point: 'If I determined that the clerk ought not to come, of course he wouldn't be allowed to come. You know that well enough, so don't talk nonsense' (ibid.). In forced intimacy for her own purposes she speaks like a man, using the familiar form of a Christian name and assuming the freedom of exchange generally barred between the sexes not freed by family connection:

'It's a very unpleasant thing, Dick –' said Miss Brass, pulling out the tin box and refreshing herself with a pinch of snuff; 'but between you and me – between friends, you know, for if Sammy knew it, I should never hear the last of it – some of the office money too, that has been left about, has gone in the same way.' (58)

On the other hand, Mrs Bagnet is an entirely sympathetic character, whose masculinity is made acceptable by her being a mother. She calls George 'old man' and 'old fellow' and when thoughts of Smallweed make his 'flesh and blood tingle', says to him, 'My advice to you, is to light your pipe, and tingle that way. It's wholesomer and comfortabler, and better for the health altogether.' Yet when she hears of the death of Jo she exclaims, 'Poor creetur!' and says it 'with a mother's pity' (*Bleak House* 49).

Such creations, the negative and positive side of the virago, reflect Dickens's own ambivalence. On a tour of Italy he met a young Englishwoman who behaved unconventionally by walking bareheaded through the streets, and who made such masculine remarks as 'Oh God what a sermon we had here last Sunday' and 'Did you ever read such infernal trash as Mrs Gore's?'. Dickens's comment is revealing; he was embarrassed by the presence of his wife and sister-in-law, without whom 'I should have thought it all very funny, and, as it was, I threw the ball back again, was mighty free and easy, made some rather broad jokes, and was highly applauded'. The young woman completed her role when she produced cigars 'and talked, and smoked, in the most gentlemanly manner I ever beheld' (Forster 1874, II, 264). Dickens was not alone in being attracted to the woman who upset the contemporary stereotype. The woman who took a masculine role might invite being 'insulted' but in the protection of respectable society she could give pleasure to the male who found himself freed from the usual inhibitions and could make 'broad jokes'. The more passive image of womanhood was protected by the exceptions, provided they behaved as good companions and did not urge public claims. Those who looked from private to social affairs were less welcome. The forthright and 'unwomanly' speech of Shorthouse's agnostic and socialist Virginia Lisle is as distasteful to her conservative author as to most of his readership. 'I have been telling Sir Percival that I am the sworn enemy of everything that is old. That I detest the social system which is the curse of civilisation. That I wish to subvert and destroy it all' (*Sir Percival* 5).

The attraction of sexual ambivalence could be more overt and more disturbing. Richard Feverel is at ease with Carola, little more than a child, who likes to ride astride like a boy and suits her speech to her preference:

> I used to when I was little, though. Not here, you know, – in the country. And ma knew of it. She didn't interfere. She wanted me to be a boy. If I call you Richard, you'll call me Carl, won't you? That's the German for Charles. In the country the boys call me Charley. Can't I ride slapping?   (*The Ordeal of Richard Feverel* 23)

This episode seems a prologue to his later entanglement with Bella Mount whose 'man-like conversation, which he took for honesty, was a refreshing change on fair lips' and who suggests, 'Call me Bella: I'll

call you Dick'. She appears in men's clothes and walks out in the
streets with him, suiting her speech to her pretence:

> 'They take up men, Dick, for going about in women's clothes, and vice
> versaw, I suppose. You'll bail me out, old fellow, if I have to make my
> bow to the beak, won't you? Say it's because I'm an honest woman and
> don't care to hide the – a – unmentionables when I wear them – as the
> t'others do,' sprinkled with the dandy's famous invocations. (38)

This perhaps can be seen as male fantasy, antedating by a generation
the exploits of Vita Sackville-West and Violet Trefusis, but there is
evidence that women sometimes affected masculine speech, even if
they seldom went so far as transvestism. To the encounter of Dickens
in Italy may be added the actress whom Munby heard on a bus in
1867, addressing a man 'with the air of one young man talking to
another' and saying, 'Jolly supper we had last Saturday week, wish
you'd been there' (Hudson 1972, 238). This is precisely the
comparison made by Miss Clack about the speech of the far from
mannish Rachel Verinder. ' "I am charmed to see you, Godfrey," she
said, addressing him, I grieve to add, in the off-hand manner of one
young man talking to another' (*The Moonstone* Second Period, 1). In
a different situation, there is similar freedom of speech and manner
when Gissing's less respectable Ida Starr overcomes Waymark's refusal
of her invitation to supper: 'Fiddlesticks! Surely you won't desert me
when I ask your protection? Come along, and pay me back another
time, if you like' (*The Unclassed* 11). Even Laura Kennedy, by no
means lacking in femininity, can use a male sporting metaphor in
speaking of the woman's position. 'A woman has a fine game to play;
but then she is so easily bowled out, and the term allowed to her is so
short' (*Phineas Finn* 75).

One of the most attractive 'masculine' women in Victorian fiction
is Marian Halcombe in *The Woman in White*, whose courage and
tenacity help the less resistant Laura to escape from her wicked
husband. On their first meeting, Hartright notices her 'large, firm,
masculine mouth' and is 'almost repelled by the masculine form and
masculine look of the features in which the perfectly-shaped figure
ended'. Later he comes to admire her direct manner of speech:

> As your friend, I am going to tell you at once, in my own, plain, blunt,
> downright language, that I have discovered your secret – without help,
> or hint, mind, from anyone else. Mr Hartright, you have thoughtlessly

allowed yourself to form an attachment, a serious and devoted
attachment, I am afraid, to my sister Laura.   (Part 1, 6, 10)

Roles and strategies

The pairing of Marion and Laura has a number of parallels in
Victorian fiction in which one woman is the stereotypical gentle
dependent heroine and the other is more forceful in speech and
action. The stronger woman is not always marked by overtly
'masculine' appearance and speech. The reader will recall Becky and
Amelia in *Vanity Fair*, Lily Dale and her 'radical' sister Bell in *The
Small House at Allington*, the very feminine but determined and
self-supporting Ethelberta and her sister Picotee in *The Hand of
Ethelberta*.

Particular interest attaches to the portrayal of such pairs by women
novelists, who may be supposed to have been better informed than
men on how they talked to each other. Shirley Keeldar and Caroline
Helstone in Charlotte Brontë's *Shirley* (1849) are thus contrasted.
How far the character of Shirley is based on Emily Brontë may remain
disputable, but this is certainly the novel in which Charlotte made
her strongest plea for woman's emancipation. Shirley, a rich heiress
and landowner, is contrasted with Caroline who has no wealth or
prospects and can look for nothing but marriage or the fate of an 'old
maid' governess. The protest is not fully resolved and both girls come
to the conventional marriage ending, but a good deal of interest is
said along the way. Shirley likes to consider herself 'Captain Keeldar'
or 'Shirley Keeldar, Esq, Lord of the Manor of Briarfield'. Mrs Pryor,
her governess, remonstrates with her: 'My dear, do not allow that
habit of alluding to yourself as a gentleman to be confirmed: it is a
strange one. Those who do not know you, hearing you speak, would
think you affected masculine manners' (12).

The conversation between Shirley and Caroline early in their
acquaintance is revealing. There is nothing overtly to suggest
difference between the girls, but Shirley continually takes, in a subtle
way, what would then have been considered a male attitude. She
asserts definite opinions about both human society and the romantic
power of nature, as against Caroline's generalities. She speaks
specifically and dismissively of men. Proposing a day's excursion she
says solicitously, 'It would not tire you to walk so far?' and being
reassured she continues,

'You would not be dull with me alone?'

'I should not. I think we should suit: and what third person is there whose presence would not spoil our pleasure?'

'Indeed, I know of none about our own ages – no lady at least; and as to gentlemen —'

'An excursion becomes quite a different thing when there are gentlemen of the party', interrupted Caroline.

'I agree with you – quite a different thing to what we were proposing.'

'We were going simply to see the old trees, the old ruins; to pass a day in old times, surrounded by olden silence, and above all by quietude.'

'You are right; and the presence of gentlemen dispels the last charm, I think. If they are of the wrong sort, like your Malones, and your young Sykes, and Wynnes [curates of Caroline's uncle], irritation takes the place of serenity. If they are of the right sort, there is still a change – I can hardly tell what change, one easy to feel, difficult to describe.'

'We forget Nature, imprimis.'

'And then Nature forgets us; covers her vast calm brow with a dim veil, conceals her face, and withdraws the peaceful joy with which, if we had been content to worship her only, she would have filled our hearts.'

(Ibid.)

Later in the novel, Shirley engages in a wonderful dialogue with her uncle who is demanding to know whom she intends to marry. Her repartee seems to bear no relationship to either the docility or the sullen defiance of a Victorian woman. It is the language of a Millament or Lady Teazle, using the single-line exchanges (*stichomythia*) characteristic of dramatic speech in a range from Greek tragedy to Restoration comedy – and one might add, Noel Coward:

'Will you, Miss Keeldar, marry a poor man?'

'What right have you, Mr Sympson, to ask me?'

'I insist upon knowing.'

'You don't go the way to know.'

'My family respectability shall not be compromised.'

'A good resolution: keep it.'

'Madam, it is you who shall keep it.'

'Impossible, sir, since I form no part of your family.'

'Do you disown us?'

'I disown your dictatorship.'

. . .

'Such obstinacy could not be, unless you were under improper influence.'

'What do you mean? There are certain phrases potent to make my blood boil – improper influence! What old woman's cackle is that?'

'Are you a young lady?'

'I am a thousand times better: I am an honest woman, and as such I will be treated.' (31)

There is a plain vitality in the final exchange which is rare in the speech of Victorian heroines; it would be good to know if it was equally rare in life.

George Eliot's Dorothea Brooke in *Middlemarch* is never so passionate and is certainly in all outward respects 'womanly'. She does, however, show through her speech as well as her actions some of the traits less often attributed to women of the time. She is intellectual and a lover of learning, full of ideas and the desire to put them into effect, definite in her beliefs, disinclined to common feminine pursuits. She is a contrast to her more domesticated sister Celia. Just before Dorothea announces her engagement to Casaubon, she and her sister are discussing him: Dorothea speaks firmly, in short and specific sentences with general ideas about the world, while Celia chatters less consequentially on the specifics of the moment. Celia speaks first:

'Is any one else coming to dinner besides Mr Casaubon?'

'Not that I know of.'

'I hope there is some one else. Then I shall not hear him eat his soup so.'

'What is there remarkable about his soup-eating?'

'Really, Dodo. Can't you hear how he scrapes his spoon? And he always blinks before he speaks. I don't know whether Locke blinked, but I'm sure I am sorry for those who sat opposite to him, if he did.'

'Celia', said Dorothea with emphatic gravity, 'pray don't make any more observations of that kind.'

'Why not? They are quite true', returned Celia, who had her reasons for persevering, though she was beginning to be a little afraid.

'Many things are true which only the commonest minds observe.'

'Then I think the commonest minds must be rather useful. I think it is a pity Mr Casaubon's mother had not a commoner mind; she might have taught him better.'   (*Middlemarch* Book 1, 5)

Dorothea is contrasted also with the selfish Rosamond Vincy, who ruins her husband Lydgate by her extravagance. Dorothea gives Lydgate both encouragement and financial help. Her speech is direct, well measured and practical:

> I have wished very much to see you for a long while, Mr Lydgate, but I put off asking you to come until Mr Bulstrode applied to me again about the Hospital. I know that the advantage of keeping the management of it separate from that of the Infirmary depends on you, or, at least, in the good which you are encouraged to hope for from having it under your control. And I am sure you will not refuse to tell me exactly what you think. (75)

Is this the speech of the many women philanthropists of the century who enabled men to have the public face of enterprises? Perhaps Angela Burdett Coutts spoke thus to Dickens about her charitable work. The gender difference is not obscured when the woman has the position of authority; in this scene Eliot notes specifically 'the searching tenderness of her woman's tone'.

Jane Eyre is not so directly contrasted with the less positive type of woman, but she has her own language strategies for talking to men. She deals with St John Rivers when he insists that they must marry if she is to accompany him on his missionary enterprise. Their dialogue conveys the brash assurance of the Victorian man that his wish will prevail, which Jane counters by coolly holding her ground and emphasising that a woman can desire both independence and romantic love but prefers to make her own distinction between them:

> 'I repeat, I freely consent to go with you as your fellow-misisonary; but not as your wife; I cannot marry you and become part of you.'
> 'A part of me you must become', he answered steadily; 'otherwise the whole bargain is void. How can I, a man not yet thirty, take out with me to India a girl of nineteen, unless she be married to me? How can we be for ever together – sometimes in solitudes, sometimes amidst savage tribes – and unwed?'
> 'Very well', I said shortly; 'under the circumstances, quite as well as if I were either your real sister, or a man and a clergyman like yourself.'
> 'It is known that you are not my sister; I cannot introduce you as such: to attempt it would be to fasten injurious suspicions on us both. And for the rest, though you have a man's vigorous brain, you have a woman's heart, and – it would not do.'
> 'It would do', I affirmed with some disdain, 'perfectly well. I have a

woman's heart; but not where you are concerned; for you I have only a comrade's constancy; a fellow-soldier's frankness, fidelity, fraternity, if you like; a neophyte's respect and submission to his hierophant: nothing more – don't fear.' (34)

Here in 1848, Bernard Shaw does not seem to be half a century away. One can understand the hostility of some reviewers to the novel, based not only on the coarse language to which they ostensibly objected. When Jane has agreed to marry Rochester, a more complex and it must be confessed less believable character than Rivers, she is both cool and provocative. Her response to his teasing uses the strategy of rhetoric and imagery to make it clear that marriage for her is not an extinction of personality. The sexual assumptions of the age are subverted as she manipulates for her own purpose the metaphors of submission. Rochester declares that he would not exchange her 'for the grand Turk's whole seraglio'.

> The eastern allusion bit me again: 'I'll not stand you an inch in the stead of a seraglio', I said; 'so don't consider me an equivalent for one; if you have a fancy for anything in that line, away with you, sir, to the bazaars of Stamboul without delay; and lay out in extensive slave-purchases some of that spare cash you seem at a loss to spend satisfactorily here.'
>
> 'And what will you do, Jane, while I am bargaining for so many tons of flesh and such an assortment of black eyes?'
>
> 'I'll be preparing myself to go out as a missionary to preach liberty to them that are enslaved – your harem inmates among the rest. I'll get admitted there, and I'll stir up mutiny; and you, three-tailed bashaw as you are, sir, shall in a trice find yourself fettered amongst our hands: nor will I, for one, consent to cut your bonds till you have signed a charter, the most liberal that despot ever conferred.'
>
> 'I would consent to be at your mercy, Jane.'
>
> 'I would have no mercy, Mr Rochester, if you supplicated for it with an eye like that. While you looked so, I should be certain that whatever charter you might grant under coercion, your first act, when released, would be to violate its conditions.' (24)

The fictional exchange reveals under the guise of fantasy the growing battle of the sexes. Within a few decades the claim to greater freedom of speech and association would characterise what Elizabeth Lynn Linton called 'The Girl of the Period'. She voiced the disquiet of many, of both sexes, when she regretted the decline of 'the fair young English girl', who showed the 'innate purity and dignity of her nature' and was 'neither bold in bearing nor masculine in mind'. By contrast, the Girl of the Period is addicted to 'slang, bold talk, or general fastness; to the love of pleasure before either love or happiness'.[5] Not all women who were discovering their rights wished for political emancipation. Trollope allows two points of view to be voiced in *The Prime Minister*. Mrs Finn regards political life as servitude, believes that 'we women have the best of it' and when asked if she will campaign for her 'rights' replies, 'Not by act of Parliament, or by platform meetings. I have a great idea of a woman's rights; but that is the way, I think, to throw them away' (11). Lady Glencora sees things differently:

> Of course I know it would be wrong that I should have an opinion. As 'man' you are of course to have your own way . . . I suppose I may have my political sympathies as well as another. Really you are becoming so autocratic that I shall have to go in for women's rights. (32)

In a later novel, Trollope lets a woman voice her feelings about inequality in the personal rather than political sphere. Mary is forbidden by her father, the Duke of Omnium, to see the commoner whom she loves and is sent to live under a chaperon in one of the Duke's houses, 'The Horns'. Her brother is taking her on a visit:

> 'How I do wish I were a man!' his sister said to him when they were in the hansom together.
> 'You'd have a great deal more trouble.'
> 'But I'd have a hansom of my own, and go where I pleased. How would you like to be shut up in a place like The Horns?'
> 'You can go out if you like it.'
> 'Not like you. Papa thinks it's the proper place for me to live in, and so I must live there. I don't think a woman ever chooses how or where she shall live herself.'
> 'You are not going to take up woman's rights, I hope.'
> 'I think I shall if I stay at The Horns much longer.'
> (*The Duke's Children* 28)

Like much of Trollope's dialogue, this reads convincingly and also gives an explicitly revealing view of Victorian tensions. Eliot's Gwendolen Harleth is a more subtle presentation of the ambivalence which many women, including George Eliot, felt about the current situation (Zimmerman 1980). Self-willed, exploiting her feminine attraction to make a rich marriage, she falls into the 'male' addiction to gambling and lets her cruel husband drown until repentance turns her into a more complaisant and womanly figure.

Children in fiction

Babies appear covertly in most Victorian fiction; George Moore in *Esther Waters* was probably the first to venture any precise description of a maternity hospital. They have their part to play, however, not only as symbols of happy marriage for the virtuous but also as objects of the fond 'baby-talk' attributed to women and eschewed by men. Bella Wilfer gives imaginary speech to her baby who is supposed to greet John's new career by saying, 'with appropriate action on the part of a very limp arm and a speckled fist: "Three cheers, ladies and gemplemorums. Hoo-ray!" ' (*Our Mutual Friend* Book 4, 12). Eleanor Bold and her sister-in-law, both self-possessed women in mixed company, indulge in prattle when alone with Eleanor's baby, in a chapter headed 'Baby Worship':

'Diddle, diddle, diddle, diddle, dum, dum, dum: hasn't he got lovely legs?' said the rapturous mother.
H'm 'm 'm 'm 'm', simmered Mary, burying her lips in the little fellow's fat neck, by way of kissing him.
'H'm 'm 'm 'm 'm', simmered his mamma, burying her lips also in his fat round short legs. 'He's a dawty little bold darling, so he is; and has the nicest little pink legs in all the world, so he has.'
(*Barchester Towers* 16)

The scene is broken by the announcement of Mr Slope, which causes Eleanor to jump up in confusion.

Once children have arrived at years of discretion the words of their parents are often formal and admonitory. We do not get many glimpses of parents speaking on a friendly equality with their offspring after early childhood. Perhaps they did not in reality; but it is more likely that the novelists develop the potential of family tensions for conflict in their plots and prefer to concentrate on the severity which Victorian parents could assume when they chose. Butler's fictional use of his own experience is of course a classic example of adult revenge; Ernest Pontifex gets the full treatment from both parents. His mother's words enable Butler to pillory both cold parenthood and evangelical piety:

> Papa does not feel that you love him with the fullness and unreserve which would prompt you to have no concealment from him, and to tell him everything freely and fearlessly as your most loving earthly friend, next only to your Heavenly Father. Perfect love, as we know, casteth out fear: your father loves you perfectly, my darling, but he does not feel as though you loved him perfectly in return. If you fear him it is because you do not love him as he deserved, and I know it sometimes cuts him to the very heart to think that he has earned from you a deeper and more willing sympathy than you display towards him.
>
> (*The Way of All Flesh* 40)

This is maliciously clever dialogue: the formal public tone of the beginning and ending are meshed with the biblical phraseology of 'perfect love casteth out fear' and 'cut to the heart', and the interpolated 'my darling' stands out as a blatantly hypocritical momentary change of register. The Anglo-Catholic Edmondstone family are more loving and share more mutual respect. Laura's mother at first censures her in terms worthy of a Pontifex:

> Laura, you seem to think you owe nothing to any one but Philip. You forget you are a daughter! that you have been keeping up a system of disobedience and concealment, of which I could not have believed a child of mine could be capable. O Laura, how you have abused our confidence!

However, Laura's penitence at once produces the response of a mother, which gives more comfort for our image of the Victorian family, 'Forgive you, my poor child! You have been very unhappy!' (*The Heir of Redclyffe* 34). When there is no controversy over conduct and duty, even fathers who are intimidating figures in public life can be playfully indulgent, like Carson with his youngest daughter when she claims indulgence as 'the only lady this morning' – 'My darling, I think you have your own way always, whether you're the only lady or not' (*Mary Barton* 6).

    As for the children themselves, the Victorians, at least in their public attitudes, regarded them with ambivalence amounting to doublethink. The Romantic notion of childhood innocence and natural goodness was still strong, not yet challenged by Freud or by novelists of the century to come. At the same time, the Augustinian and Calvinist view of human depravity was not confined to extreme Evangelicals. Children were liable to lose their innocence very easily and needed to be protected against the world and against their own propensity to evil. This was especially so for girls, for whom one false step could be social disaster as well as spiritual peril. It is the more surprising that in the major novels children often speak naturally and convincingly. The discrepancy of dialogue between great and inferior writers is nowhere more apparent than in the speech of children.

Small children prattle inconsequentially as they have always done and show difficulties in pronunciation of some sounds. Little Polly Home feels 'Dedful miz-er-y' (*Villette* 3) and a small boy teased to smoke his grandfather's pipe says, 'I s'ant puff any more puffs' (*Wives and Daughters* 59). A striking contrast in parental attitude appears in the cases of two children who cannot manage the sound /k/ and instead produce /t/ – one of the most common childish substitutions. Ernest Pontifex is bullied and beaten by his father for saying 'tum' instead of 'come' (*The Way of All Flesh* 22) but Esther Waters's little Jackie is not even rebuked when he calls, 'Tum for a walk, mummie, tum along' (19). Children can also be disconcerting in their naive directness. Shandon's youngest child, who 'could hardly speak plain', calls Bungay 'Mr Bundy' and asks him, 'If you're rich, why don't you take papa out of piz'n?' (*Pendennis* 31).

Dickens has a less sure touch with the speech of Paul Dombey, who at the age of five is highly articulate in challenging Mrs Pipchin's moral tale about the boy who was killed by a bull for asking questions:

> 'If the bull was mad,' said Paul, 'how did *he* know that the boy had asked questions? Nobody can go and whisper secrets to a mad bull. I don't believe that story'.　　　　　　　　　　　　(*Dombey and Son* 8)

However, it is fair to add that Dickens has, a few pages earlier, explained that there were times when Paul 'looked (and talked) like one of those terrible little beings in the fairy tales, who, at a hundred and fifty or two hundred years of age, fantastically represent the children for whom they have been substituted'. Certainly he wrung the hearts of many readers who could accept the convention of Paul's prolonged dying speeches with such gems as 'How fast the river runs between its green banks and the rushes, Floy! But it's very near the sea. I hear the waves! They always said so!' (16). It is in passages like these that we have to take the Victorian novelists and their public on their own terms and try to see what the text was saying to those whose presuppositions were in some matters different from ours. Later in his career, Dickens almost seems to be sending up his own earlier creations when he writes of moral tales for children in which 'Little Margery . . . severely reproved and morally squashed the miller, when she was five and he was fifty' (*Our Mutual Friend* Book 2, 1).

Older children speak in short sentences with simple vocabulary, even when precocious in their manner like Catherine Linton: 'The pony is in the yard, and Phoenix is shut in there. He's bitten – and so is Charlie. I was going to tell you all about it, but you are in a bad temper, and don't deserve to hear' (*Wuthering Heights* 18). Egbert Pardiggle vents on Esther his indignation at his mother's escheating of his pocket-money in simple but forceful terms: 'O then! Now! Who are you! *You* wouldn't like it, I think? What does she make a sham for, and pretend to give me money, and take it away again?' (*Bleak House* 8).

The gender differences shown in the speech of their seniors are less apparent between boys and girls. They did not mix as freely as they do today, and conversation outside the family circle is generally single sex. Boys are direct, enthusiastic, prone to mischief and physical activity, traits which at that age can transcend class, as between Tom Tulliver and Bob Jakin. Their fight over a halfpenny ends with Tom's simple statement, 'There the halfpenny lies. I don't want your halfpenny; I wouldn't have kept it. But you wanted to cheat: I hate a cheat. I shan't go along with you any more' (*The Mill on the Floss* Book 1, 5). There is an equally straightforward dialogue when young Ripton objects to being called a fool by Richard Feverel. His challenge to repeat it, 'Do it and see', is taken up and he hits Richard; the response is simple:

'Shall we fight here?' he said.
   'Anywhere you like', replied Ripton.
   'A little more into the wood, I think. We may be interrupted.'
                                  (*The Ordeal of Richard Feverel* 2)

Much sadder are the preternaturally old children, worldly wise beyond their years. They often speak for the pressure of reality upon the poor, among whom childhood was brief and soon lost in the need to add to the family income. Shandon's child, quoted above, already understands trouble. The streetwise Charley who befriends Mary Barton in Liverpool is knowing and articulate beyond his years, with a masculine contempt for women's intelligence when she asks him what she can do to catch the ship on which Will is sailing:

> 'Do!' said the boy impatiently, 'why, have I not told you? Only women (begging your pardon) are so stupid at understanding about anything relating to the sea; – you must get a boat, and make all haste, and sail after him, – after the *John Cropper*. You may overtake her, or you may not. It's just a chance; but she's heavy laded, and that's in your favour. She'll draw many feet of water.' (27)

Charley's nautical knowledge is more convincing than his fluent command of language; but he is a device of the plot and not a developed character. Little Jude, 'Father Time', is a much more significant old-young boy, perhaps no more convincing on a realistic plane but effective in voicing thoughts which adults cannot so simply verbalise; when thunder accompanies the Doctors 'in blood-red robes' at Christminster he whispers, 'It do seem like the Judgment Day!'. Sue has to agree with his feeling 'It would be better to be out o' the world than in it, wouldn't it?' He becomes a real child when he bursts out 'I won't forgive you, ever, ever! I'll never believe you care for me, or father, or any of us any more!' (*Jude the Obscure* Part 6, 1, 2). The reality of the preternaturally old child was less picturesque and solemn. The company of the streets bred speech that was both harsh and succinct. Greenwood records his conversation with a girl of about ten whose infant brother was sitting on the footpath as she played. He asked, 'Can't he walk?' 'How can he when he's got the rickets?' replied the knowing female in tones that betokened her pity for my ignorance; 'can't you step over him, stoopid? Bat up. Poll, keep the pot a-bilin' (Greenwood 1881, 143).

As in other types of dialogue, a sense of reality was not conveyed by all novelists. George Eliot was scathing about children in fiction who speak too formally and wisely, singling out one character of four and a half years who pontificates in 'Ossianic fashion'.[6]

Notes

1.   The situation does not seem to have been much different in the early twentieth century, at least in some circles. The eponymous heroine of

Virginia Woolf's *Mrs Dalloway* (1925) could never remember the difference between the Albanians and the Armenians, and Mrs Ramsey in *To the Lighthouse* (1927) had difficulties with square roots. Lady Slane in Vita Sackville-West's *All Passion Spent* (1931) kept into old age her resentment about her brothers' superior education. These fictional characters would of course have been born well back in the nineteenth century.

2.   Bulwer's use of Greek words – 'the fitting and the good (or beautiful)' – in a book intended for general readership, bears out what was said in Chapter 2 about the widespread understanding of classical languages in the nineteenth century.

3.   Kingsley seems to recognise that the Victorian cult of chivalry, which was shared by writers of more than one social and religious opinion, often worked to the disadvantage of women by assuming that they could not survive without male protection. See Chapman (1986), 51f.

4.   The reference is to the Married Woman's Property Act, passed in 1882, which Amy calls, 'A Splendid Act of Parliament'.

5.   Linton's first article with this title appeared in the *Saturday Review* on 14 March 1868, and was followed by others eventually published in volume form. Her attack aroused much controversy, including a rebuttal from the feminist Edith Simcox.

6.   In her review 'Silly novels by lady novelists', *Westminster Review* **66**, October 1856. The culprit in this instance was Henrietta Lascelles in her novel *Compensation*.

CHAPTER 8
Class and occupational speech

Aristocratic speech

Victorian novelists sometimes draw attention to varieties of speech which are not marked by sub-standard or regional features, but are confined to a limited section of the population. While social class is often shown by deviance which marks the speaker as uneducated, the speech of members of the upper class may also differ from the unmarked standard used for the majority of fictional characters.

It was a period of concern about the true extent of the aristocracy and the nature of the aristocrat. The term was used freely and had as its core the holders of hereditary titles and their families. But the parameters, as in many contemporary concerns, were not so clear as they had been in the past. There were ancient families without title, like Trollope's Thornes and Dunstables, who thought themselves in no way inferior to the peerage, and in fact superior to those recently ennobled. The peerage itself had grown considerably over the past two generations and its members were apprehensive of further expansion. The threat to create a substantial increase in the House of Lords had been effective in securing the passage of the Catholic Emancipation Act in 1829, and again of the First Reform Act in 1832.

At the same time, the aristocracy still enjoyed great national prestige. In the absence of other charismatic figures such as sportsmen and media stars, their doings were watched and discussed, their social gatherings regarded as a public spectacle and their scandals received with satisfaction which released jealousy as well as prurience. Thomas Hughes describes the evening of a fashionable ball in Mayfair. After the lesser attraction when the canopy was put over the steps:

> The crowd collected again round the door – a sadder crowd now to the eye of any one who has time to look at it; with sallow, haggard-looking men here and there on the skirts of it, and tawdry women joking and

> pushing to the front, through the powdered footmen and linkmen in
> red waistcoats, already clamorous and redolent of gin and beer, and
> scarcely kept back by the half-dozen constables of the A division, told
> off for the special duty of attending and keeping order on so important
> an occasion.   (*Tom Brown at Oxford* 38)

Members of the aristocracy can of course be thorough villains. They
may be titled like Lord Steyne and Lady Kew, or they may be lesser
persons whose badness consists in taking advantage of their class
superiority, like Steerforth and Harthouse. More often, however,
upper-class characters represent the dreams of the middle class; as
Humphry House pointed out, the many Victorian assertions of
essential nobility and the right to honour in shared humanity were
directed not at the elevation of the working class but by bourgeois
claims to be reckoned among the highest in the land (House 1941,
153). Thackeray's *Book of Snobs* (1848) was satire that came
uncomfortably near to the truth about imitative pretensions to
gentility.

Nevertheless, the novelists often satirise upper-class speech. There
are recurrent patterns of deviance, mainly but not exclusively among
the titled characters, which could please the envy that was mixed
with middle-class aspiration. Some of these depict survivals of old
speech forms, preserved in the closed circle of higher social life and
sometimes made a defence against the lower orders. In lexis, some
elements of fashionable slang have already been discussed. In
articulation, slow, drawling speech, with elision of many unstressed
elements, is the basic characteristic. It suggests languor and laziness,
disinclination to make any effort, protected by the system within
which no effort is required. Lord Verisopht lives up to his name as
soon as he speaks: 'My ears did not deceive me, and it's not
wa-a-axwork' (*Nicholas Nickleby* 19). The 'debilitated cousin' of Sir
Leicester Dedlock shows the type with Dickensian exaggeration, the
detached, uninvolved nature of the speaker being further suggested by
free indirect style:

> A languid cousin with a moustache, in a state of extreme debilitation,
> now observes from his couch, that – man told him ya'as'dy that
> Tulkinghorn had gone down to t'that iron place t'give legal 'pinion
> 'bout something; and that, contest being over t'day, 'twould be highly
> jawlly thing if Tulkinghorn should pear with news that Coodle man
> was floored.   (*Bleak House* 40)

Elsewhere Dickens suggests lazy detachment rather by short sentences and a general impression that the speaker finds it too much trouble to develop his thought. Young Barnacle speaks 'in a nasal way that was a part of his general debility'. 'I want to speak to you, Gowan. I say. Look here. Who is that fellow?' (*Little Dorrit* Book 1, 17).

Other novelists use a similar device; Sir Francis Clavering combines the laconic tone with phonemic deviance:

> 'Good fellow, Strong – ain't he, Miss Bell?' Sir Francis would say to her. 'Plays at *écarte* with Lady Clavering – plays anything – pitch and toss, pianoforty, cwibbage if you like. How long do you think he's been staying with me? He came for a week with a carpet-bag, and gad, he's been staying here thwee years. Good fellow, ain't he? Don't know how he gets a shillin' though, by Jove I don't, Miss Lauwa'.   (*Pendennis* 22)

Clavering's principal phonemic peculiarity is one which novelists use for aristocratic speech throughout the period: the substitution of *w* for *r* is as distinctive a signal as the v/w switch of the cockney. It is another 'lazy' pronunciation, the bi-labial continuant replacing the vibration and tongue-placement of the expected consonant. It assists instant recognition of the character of Lord Mutanhead and reinforces the effect of his name, when he appears at Bath: 'Gwacious Heavens!' said his Lordship. 'I thought evewebody had seen the new mail cart; it's the neatest, pwettiest, gwacefullest thing that ever wan upon wheels – painted wed, with a cweam piebald' (*Pickwick Papers* 35). Gaskell comments quietly upon the habit – 'Miss Browning had gone in the chariot (or "chawyot" as Lady Cumnor called it; – it rhymed to her daughter, Lady Hawyot – or Harriet, as the name was spelt in the *Peerage*)' (*Wives and Daughters* 2). It was an accepted signal wherever aristocratic speech was to be ridiculed in print.[1] A lisp is another mark of the effete aristocrat: Lord Fitzheron 'lisped, in a low voice' (*Sybil* Book 1, 1). Thackeray's Lord Cinqbars says of a pretended duel, 'There wath no ballth in the pithtolth' (*A Shabby Genteel Story* 1840, 9). There are other phonemic deviances too; the Honourable Peter Brayder exclaims, 'Infahnally philosophic!' (*The Ordeal of Richard Feverel* 36).

The affected 'debilitated' tone used by novelists for men of fashion is witnessed by Bulwer-Lytton, who objects that 'hesitating, humming and drawling are the three Graces of our conversation':

We are at dinner: a gentleman, 'a man about town,' is informing us of a misfortune that has befallen his friend: 'No – I assure you – now err – err – that – er – it was the most shocking accident possible – er – poor Chester was riding in the Park – er – you know that grey – er – (substantive dropped, hand a little flourished instead) – of his – splendid creature! – er – well sir, and by Jove – er – the – (no substantive, flourish again) – took fright, and – e – er' – here the gentleman throws up his chin and eyes, sinks back exhausted into his chair, and after a pause adds, 'Well, they took him into – the shop – there – you know – with the mahogany sashes – just by the Park – er – and the – er – man there – set his – what d'ye call it – er – collar-bone; *but* he was – er – ter-ri-bly – terribly' – a full stop. The gentleman shakes his head, – and the sentence is suspended in eternity.

(Bulwer-Lytton 1833, 156f)

As the early Victorians carried on some elements of Regency aristocratic speech, so the drawl was heard more widely later in the century. By the seventies it was characteristic of middle-class affectation rather than aristocratic languor. A cartoon in *Punch* has a 'Captain Drawle' saying to the stage manager at an amateur dramatic rehearsal 'Well – er – my Dear fellow – er – er – it's your own house, you know – you can stand where you like!' and Du Maurier has one of his young aesthetes with the displaced *r*: 'I weally could't go down to suppah with a young lady who wears mauve twimmings in her skirt, and magenta wibbons in her hair!' (*Punch* 10 April 1875; 17 February 1877).

Lexical items are freely used to characterise aristocratic speakers. Various pronunciations of 'devil' and 'devilish' are frequent: 'What the deyvle', drawls Lord Verisopht (*Nicholas Nickleby* 19); 'I have been in a devilish state of depression', says Cousin Feenix (*Dombey and Son* 51). Gissing commented on this character, 'His talk does not seem to me exaggerated, and it is unusually interesting' (Gissing 1898, 101). The polite 'your servant' is affected by the pretentious elements of the middle class and seems to belong to them rather than to the aristocrats who had used it in the previous century. Dickens gives it to the uneducated genteel like Omer the undertaker, and Micawber uses it, distantly, to Mrs Heep (*David Copperfield* 21, 17). Honest country characters also use it, and it seems to mark one of the survivals of older usage in rustic speech; it is said by John Browdie to Nicholas (*Nicholas Nickleby* 13) and by Bob Jakin to Tom Tulliver, with the eighteenth-century pronunciation, 'sarvant' (*The Mill on the Floss* Book 3, 5).

The familiar speech of upper-class characters is not always debilitated. There is also the convention of making it hearty and full of sporting metaphors, a style which shows the confidence and vigour of a privileged class. Thus Lord Heddon suits his speech to his opinions:

> You hold that the young grocer should have a soul above sugar. It won't do! Take my word for it, Feverel, it's a dangerous experiment, that of bringing up flesh and blood in harness. No colt will bear it, or he's a tame beast. And look you: take it on medical grounds. Early excesses the frame will recover from: late ones break the constitution. There's the case in a nutshell.   (*The Ordeal of Richard Feverel* 18)

The Marquis of Clare uses another sporting metaphor about a pretty girl, 'I would not mind taking fairly long odds that she bowls you over in five minutes' (*Sir Percival* 4).

The aristocrat can take a patronising tone towards those of lower status, regarding it as a duty of rank to give instruction in the proper conduct of life. Lady Cumnor tells Cynthia:

> You must conduct yourself with discretion in whatever state of life it pleases God to place you, whether married or single. You must reverence your husband, and conform to his opinion in all things. Look up to him as your head, and do nothing without consulting him . . . Keep strict accounts; and remember your station in life.
>
>   (*Wives and Daughters* 57)

Lady Lufton is outwardly more genial but equally dictatorial in her message:

> Just explain to her that any young lady who talks so much to the same young gentleman will certainly be observed – that people will accuse her of setting her cap at Lord Lufton. Not that I suspect her – I give her credit for too much proper feeling: I know her education has been good, and her principles are upright. But people will talk of her.
>
>   (*Framley Parsonage* 13)

The convention that an aristocrat speaks with a remote and affected tone can be turned to good effect for revelation of underlying character. When Lord Mountfaucon speaks earnestly to Lucy, Meredith comments, 'Lord Mountfaucon had never spoken in this way before. He spoke better too. She missed the aristocratic twang in his voice, and the hesitation for words, and fluid lordliness with which he rolled over difficulties in speech' (*The Ordeal of Richard Feverel* 40).

Lower-class speakers sometimes imitate aristocratic features as part of their cult of superiority to their neighbours and aspirations to higher status. Bantam, the Master of Ceremonies at Bath, affects the aristocratic drawl and general inanity of speech – 'Never in Ba-ath! He! he! Mr Pickwick, you are a wag. Not bad, not bad. Good, good. He! he! he! Re-markable' (*Pickwick Papers* 35). Foker is a youth 'of whom you would hesitate to say which character in life he most resembled, and whether he was a boxer *en goguette*, or a coachman in his gala suit'. He too takes a laconic tone, with omission of pronouns and lexical repetition, when he speaks of his school: 'Beastly old hole . . . Hate it. Hate the Doctor: hate Towzer, the second master; hate everybody there. Not fit place for a gentleman' (*Pendennis* 3). Mantalini uses the aristocrat's sprinkling of oaths, with the short /a/ raised to /e/ in a style fashionable at an earlier time, affected in his own and later to become a cockney feature[2]: 'demmit, how d'ye do? . . . I will twist his demd nose off his countenance' (*Nicholas Nickleby* 17). Thackeray shows the shift as a variant on the minced oath *Gad*: the 'Dining-out Snob' Guttleton exclaims 'Good Ged! what the deuce do the Forkers mean by asking *me* to a family dinner?' (*The Book of Snobs* 20). The Coketown manufacturers 'liked fine gentlemen' and 'yaw-yawed in their speech like them' (*Hard Times* Book 2, 2).

The titled nobility appear frequently in Victorian fiction, disproportionately to their overall number but representing their importance in the minds of middle-class readers. Apart from the deliberate caricature of affectation, they show few special class features but speak with the idiolects proper to their imagined characters. The novelists did not spend much time in aristocratic circles, and the use of a title does not often show more than importance in the hierarchy of the plot, with a concomitant tendency to command and organise. Sir Leicester Dedlock is proud and reserved, laconic in speech: 'Officer . . . you know your duty. Do your duty; but be careful not to overstep it. I would not suffer it. I would not endure it' (*Bleak House* 54). There is irony in the stroke which later robs him of the speech which he had seemed to use grudgingly. In contrast, Thackeray makes Lord Kew relaxed and casual; his reply to the angry Barnes's, 'By Jove, he shall answer for it!' is 'I daresay he will, if you ask him, but not before ladies. He'd be afraid of frightening them. Poor Jack was always as gentle as a lamb before women' (*The Newcomes* 1855, 29). Lord de

Guest in *The Small House at Allington* is genially condescending. Lord Mountclere is simply the classic old man seeking a young wife: 'I implore that the marriage may be soon – very soon'; and his younger brother is a bullying snob – 'The suggestion is as delicate as the – atmosphere of this vile room. But let your ignorance be your excuse, my man' (*The Hand of Ethelberta* 39, 41). All these and many more are successful as characters but they do not collectively build up a record of aristocratic speech.

Occupational speech

Other group styles are associated with professions and trades. The increasing complexity of the nineteenth-century economy was producing more diverse occupations to be another factor in uncertainties about social status. Occupational speech is marked in the novels mainly by lexical items connected with special interests: this would be true in reality, where syntax and pronunciation were determined by education and environment. Occupational features are combined in fiction with sub-standard pointers or with standard speech as appropriate to the character.

Victorian fiction covers a wide range of occupations, reflecting contemporary society. Not all are given a distinctive idiolect, and many appear only briefly. The novelists concentrate their interest on occupations which were prominent in the public eye or which readers were likely to encounter in their lives. Special features are generally used to show the character in an occupational role, but sometimes are carried over into private conversation where they help to 'place' the character and to increase the comic or serious potential.

Members of the legal profession had been portrayed in literature since Chaucer's Man of Law. The rule of law was a cherished feature of British life, respected, feared by those who fell into its clutches, ridiculed as much as it was reverenced. Dickens, experienced in his early years as a court reporter, leads the way in the portrayal of legal characters. They range from Dodson and Fogg's clerk Jackson to the astute and successful Tulkinghorn. In general they are marked by their use of the legal jargon which Dickens had heard in and around the courts. Thus Jackson combines technical language with sub-standard pronunciation – 'It's only a *subpoena* in Bardell and Pickwick on behalf of the plaintiff ... It'll come on, in the settens after Term; fourteenth of Febooary, we expect; we've marked it a special jury case, and it's only ten down the paper' (*Pickwick Papers* 31). Serjeant Buzfuz makes his effect by reiterated court phrases – 'my learned friend', 'gentlemen of the jury', 'I shall show you', 'I shall prove to you'.

In general, minor legal characters have a heavy incidence of legal language which quickly establishes their place in the novel. Members of the lower branches of the profession are often shown as grasping and opportunist. The attorney Dockwrath responds to being called 'a mean, low, vile scoundrel' by saying to his clerk, 'Adams, just take a note of that'. This is reminiscent of Dodson and Fogg when Pickwick attacks them verbally – 'You won't forget these expressions, Mr Jackson?' (*Orley Farm* 20, *Pickwick Papers* 20). More developed characters have their own idiolect, with a sprinkling of legal phraseology. Jaggers is himself more than he is a lawyer, with his staccato, overbearing manner of speech: '*You* thought! I think for you; that's enough for you. If I want you, I know where to find you; I don't want you to find me. Now I won't have it. I won't hear a word' (*Great Expectations* 20). By contrast, Tulkinghorn uses legal phraseology in a suave and leisurely manner which reflects his craftiness:

> 'As a few fresh affidavits have been put upon the file,' says Mr Tulkinghorn, 'and as they are short, and as I proceed upon the troublesome principle of begging leave to possess my clients with an new proceedings on a cause;' cautious man, Mr Tulkinghorn, taking no more responsibility than necessary; 'and further, as I see you are going to Paris; I have brought them in my pocket.'   (*Bleak House* 2)

Minor legal figures in the same novel, Kenge, Vholes and Snagsby, are presented through the idiolect suitable to their personalities rather than with extensive legal reference.

The legal style can be humorous when it is carried into private affairs. The law clerk Guppy prefaces his proposal to Esther Summerson with due caution: 'What follows is without prejudice, miss?' he asks, and continues:

> It's one of our law terms, miss. You won't make any use of it to my detriment at Kenge and Carboy's, or elsewhere. If our conversation shouldn't lead to anything, I am to be as I was, and am not to be prejudiced in my situation or worldly prospects. In short, it's in total confidence.   (*Bleak House* 9)

Dickens has the richest array of legal characters. Other novelists generally use them more sparingly and confine them to actual legal matters. Trollope's barrister Mr Wharton has scarcely any linguistic signs of his profession; Mr Chaffanbrass in court is marked by a bullying sarcasm reminiscent of Buzfuz – 'Come, sir, out with it. If I don't get it from you, I shall get it from somebody else. You've been very plain-spoken hitherto. Don't let the jury think your heart is failing you at last' (*Orley Farm* 78). The drama of Lady Mason's trial is made effective by the contrast between Chaffanbrass and the emotive but restrained oratory of Furnival, the defending counsel:

> Gentlemen of the jury, there sits my client with as loving a friend on one side as ever woman had, and with her only child on the other. During the incidents of this trial the nature of the life she has led during the last twenty years – since the period of this terrible crime with which she is charged – has been proved before you. I may fearlessly ask you whether so fair a life is compatible with the idea of guilt so foul?   (Ibid.)

Barristers and judges in court are generally marked by an admonitory or bullying style of speech, with legal phraseology interspersed; the barrister who cross-examines Mary Barton:

> Now, young woman, remember you are upon your oath. Did you ever tell the prisoner at the bar of Mr Henry Carson's attentions to you? Of your acquaintance, in short? Did you ever try to excite his jealousy by boasting of a lover so far above you in station? (32)

The magistrate who sentences Ernest Pontifex enjoys himself with an ironical (and Butlerian) survey of the educational system before his peroration:

> Nevertheless, not only does it appear that your mind is as impure as though none of the influences to which I have referred had been brought to bear upon it, but it seems as if their only result had been this – that you have not even the common sense to be able to distinguish between a respectable girl and a prostitute.   (*The Way of All Flesh* 62)

This is speech used for authorial comment rather than establishment of character. Moore, too, has a point to make when he observes that the judge sentencing Sarah for stealing to pay for gambling enjoys a bet and a drink but expresses himself in deprecatory terms:

> For my part I fail to perceive any romantic element in the vice of gambling. It springs from the desire to obtain wealth without work, in other words, without payment; work, whether in the past or the present, is the natural payment for wealth, and any wealth that is obtained without work is in a measure a fraud committed upon the community. Poverty, despair, idleness, and every other vice spring from gambling as naturally, and in the same profusion, as weeds from a barren land. Drink, too, is gambling's firmest ally.   (*Esther Waters* 39)

Although Butler and Moore have set up targets to suit their purposes, the recorded judicial language of the period proves that they have not departed from realism into parody. Here is the judge sentencing Oscar Wilde and Alfred Taylor in 1895:

> I hope, at all events, that those who sometimes imagine that a judge is half-hearted in the cause of decency and morality because he takes care that no prejudice shall enter into the case, may see that this is consistent at least with the utmost sense of indignation at the horrible charges brought home to you. It is no use for me to address you. People who can do these things must be lost to all sense of shame, and one cannot hope to produce any effect upon them.   (Hyde 1948, 339)

The Parliamentary style, familiar through newspaper reports of proceedings, was of interest to those whose lives were increasingly affected by central legislation. Parliamentary powers were impinging more than ever before on private lives, and politics had became a recognised profession. Members of Parliament in general are not highly esteemed by the novelists; the brief appearance of Mr Gregsbury at the beginning of *Nicholas Nickleby* is marked only by the complacent clichés which were to appear later in the speech of Podsnap. Dickens does not make much use of politicians as characters; Disraeli naturally does a great deal more with the people he knew well, but often his politicians' words are reported only to create the appropriate atmosphere for his plot, as when there is an unexpected division of the House:

> Send to the Carlton; send to the Reform; send to Brook's. Are your men ready? No; are yours? I am sure I can't say. What does it mean? Most absurd! Are there many fellows in the library? The smoking-room

is quite full. All our men are paired till half-past eleven. It wants five minutes to the half-hour. What do you think of Trenchard's speech? I don't care for ourselves; I am sorry for him. Well, that is very charitable. Withdraw, withdraw; you must withdraw.   (*Sybil* Book 4, 3)

Even when Disraeli gives a political figure direct speech, the special effect is mainly lexical, contained in an intimate upper-class register: 'You will go down on Friday; feed the notabilities well; speak out; praise Peel; abuse O'Connell and the ladies of the Bed-chamber; anathematise all waverers; say a good deal about Ireland; stick to the Irish Registration Bill, that's a good card' (*Coningsby*.1844, Book 8, 3).

Trollope has an ear for political as for other speech, but it is not his strongest area of dialogue. When his politicians speak in the House, it is usually with the formal language of *Hansard*, given in reported speech for a locationary effect: 'A candidate had been brought forward, he said, by those interested in the Duke's affairs. A man whom he would not name, but who he trusted would never succeed in his ambition to occupy a seat in that House, had been brought forward' (*The Prime Minister* 57). In private talk, the use of appropriate language gives the reader a sense of eavesdropping on high affairs, although in fact nothing substantial is being said:

> 'We have not had a majority against us this Session on any Government question.'
> 'But we have had narrowing majorities. What will the House do as to the Lords' amendments on the Bankruptcy Bill?'
> 'Grogram says they will take the amendments.'
> 'And if they don't?'
> 'Why then,' said Mr Monk, 'the Lords must take our rejection.'
> 'And we shall have been beaten,' said the Duke.   (Ibid. 66)

Sometimes Trollope is content with a few technical words, familiar to his readers, to remind them that the speaker is a politician. 'The election will not come on till November, and you must look about you. Both Mr Monk and Lord Brentford seem to think you will be in the House' (*Phineas Finn* 47).

Novelists who did not come so close to political life have to be content with lexical items as the sole indicator: 'It is impossible for a noble to lead a democracy. The moment you begin to reason and argue with people, you may as well be a socialist at once! I was terribly near getting into office once: had the Buck-hounds offered me!' (*Sir Percival* 113).[3]

Doctors are characterised in speech by mention of their professional work. The effect may be purely comic, to set a situation, as at Bob Sawyer's party when Hopkins speaks:

> 'Rather a good accident brought into the casualty ward.'
>
> 'What was that, Sir?' inquired Mr Pickwick.
>
> 'Only a man fallen out of a four pair of stairs' window; – but it's a very fair case – very fair case indeed.'
>
> 'Do you mean that the patient is in a fair way to recover?' inquired Mr Pickwick.
>
> 'No,' replied Hopkins, carelessly. 'No, I should rather say he wouldn't. There must be a splendid operation though, tomorrow – magnificent sight if Slasher does it.'   (*Pickwick Papers* 32)

Black humour about medical matters is universal; Henry Kingsley give a similar brief glimpse of medical students commenting on a man as he passes:

> 'By Gad! what preparations that fellow would cut up into.'
>
> 'Ah!' said another, 'and wouldn't he cuss and d— under the operation neither.'   (*Ravenshoe* 59)

Sometimes medical language simply gives verisimilitude to the brief appearance of a doctor, like the surgeon who attends Cavalletto – 'there's a compound fracture above the knee, and dislocation below. They are both of a beautiful kind' and in the same novel the physician who 'can find nothing the matter with Mr Merdle. He has the constitution of a rhinoceros, the digestion of an ostrich, and the concentration of an oyster' (*Little Dorrit* Book 1, 13; 20). A doctor who is a major character uses the language of his profession when it is called for by the plot, like Gaskell's Gibson whose main function is to be a father and stepfather, but who can say, 'if he has got aneurism of the aorta his days are numbered' (*Wives and Daughters* 35). Lydgate, the most fully developed of medical characters, is given technical credibility largely by authorial comment on his study and theories. His conversation contains little medical language, and that only of the simplest; 'With our present medical rules and education, one must be satisfied now and then to meet with a fair practitioner'; 'the symptoms are worse' (*Middlemarch* 17, 70). The point is that Lydgate is important for himself and as the husband of Rosamond; he is not introduced like Bob Sawyer to exemplify the humour of the medical man in lay company. When the Middlemarch doctors are together their only medical shop-talk is about how drugs should be bought and dispensed (ibid. 45). Similarly, Candy and his mysterious assistant Ezra Jennings in Collins's *The Moonstone* speak in general terms about medical cases, with occasional phrases like 'physiological principle' to give verisimilitude.

Schoolmasters had been experienced by most readers of novels and are generally presented with a view to the laughter evoked by what is feared in reality. There are benevolent specimens like Marton and Dr Strong but more often the effect is satirical. Squeers and McChoakumchild are monstrous caricatures presented to express Dickens's views about the ill-treatment of the young. The Doctor who despairs of Arthur Pendennis at Grey Friars School is similarly used to make a point; his language, with legal instead of scholastic jargon, could serve for a fictional judge passing sentence:

> Your idleness is incorrigible and your stupidity beyond example. You are a disgrace to your school, and to your family and I have no doubt will prove so in after-life to your country. If that vice, sir, which is described to us as the root of all evil, be really what moralists have represented (and I have no doubt of the correctness of their opinion), for what a prodigious quantity of unhappy future crime and wickedness are you, unhappy boy, laying the seed! Miserable trifler! A boy who construes *and*, instead of *but*, at sixteen years of age, is guilty, not merely of folly, and ignorance and dullness inconceivable, but of crime, of deadly crime, of filial ingratitude, which I tremble to contemplate. (2)

Butler is more convincing with his Doctor Skinner, less obviously a schoolmaster but neatly presented as pompous and self-indulgent. Another caricature of the pedant appears in his censure of Ernest 'because he pronounced Thalia with a short i . . . "and this to me" he thundered, "who never made a false quantity in my life" '. His idiolect is more apparent when he is considering his next meal, rejects all suggestions and says, 'Stay – I may presently take a glass of cold water and a small piece of bread and butter'. (The dramatic 'stay' may derive from a specific reminiscence by Butler; it is used also by the Principal of the Deformatory School in Erewhon – 'But stay – yes – that will do very nicely' (*Erewhon Revisited* 13).) After this, Skinner eats indulgently and then speaks in the idiom of question and answer associated with the Evangelicals and perhaps derived more directly from Chadband – though Butler elsewhere in the same novel describes Dickens as 'literary garbage':

> 'And what shall it be to drink?' he exclaimed persuasively. 'Shall it be brandy and water? No, it shall be gin and water. Gin is the more wholesome liquor.'   (*The Way of All Flesh* 30, 27)

Stelling in *The Mill on the Floss* shows little distinctive idiolect but speaks in tone of his age and class, as when he gives his opinion of girls: 'They've a great deal of superficial cleverness; but they couldn't go far into anything. They're quick and shallow' (Book 2, 1).

Bradley Headstone in *Our Mutual Friend* is one of the most developed and interesting of schoolmaster characters. Dickens does not give him the caricatured pedantry of the comic teacher but rather emphasises the inner anxiety of a man who has achieved by hard learning a better position than his origins would make likely. His self-doubt mingled with dogged attention to his goal is shown when he is first attracted to Lizzie Hexam. Her brother Charlie has said that he may come to be ashamed of his sister's ignorance:

> 'Yes,' said Bradley Headstone in a slurring way, for his mind scarcely seemed to touch that point, so smoothly did it glide to another, 'and there is this possibility to consider. Some man who had worked his way might come to admire – your sister – and might even in time bring himself to think of marrying – your sister – and it would be a sad drawback and a heavy penalty upon him, if, overcoming in his mind other inequalities of condition and other considerations against it, this inequality and this consideration remained in full force.'   (Book 2, 1)

This is the mature Dickens at his best; the formal cadence at the end of Headstone's speech shows the attempt at self-possession after the groping conjecture with which he begins, emphasised by the hesitancy over 'your sister' instead of the personal name which convention would not allow him to use of a woman only recently met. Behind his words lies the anguish of many who were torn between social classes as a result of their own ability or good fortune.

The industrial manufacturer was a type who upset the traditional class structure. Rich and influential in his own neighbourhood, and a force in the changing economy of the nation, he was generally of humble origin. His sons and daughters might receive a good education and acquire social graces, but he was himself a man whom polite society could neither fully accept nor exclude. Disraeli's Millbank in *Coningsby* is one of the first manufacturers in fiction, and his part in the plot is largely to produce a son who goes to Eton with the aristocratic hero and a daughter whom the hero marries. Disraeli emphasises his abrupt, forceful manner when Coningsby, as yet unknown to him, comes to his mill: ' "He can see the works at the proper times", said Mr Millbank, somewhat pettishly; "tell him the regulations" ' (Book 4, 3). He becomes courteous when he learns who his visitor is, with a shift of verbal manner which suggests a man able to move easily between classes: 'I am sorry that you should have been received at this place with so little ceremony, sir, but if your name had been mentioned you would have found it cherished here.'

The most famous confrontation of old aristocracy with new capitalism is the meeting of Sir Leicester Dedlock and Rouncewell in *Bleak House*. Rouncewell's son wants to marry a girl in the service of Sir Leicester. His wish to give her some education seems dangerously subversive to the baronet who can imagine no better training than being in his household. The two men talk without true comprehension of each other, a confrontation of the old and the new. Dickens makes Rouncewell highly articulate, politely forceful and self-confident, the very voice of those who knew that a generation was changing the economic and social structure of Britain:

> I have lived on workman's wages, years and years, and beyond a certain point have had to educate myself. My wife was a foreman's daughter, and plainly brought up. We have three daughters, besides this son of whom I have spoken; and being fortunately able to give them greater advantages than we had ourselves we have educated them very well; very well. It has been one of our great cares and pleasures to make them worthy of any station. (28)

Gradgrind and Bounderby in *Hard Times* are much less sympathetic characters and, as their names suggest, caricatures of their types. Gradgrind speaks smoothly and pedantically; he ponders on the unwelcome signs of imagination in his children:

> Whether any instructor or servant can have suggested anything? Whether Louisa or Thomas can have been reading anything? Whether, in spite of all precautions, any idle storybook can have got into the

house? Because, in minds that have been practically formed by rule and line, from the cradle upwards, this is so curious, so incomprehensible!

Bounderby by contrast is the self-made man who prides himself on an even more lowly childhood than the reality. His idiolect is aggressive, staccato and self-consciously coarse. He expresses his views on 'idle imagination' in different terms from Gradgrind:

> A very bad thing for anybody, but a cursed bad thing for a girl like Louisa. I should ask Mrs Gradgrind's pardon for strong expressions, but that she knows very well I am not a refined character. Whoever expects refinement in *me* will be disappointed. I hadn't a refined bringing up.
>
> (Book 1, 4)

Gaskell's Thornton is a likeable man in notable contrast to these two. The novel in which he appears, *North and South*, was published a year after *Hard Times*; there is no reason to suppose that she was trying to correct Dickens's presentation, though, living in Manchester, she probably knew more of the manufacturer type than he did. Thornton has no strong idiolect but he too is direct and confident in his position. He speaks of the way he has reduced the smoke from his factory chimneys:

> Mine were altered by my own will, before Parliament meddled with the affair. It was an immediate outlay, but it repays me in the saving of coal. I'm not sure whether I should have done it, if I had waited until the Act was passed. At any rate, I should have waited to be informed against and fined, and given all the trouble in yielding that I legally could. (10)

The speech of Robert Moore in *Shirley* has no special characteristics beyond those occasioned by his radical and 'advanced' sentiments. In general, the novelists are more interested in presenting the social impact of manufacturers as a new and partly threatening set of men. Despite their regional placing, they do not usually speak in dialect, which is left to the workmen who have become their social inferiors.

The police force was a recent innovation, generally respected, and little parodied in comparison with the legal system which it served. Dickens's Inspector Bucket is one of the few developed portraits of policemen in Victorian fiction. He speaks with quiet and shrewd authority using some of the style of his occupation. When he is arresting George: 'You've been seen hanging about the place, and you've been heard more than once in a wrangle with him, and it's possible – I don't say it's certainly so, mind you, but it's possible – that he may have been heard to call you a threatening, murdering, dangerous fellow' (*Bleak House* 49). His speech is interesting as that of a new type of man, without much formal education but rising to a position of authority in society through the new national structures which were replacing the diversity of local custom. The other famous Victorian fictional detective, Sergeant Cuff in *The Moonstone*, is marked more by grave and measured speech than by any idiolect of his calling. 'Her ladyship has smoothed matters over for the present very cleverly,' said the sergeant. 'But *this* family scandal is of the sort that bursts up again when you least expect it' (First Period, 22).

Generally the police appear briefly when the plot requires their intervention and speak in appropriate language. 'Shall I take him to the lock-ups for assault, sir?' asks the policeman who intervenes when Jem strikes Harry Carson (*Mary Barton* 15). The Superintendent who calls on old Carson after the murder of Harry has no specific speech pointers to his job. The police officer may be a silent actor, like the one who watches Lopez in the Silverbridge election, 'very slowly making his way along the pavement' (*The Prime Minister* 34). Working men do not get the respectful 'sir' accorded to Harry Carson, but the tone of reproof is friendly enough when Jude is caught in reverie at Christminster – 'You've been a-settin' a long time on that plinth-stone, young man. What med you be up to?' His radical speech outside the 'Commemoration' gets a harsher rebuke – 'Keep yer tongue quiet, my man, while the procession passes' (*Jude the Obscure* Part 2, 1; Part 6, 1).

Non-fictional record of police speech partly supports the brief appearances in fiction. Kirwan gives a police sergeant a bullying, interrogative tone, with a cockney accent as broad as the derelicts whom he is questioning:

'I don't want ye partikler, I don't; but stop yer jaw and keep a civil tongue in your head will ye,' said the sergeant. 'Whose gal is that ere a toasting the taty with the skiver?'

An inspector at the races has very slightly deviant speech as he points out a notorious courtesan:

> That's her, Sir, as is sitting back in the front seat with a plate of
> chicken on her lap, with the golden butterflies in her lace bonnet, and
> the splendid diamond cross hanging from her neck – that's the gal with
> the blue eyes and auburn hair.   (Kirwan 1870, 66, 190)

Mayhew makes less attempt at accurate reporting in terms of heard
speech and is content to give the message more formally: 'That
woman', said the sergeant, 'is one of the lowest class we have; she is
not only a common prostitute herself, and a companion of ruffians
and thieves, but the servant of prostitutes and low characters as
debased as herself, with the exception of their being waited upon by
her' (Mayhew 1862, 63f).

Waiters were encountered fairly frequently with the greater
mobility of life and the gradual increase in habits of public eating.
The job was essentially male for much of the period; Munby records
dinner at a restaurant with 'a staff of quiet and well-conducted
waitresses' (his emphasis) as a novelty in 1872 (Hudson 1972, 307).
Waiters are usually part of the background for more central characters;
Dickens inevitably gives them a personal touch, as with the waiter
who consumes most of young David Copperfield's meal, but whose
language is that of the typical Dickensian 'fly' character rather than
distinctive of his occupation. William Potkins in *Great Expectations* is
little more than a silent audience for Pumblechook. The harassed
waiter at the 'Cat and Fiddle' has the reply, 'Yes sir – directly,
directly', in unbroken descent from the 'Anon, anon, sir' of
Shakespeare's Francis at the Boar's Head in *1 Henry IV* (*Sybil* Book 2,
10). Waiters' language that extends beyond a promise of service is
usually weary and defensive; when a dispute breaks out about an
interloper in the 'commercial room' – ' "The gent said as he was
'mercial", said the poor man. "Was I to go and contradict a gent and
tell him he wasn't when he said as how he was?" ' (*Orley Farm* 6).

Major characters generally show few occupational speech features.
The wide range of trades and occupations in the novels is often in
brief appearances which give little scope or need for more than a few
lexical features appropriate to the character and make it difficult to
pass any judgement on their credibility. Sometimes it is possible to
compare fictional speech with real observation. Trumbull the
auctioneer in *Middlemarch* apes gentility and betrays his commercial
outlook by his regard for the monetary value of cultural possessions: 'I
am a great bookman myself. I have no less than two hundred volumes

in calf, and I flatter myself they are well selected. Also pictures by Murillo, Rubens, Teniers, Titian, Vandyck, and others' (32). When he is conducting a sale his idiom is brisker; Ladislaw offers five pounds for a picture:

> Ah! Mr Ladislaw! the frame alone is worth that. Ladies and gentlemen, for the credit of the town! Suppose it should be discovered hereafter that a gem of art had been amongst us in this town, and nobody in Middlemarch awake to it. Five guineas – five seven-six – five ten. Still, ladies, still! It is a gem, and 'Full many a gem' as the poet says, has been allowed to go at a nominal price because the public knew no better.
>
> (60)

This reveals authorial imagination developing what could be heard in the contemporary world; Greenwood records an auctioneer at a bankrupt sale:

> 'Lot 28', says the auctioneer, 'is an inlaid worktable and a velvet-covered settee; what shall I say for lot 28? Ten shillings, eleven, twelve, twelve, twelve! Any advance upon twelve? Why, gentlemen, the worktable is worth thrice the money!' (Greenwood 1881, 155f)

Sailors are traditionally decent characters in English fiction, from Commodore Trunnion through Captain Wentworth and beyond. Soldiers, on the other hand, tend to be less approved; sailors were the continual defence of Britain's island independence and trade, and were out of sight for most of their working lives. Soldiers were more generally present and in the popular mind were associated with repression and the putting down of demonstrations. Captain Cuttle, probably the best loved of sailors in Victorian fiction, is a Dickensian original whose idiolect depends as much on his ill-remembered quotations and his recurrent 'When found, make a note of ', as on his nautical expressions. The latter serve largely to create humour through the incomprehension of his hearers:

> 'Keep her off a point or so!' observed the Captain, in a contemplative voice.
> 'What did you say, Captain Cuttle?' inquired Walter.
> 'Stand by!' returned the Captain, thoughtfully. (*Dombey and Son* 15)

Mrs Bayham Badger's more improbable nautical speech is funny in its incongruity; the information that her first husband was a sailor explains the idiolect, instead of the idiolect giving credibility to the character: 'The dear old Crippler!' said Mrs Badger, shaking her head. 'She was a noble vessel. Trim ship-shape, all a taunto, as Captain Swosser used to say. You must excuse me if I occasionally introduce a nautical expression; I was quite a sailor once' (*Bleak House* 13).

Gaskell's Will Wilson seems to be a sailor largely because he is a likeable character and is destined to make a dramatic return from the sea in order to give evidence. His speech is nautical in content and a few technical phrases but is not otherwise distinguished from the non-standard usage of his class:

> It were Jack Harris, our third mate, last voyage, as many and many a time telled us all about it. You see he were becalmed off Chatham Island (that's in the Great Pacific, and a warm enough latitude for mermaids, and sharks, and suchlike perils). So some of the men took the long boat, and pulled for the island to see what it were like.
>
> (*Mary Barton* 13)

Hardy uses speech to more purpose, but perhaps with some exaggeration, in Bob Loveday, who carries his nautical idiom into private life. 'Let me pilot 'ee down over these stones', he says to Anne; and again, tells her that he 'admired you as a sweet little craft',[4] and of women in general, 'any little vulgar action unreaves their nerves like a marline-spike' (*The Trumpet Major* 1880, 19). This kind of thing is effective in a casual reading but begins to seem forced on scrutiny. It may be concluded that the constant absence of sailors at sea meant that most people saw and heard little of them; there seems to be a literary convention of nautical idiom, spread through melodrama and popular stories into the novel. Brief encounters were richness for the novelist with a retentive ear. Dickens records the 'absence of knowledge of anything but English' in the crew of the ship on which he sailed from Genoa and relates how the chief officer dismisses a boatload of musicians in the harbour by speaking 'in this explicit and clear Italian to the principal performer – "Now, Signora, if you don't sheer off you'll be run down, so you had better trice up that guitar of yours and put about" '. (Forster 1874, III, 61).[5] Often a sailor exemplifies bluff good humour and honesty rather than showing any signs of his calling. Thus Meredith's Admiral Baldwin speaks like a typical country gentleman: 'Ah! he's a good whip, men say. Keeps first-rate stables, hacks and bloods. Esslemont hard by will be the place for the honeymoon, I guess. And he's a lucky dog, if he knows his luck' (*The Amazing Marriage* 1895, 13).

Soldiers, more frequently encountered by the novelists and their readers in all classes of society, generally have less distinctive speech idiom. This is understandable; mixing more with others and not confined to their own society for long periods as sailors were, they were less likely to develop their own jargon beyond the needs of duty. Dobbin, George Osborne, Rawdon Crawley, Major Pendennis and Colonel Newcome speak according to their education and position in society rather than their calling. Sergeant Troy is in the tradition of the treacherous and damaging soldier, but his speech does not generally follow the externals of his uniform and swordplay; he is shown as a man of some education who is considered to have come down in the world. Captain Brown in Gaskell's *Cranford* (1853) is a thoroughly good type, who meets an early and heroic civilian death; apart from a certain bluntness which can agitate the ladies, there is little of the soldier in his speech.

These are important and developed characters; others may be presented more as soldiers than as vital agents in the relationships of the novel. Captain Strong is caricatured for his insistent soldiership and speaks accordingly – 'quitted the service ... we marched through Diebitsch's lines ... he would have pounded the stock-jobbing Pedroites ... Alava offered me a regiment' (*Pendennis* 22). This is the humour of Ancient Pistol rather than natural dialogue. The Bagnets have named their children Quebec, Malta and Woolwich but neither they nor George use much military language, apart from reference to campaign experiences. When George puzzles over a letter, his burst of military metaphor is comic rather than convincing: 'Now what may this be? Is it blank cartridge or ball? A flash in the pan, or a shot?' (*Bleak House* 34). Major Bagstock, a character of some importance, is well characterised as sly and blustering but shows few speech indicators of his former calling: 'Old Joe, sir, needn't look far for a wife even now, if he was on the look-out; but he's hard-hearted, Sir, is Joe – he's tough, Sir, tough, and de-vilish sly!' (*Dombey and Son* 7). Here the last phrase suggests aping the aristocratic drawl rather than military style. Captain Dowler in *Pickwick Papers* speaks aggressively but with little military jargon.

In *The Trumpet Major*, having set up one brother as a sailor, Hardy had to give credibility of idiom to the other who is a soldier. John

Loveday uses little military idiom in his private conversations, though he has memorised the official regulations:

> By the orders of the War Office, I am to exert over them (that's the government word) – exert over them full authority; and if any one behaves himself towards me with the least impropriety, or neglects my orders, he is to be confined and reported.   (*The Trumpet Major* 11)

Loveday's reticence about military jargon, except in direct quotation, is humorously contrasted with the pompous Volunteer officer Festus Derriman who becomes confused about his drill: 'I should pull off my right glove and throw back my goatskin; then I should open my priming-pan, prime and cast about – no, I shouldn't, that's wrong; I should draw my right pistol, and as soon as loaded, seize the weapon by the butt.' The drill sergeant – 'I have only been in the army three week myself, and we are all liable to mistakes' does not manage any better – 'Tention! to the right – left wheel, I mean, no, no, – right wheel.' Miller Loveday picks up some of the military language with cheerful imprecision: "Tis only my son John's trumpeter chaps at the camp of dragoons just above us, a-blowing Mess, or Feed, or Picket, or some other of their vagaries' (Ibid. 7, 23, 17.). Hardy shows more familiarity than do most of his contemporaries with military phraseology. In his boyhood he had listened to men with memories of the Napoleonic years, which always fascinated him until he forsook the novel and wrote his verse epic *The Dynasts*.

Notes

1. For example, an affected young man, described in the caption as 'First Cock Sparrow' exclaims, 'What a miwackulous Tye, Fwank! How the doose do you manage it?' (*Punch* 25 July–December 1853, 18).

2. The broad cockney Drinkwater in Shaw's *Captain Brassbound's Conversion* (1899), says *vennity* for 'vanity', *bleck* for 'black' and *kepn* for 'captain'.

3. The Mastership of the royal pack of Buckhounds was an honour granted to a peer until both pack and title were abolished in 1901. Disraeli's Lord Marney 'wanted the Buck-hounds' if his party came into power (*Sybil* Book 4, 12).

4. This may have been something of a cliché for nautical characters. In
    Douglas Jerrold's melodrama *Black-eyed Susan* (1829) the hero calls his
    wife 'as sweet a litle craft as was ever launched' (III. ii).

5. This is reminiscent of Mrs Plornish speaking to Cavalletto; she 'attained
    so much celebrity for saying "Me ope your leg well soon", that it was
    considered in the Yard but a very short remove indeed from speaking
    Italian' (Little Dorrit Book 1, 25).

CHAPTER 9
Allusion and quotation

A striking difference between Victorian and present-day conversation is the decline in allusion or direct quotation derived from written sources. Fictional characters often speak in a way which aids direct communication between them but which may seem forced, and sometimes incomprehensible, to the modern reader. The higher educational curriculum, innocent of science and technology and, until late in the century, even of such 'modern' subjects as English, was grounded on the classics. Those who had passed through the grammar schools, public schools and universities were bonded by the memory, however faded, of what they had learned in their youth:

> Knowledge of the classics was still a universal passport. It opened the doors of intellectual society. On the solid foundation of common effort and allusion, the culture of a gentleman rested. Statesmen quoted Latin in the Commons, and even on the hustings: and busy men of the world found relaxation in the evenings or on holiday in re-reading the authors of the old pagan world whom they had first encountered at school or college. (Bryant 1940, 39)

The emphasis in this is on *men* in the male rather than generic sense, but women were not entirely excluded from the club. Girls' schools proliferated over the last quarter of the century, but even earlier the governess would impart knowledge of classical myths and history, if not of the languages. Agnes Grey and her sister are taught Latin by their clergyman father. Learned women like Harriet Martineau and George Eliot were comparatively few but many picked up their knowledge from general conversation or by sitting in on their brothers' lessons, even if they met the disdain of Tom Tulliver to Maggie – 'Girls can't learn Latin'. When Kingsley produced his redaction of Greek myths in *The Heroes* in 1855, he wrote in the Preface to his young readers:

Those of you who are boys will, perhaps, spend a great deal of time in reading Greek books; and the girls, though they may not learn Greek, will be sure to come across a great many stories taken from Greek history.

Such knowledge was of course mainly limited to the more privileged classes, although the appetite and capacity of many working men for education was remarkable. Well-read artisans who appear in the novels, like Kingsley's Alton Locke and Butler's tinker Shaw in *The Way of All Flesh*, were found in reality. It is not only highly educated fictional characters who draw on literary sources. Such allusion did not seem affected or forced. It was reference to a shared code; what had already been memorably expressed in the past could serve the needs of the present. There was something archetypal about literary sources which accorded well with the widespread Victorian nostalgia for the past and the glorification of chosen periods of history as the golden age which had its lessons for the nineteenth century. Ability to recognise and perhaps expand an allusion gave to speech a dimension which it has lost.

Classical allusions

Allusions are often lightly casual, to reinforce a conversational point, and here women are as articulate as men. Catherine Linton exclaims that any who try to separate her from Heathcliff will 'meet the fate of Milo' (*Wuthering Heights* 9). Signora Vesey-Neroni contrasts the sensitive Arabin with the men who 'not so highly tempered sever the everyday Gordian knots of the world's struggle'. She has no difficulty in picking up and capping Slope's saying that his old letters 'are burnt on a pyre, as Dido was of old'. 'With a steel pen stuck through them of course, to make the simile more complete. Of all the ladies of my acquaintance I think Lady Dido was the most absurd. Why did she not do as Cleopatra did? Why did she not take out her ships and insist on going with him?' (*Barchester Towers* 38, 27). Jude, an autodidact, draws on the classics when he feels the threat of his last illness, 'As Antigone said, I am neither a dweller among men or ghosts' (*Jude the Obscure* Part 6, 9).

Ginevra Fanshawe, although scornful of formal education, refers to a doctor as 'Esculapius' (*Villette* 24). Such passing use of classical sobriquets is frequent and appears in a variety of social groups. In the

squalid minor theatrical world of Costigan, everyone accepts the way
in which Bows calls Miss Costigan 'Hebe' when she enters with some
wine (*Pendennis* 11). A clergyman's wife, promising not to speak of
widowhood, says, 'I will not even refer to Dido or Zenobia'
(*Middlemarch* 55). The middle-class Edmondstones have no problems
when Guy says of a normally inseparable couple, 'The fidus Achates
was without his pious Aeneas' (*The Heir of Redclyffe* 5). The
hack-writer Biffen, learning of Reardon's improved salary, exclaims,
'By Plutus! That's good hearing' (*New Grub Street* 250).

In higher social circles women and men make more frequent
references and draw the allusion into their conversation. When Lady
Glencora is working for her husband's political party, ' "One has
always to be binding one's fagot," she said to Mrs Finn, having read
her Aesop not altogether in vain.' Mrs Finn picks up the point and
replies, 'Don't bind your fagot too conspicuously.' The Duke himself,
when it is suggested that he should return to politics after losing office
says, 'Caesar could hardly have led a legion under Pompey' (*The Prime
Minister* 27, 72). Sometimes character is revealed by an extended
classical reference which develops a simple allusion to the point of
pretentiousness. When Richard likens a woman seen in the park to
the Roman war-goddess Bellona, Adrian takes him up:

> 'Bellona?' returned the wise youth. 'I don't think her hair was black.
> Red, wasn't it! I shouldn't compare her to Bellona; though, no doubt,
> she's as ready to spill blood. Look at her! She does seem to scent
> carnage. I see your idea. No; I should liken her to Diana emerged from
> the tutorship of Master Endymion, and at nice play among the gods.
> Depend upon it – they tell us nothing of the matter – Olympus shrouds
> the story – but you may be certain that when she left the pretty
> shepherd she had greater vogue than Venus up aloft.'
>
> (*The Ordeal of Richard Feverel* 37)

Such a response would have been impossible fifty years later and
would have been shouted down if attempted. It is a sign of the
familiarity which could find analogues for new experience in shared
memory. Farebrother, an ordinary country clergyman, can say to
Lydgate,

> I am not a mighty man – I shall never be a man of renown. The choice
> of Hercules is a pretty fable; but Prodicus makes it easy work for the

hero, as if the first resolves were enough. Another story says that he came to hold the distaff, and at last wore the Nessus shirt.

(*Middlemarch* 18)

When Gibson, a country doctor, needs to warn his apprentice against sharing a secret, he relates at length the story of King Midas's barber and the reeds (*Wives and Daughters* 5). Dialogue continually reveals how the Victorians would draw on this store of common knowledge to aid communication.

Allusions to English literature

English literature was not considered an academic subject until comparatively late in the nineteenth century, but it was widely read by both sexes. Admiration for Shakespeare was at its height, though he might be read only in Thomas Bowdler's expurgated *Family Shakespeare* edition (1818). Milton and Bunyan were approved for their Protestantism; any theoloigical deviations in their work seem to have caused little concern. Eighteenth-century and Romantic writers were well known; Tennyson was the most admired of contemporary poets. The habit of quotation and allusion engendered by classical study extended to English texts.

Lady Glencora knows her Shakespeare as well as her Aesop: 'Othello's occupation will be gone', she says when her husband is losing office. When she likens herself to another Shakespearean character, her confidante Mrs Finn picks up and extends the analogy as quickly as she had the classical one:

'I was the Lady Macbeth of the occasion all over; – whereas he was so scrupulous, so burdened with conscience! As for me, I would have taken it by any means. Then it was that the old Duke played the part of the three witches to a nicety. Well, there hasn't been any absolute murder, and I haven't gone quite mad.'
   'Nor need you be afraid, though all the woods of Gatherum should come to Matching.'   (*The Prime Minister* 72, 80)

Her husband the Duke also has a liking for *Macbeth*, encouraging his son to speak in Parliament with 'but screw your courage to the sticking place, And we'll not fail' – not a happy allusion, since this is Lady Macbeth's exhortation to the murder of Duncan (*The Duke's Children* 67). While a present-day speaker with an academic background might well make a passing allusion to *Macbeth*, such an extended analogy is unlikely to be heard and the dialogue is revealing not only about the extent of knowledge but also of Victorian leisure to pick up and develop a conversational point.

Literary reference can be useful in tense as well as relaxed relationships. When Slope is skirmishing with Signora Vesey-Neroni, they communicate through mingled classical and Shakespearean allusion; their silent understanding of one another is conveyed through the names that have become part of the cultural tradition:

'True love is always despondent or tragical. Juliet loved, Haidee loved, Dido loved, and what came of it? Troilus loved and ceased to be a man.'

'Troilus loved and was fooled', said the more manly chaplain. 'A man may love and yet not be a Troilus. All women are not Cressids.'

'No, all women are not Cressids. The falsehood is not always on the woman's side. Imogen was true, but how was she rewarded? Her lord believed her to be the paramour of the first he who came near her in his absence. Desdemona was true and was smothered. Ophelia was true and went mad. There is no happiness in love, except at the end of an English novel.'   (*Barchester Towers* 27)

Recourse to literary characters in order to make a point covertly is had also by Mary Garth when Fred Vincy is pursuing her. He says:

'I suppose a woman is never in love with any one she has always known – ever since she can remember; as a man often is. It is always some new fellow who strikes a girl.'

'Let me see,' said Mary, the corners of her mouth curling archly; 'I must go back on my experience. There is Juliet – she seems an example of what you say. But then Ophelia had probably known Hamlet a long while; and Brenda Troil – she had known Mordaunt Merton ever since they were children; but then he seems to have been an estimable young man; and Minna was still more deeply in love with Cleveland, who was a stranger. Waverley was new to Flora MacIvor; but then she did not fall in love with him. And there are Olivia and Sophia Primrose, and Corinne – they may be said to have fallen in love with new men. Altogether, my experience is rather mixed.'   (*Middlemarch* 14)

This is very revealing in several ways. Two young people, neither of them presented as scholars, are able to share allusions from Shakespeare, Scott and Goldsmith. Under the cover of literary reference, things can be said which the convention of the time restrained between the sexes; the conversation which was becoming personal is distanced without losing its theme. Further, and this is true of all such passages of dialogue, the reader is subliminally persuaded of the 'reality' of characters who can themselves refer to characters of fiction.

Shared literary knowledge can cover an awkward social situation. Lily Dale lightly describes Crosbie to her sister as 'an Apollo'. Their brother Bernard hears the word as he enters with Crosbie and starts to question Lily about it. Crosbie, who has heard nothing, quotes from *Love's Labour's Lost* in a tactful attempt to ease the tension. ' "As sweet and musical as bright Apollo's lute string with his hair," said Mr Crosbie, not meaning much by the quotation, but perceiving that the two girls had been in some way put out' (*The Small House at Allington* 2).

The ordinariness of the speaker and listeners makes the detailed literary reference remarkable. In more literary circles, such allusions come as part of the whole presentation and are less striking. The hacks of *New Grub Street* continually exchange allusions and quotations. The death of Alfred Yule is likened to the end of Milton: 'He died in the country somewhere, blind and fallen on evil days, poor old fellow'. Jasper Milvain is more modern when he says sarcastically to his sister, 'Oh, if you can be a George Eliot, begin at the earliest opportunity'. He has to confess ignorance when Marian Yule quotes from Tennyson's *Idylls of the King*, but he is able to quote appositely from 'The Northern Farmer' about marrying where money is (1, 3, 37).

Tennyson is a favourite for quotation, particularly when the Arthurian poems support the medievalist enthusiasm which places some characters in the prevailing fashion. Shorthouse's *Sir Percival* is built around the Holy Grail theme; characters read and quote copiously from Malory. Constance, the narrator of the story, is better acquainted than Percival with Malory's Victorian adapter:

'Do you like Tennyson, Sir Percival?' I said.
    He looked perplexed for a moment, then he said, 'Oh, yes. I have read his poems. I like them very much.'
    'Do you like the "Idylls of the King" ?'
    'Yes,' he said, rather doubtfully: 'I don't think I have read them all.'
                                                                                                (3)

The young people in *The Heir of Redclyffe* act out a fantasy based on
the German romance *Sintram* (1814) by de la Motte Fouqué, but they
also know their Tennyson. When the novel was published in 1853,
'Locksley Hall', now often cited as a bad specimen of Victorian
evolutionary optimism, was new and challenging. Philip Morville is
shaken by it: 'There is nonsense, there is affectation in that, Laura;
there is scarcely poetry, but there is power, for there is truth.' Later he
makes use of the poem, as Mary Garth does with other allusions, to
present his own feelings without open avowal. 'I would not say a word
if he were worthy, but Laura – Laura, I have seen Locksley Hall acted
once; do not let me see it again in a way which – which would give
me infinitely more pain' (3, 8). Predictably, and no doubt speaking for
Charlotte Yonge his creator, the priggish Philip does not approve of
Guy's reading and quoting Byron: 'It is bad food for excitable minds.
Don't let it get hold of you.' Later he relents so far as to say that his
warning against Byron 'applied to his perversions of human passion,
not to his descriptions of scenery' (6, 29). Such literary preferences
can expound character types; Signora Vesey-Neroni, quoted above,
alludes approvingly to *Don Juan*, but Lord Cumnor gets into trouble
with his wife for quoting from *Childe Harold*, even though he is
mistaken about the authorship:

'To make a Roman holiday. Pope, or somebody else, has a line of poetry
like that. To make a Roman holiday,' he repeated, pleased with his
unusual aptitude at quotation.
    'It's Byron, and it's nothing to do with the subject in hand. I'm
surprised at your lordship's quoting Byron, – he was a very immoral
poet.'   (*Wives and Daughters* 12)

In an interesting kind of intertextuality, characters in novels may
quote from contemporary or recent fiction. The characters of
Dickens had already become standard figures. Bracebridge calls for
a drink, ' "to take the taste of it out of my mouth", as Bill Sikes has
it', and replies casually, 'Mr Jingle dines everywhere, except at home'
to Lancelot's question about his evening plans (*Yeast* 5). Phineas Finn
refers to the superannuated Regency dandy in *Bleak House* when he
castigates the taste for external show by telling the House of
Commons, 'Turveydrop and deportment will suffice for us against any
odds' (*The Duke's Children* 26). A ruined doctor can say, 'I am
physically weak, and, to quote Mrs Gummidge, "things go contrairy

with me" ' (*New Grub Street* 29). If this should seem forced, we can compare the factual testimony of Greenwood when an agitated man hails a cab late at night and the cabman, recognising a childbirth emergency, says, 'Mrs Gamp, I'll wager' (Greenwood 1881, 110). Attempts to improve the lot of the rural poor make Lancelot think of Mr Lyle in Disraeli's *Sybil* (*Yeast* 13). Violet in Charlotte M. Yonge's *Heartsease* (1854) enjoys *Mary Barton*; although her husband 'calls such books trash', his brother comments, 'he reads them, though' (4).

Biblical allusions

The use of the religious register in dialogue has already been considered, including pious but garbled biblical references. Allusions to the Bible were often made in more secular contexts, drawing on it as a source of shared reference rather than of faith. Here the classes were on more of an equality; the Bible, in the Authorised Version, was heard by all who attended Anglican or Protestant places of worship, in the denominational free schools as well as the fee-paying ones, and frequently by the whole household at family prayers. When Ruskin was a child the Bible was read from beginning to end, and then started again; and his family, though strongly Evangelical, was not exceptional.

Some biblical names had entered into the language with little regard for their original context. 'Hold your tongue, you Jezebel', says Ralph Nickleby to Mrs Snawley (*Nicholas Nickleby* 59), and the same word is used in a very different fictional and social context when Mrs Proudie says to Slope of Signora Vesey-Neroni, 'I am surprised that you should leave my company to attend on such a painted Jezebel as that' (*Barchester Towers* 11). John Graham warns his mother that one day 'I shall go forth like Jacob or Esau, or any other patriarch, and take me a wife' (*Villette* 20). Lopez, speaking to his wife, makes a cynical reference which accords with his character. 'You know that the Israelites despoiled the Egyptians, and it was taken as a merit on their part. Your father is an Egyptian to me, and I will despoil him' (*The Prime Minister* 53). Pious Dorothea is equally in character when she explains her plans for improving labourers' cottages – 'instead of Lazarus at the gate, we should put the pig-sty cottages outside the park gate' (*Middlemarch* 3). Sue Bridehead says that going from Kennetbridge to Christminster 'is like coming from Caiaphas to Pilate' (*Jude the Obscure* Part 6, 1). The servant Liddy, seeing the labourers coming for their wages, exclaims 'The Philistines be upon us' (*Far from the Madding Crowd* 9). Ability to pick up and extend a reference can give force to an argument. When the widowed Ethelberta Chickerel's mother-in-law says to her, 'I have been a Naomi to you in everything', Ethelberta replies, 'I do own that you have been a very good Naomi to me thus far; but Ruth was quite a fast widow in comparison with me, and yet Naomi never blamed her. You are unfortunate in your illustration' (*The Hand of Ethelberta* 10). Even Jorrocks's friend Green, frequently confused in his speech references, recalls that Nimrod was 'the mighty 'unter before the Lord' (*Jorrocks's Jaunts and Jollities* 1838, 12).

The phrases of the Authorised Version are used as interpolations in speech which are accepted without remark. Izz Huett, who admits to having 'an ear at church for pretty verses', saucily reminds Tess that there is 'A time to embrace and a time to refrain from embracing' – quoting from *Ecclesiastes* (*Tess of the D'Urbervilles* 23). Jude, once a devout Bible student and now unbelieving, still uses such language naturally when he says to Sue, 'I am in terror lest, if you leave me, it will be another case of the pig that was washed turning back to his wallowing in the mire' (*Jude the Obscure* Part 6, 3). Everett Wharton, never notably pious, finds it equally natural when admitting his financial dependence on his father, to say 'it was simply kicking against the pricks to speak as I did' (*The Prime Minister* 35). The biblical echo can be sardonic, as when Dare in *A Laodicean* refers to the *Book of Job* and tells his father that he comes 'From going to and fro in the earth, and walking up and down in it, as Satan says to his Maker' (Book 2, 5). There is a pleasant authorial irony when Vincy, having accused Bulstrode of excessive religiosity, fears that his wife will 'consider it your fault if we quarrel because you strain at a gnat in this way' (*Middlemarch* 13).

It is often the casual, and to the modern reader improbable, nature of the allusion which gives it credibility. The lighthearted comment, which might have been offensive to the very pious, shows how religious awareness permeated people's minds. Paul Emanuel characterises the inviolate confidence of Englishwomen by saying, 'I believe, if some of you were thrown into Nebuchadnezzar's hottest furnace you would issue forth untraversed by the smell of fire' (*Villette* 19). Stephen Guest teases Lucy that the local Rector 'has been preaching against buckram, and you ladies have all been sending him a round-robin saying – "This is a hard doctrine; who can bear it?"'

(*The Mill on the Floss* Book 6, 1). Squire Lavington abuses his radical gamekeeper with 'What right has the fellow to speak evil of dignities?' – 'quoting the only text in the Bible which he was inclined to make a "rule absolute" ' (*Yeast* 11). In a different social milieu, John Barton hopes to see his daughter 'earning her bread by the sweat of her brow, as the Bible tells her she should do' rather than become a lady (*Mary Barton* 1).

Foreign phrases in conversation

The use of foreign words and phrases in conversation was frequent among educated speakers, though it was often disapproved by arbiters of language. The extreme Saxonism of men like William Barnes was shared by few, although the author of *The Habits of Good Society* published in 1859 asserts that 'the best speakers will never use a Latin word where an Anglo-Saxon one will do as well: "buy" is better than "purchase", "wish" than "desire" and so on' (cit. Phillipps 1984, 53).[1] There was considerably more support for the view that modern English should be unsullied by extracts from other tongues. National and Imperial pride, and expectation that English was becoming an international language, supported claims that it was sufficient in its own strength to express any ideas. The vehemence of some of the opposition to foreign expressions suggests that their use was frequent in some quarters, and this is borne out by the evidence of fictional dialogue. Harrison's objection, levelled at writing as well as speech, is typical. Agreeing that foreign loan-words may sometimes be necessary to identify new referents, he continues:

> But it is very different from that silly pedantic affectation of interlarding our language with foreign terms, when there is no occasion for it . . . We wish not the manly form of our language to be tricked out in a coat of many colours. It has arrived at vigorous and manly proportions, and spurns from it that officiousness, which would hide its dignity under a load of foreign frippery.   (Harrison 1848, 378)

A newspaper article in 1863 headed 'English for the English' warned of a 'serious assault on the purity of the English language' and described the use of foreign terms as 'a vicious kind of slang utterly unworthy to be called a language' (*Leeds Mercury* 12 November 1863, cit. Crowley 1989, 75)

French was the principal and almost the sole offending language; others are rarely used except for such technical expression as Italian musical terms. When Cynthia Kirkpatrick calls Molly Gibson 'cuishla ma chree' she is quoting from an Irish ballad rather than showing any knowledge of Gaelic (*Wives and Daughters* 45). The same phrase with slight variation is used to add credibility to an Irish girl who greets an orphaned baby as 'Acushla ma chree' (*Ravenshoe* 3). The worldly Colonel Bracegirdle replies to a question with '*Quien sabe?* said the Spanish girl, when they asked her who was her child's father' (*Yeast* 6). French retained some of its esteem from the eighteenth century when it had been the leading European language of fashion and diplomacy. It was still the modern language most usually taught, though as an 'accomplishment' rather than as a serious component of education. A sprinkling of French was used by the nobility, often with no additional semantic value but rather as a sign of a shared fashionable code. 'A great Whig dame' talking of political plans says, 'Lady Charlotte has heard something: *nous verrons*' (*Sybil* Book 4, 12). Lady Glencora agrees that things have been 'Pas si mal' (*The Prime Minister* 11). Mrs Henry Wood makes Lady Levison wonder how a disgraced nephew can return to England – ' "Unless, indeed, he comes *en cachette*" – "En cachette, of course", replied Mr Carlyle' (*East Lynne* Part 2, 4).

Foreign phrases are still more frequent in the class depicted and satirised by Thackeray, earnestly striving to be associated with the highest. Major Pendennis uses a great deal of French in his conversation. Over a short period he speaks of 'an *affaire de cœur*', exclaims *mon Dieu!*, describes a man as 'another *soupirant*', which is too much for Foker who asks 'Another *what?*' and has to be given the gloss 'another admirer'. He says that his nephew's opinions 'one must not take *au pied de la lettre*' and declares himself *épris* by Miss Fotheringay's performance. He philosophises 'All women are the same. *La petite se console*' and recalls reading French tragedy at school (*Pendennis* 8, 10, 11, 55). The words he uses would be familiar to most of his class – Foker's question puts him at once in a lower order – and do not suggest a deep knowledge of the language. They also serve to bowdlerise references which might be even marginally sexual or blasphemous. In the same novel, Blanche Amory's French interpolations are even more affected and artificial and bring a deserved reaction from one of her admirers:

'Are you going to *bouder* me at present?' Blanche asked. 'Major, scold
your *méchant* nephew. He does not amuse me at all. He is as *bête* as
Captain Crackenthorpe.'

'What are you saying about me, Miss Amory?' said the guardsman
with a grin. 'If it's anything good, say it in English, for I don't
understand French when it's spoken so devilish quick.' (58)

French phrases were not confined to the affectations of the rich
and would-be fashionable but were also used by the professional
middle class. Dr Gibson's wife echoes Major Pendennis in describing a
'charming young man' as a *soupirant* (*Wives and Daughters* 60). The
honest Anglican priest Campbell says 'a luxury is in its very idea a
something *recherché*' (*Loss and Gain* 18). Mrs Grantly tells her
husband that he is so matter-of-fact that 'one can't trust oneself to
any *façon de parler*' (*Barchester Towers* 20). The pious Argemone fears
that Lancelot will 'become more and more *morne* and self-absorbed'
(*Yeast* 3). In the same novel Colonel Bracegirdle seems to regard a
French word as more suitable for women of a different sort – 'to form
liaisons, as the Jezebels call them' (2). Doria Forey exclaims, 'How
triste!' to an 'enamoured' curate (*The Ordeal of Richard Feverel* 4).
Even Charlotte M. Yonge's studiedly unaffected characters can
indulge in it. 'Et pourquoi?' asks Charles Edmonstone when he is
offended by a statement and Amy defends the absent Guy with 'Les
absens ont toujours tort' (*The Heir of Redclyffe* 7, 26). This last, a
quotation from Destouches, seems to have been a popular phrase to
check gossip behind people's backs; Cynthia Fitzpatrick uses a reverse
application to defend herself when she is blamed for misleading the
absent Roger Hamley: 'We used to say in France that *les absens ont
toujours tort*, but really it seems as if here –' (*Wives and Daughters* 36).
At another time she resents being taken *au grand sérieux* (34). Her
mother receives mild authorial censure because she 'delighted' to
speak of *objets d'art* in the drawing room (39).

Others are less certain of their pronunciation and represent yet
another aspect of contemporary striving for the gentility which
seemed to include use of foreign words and phrases. Jorrocks
apologises for the smallness of his 'sally-manger, as we say in France'
and banishes from his table such foreign dishes as 'blankets of woe'
and 'orse douvers' (*blanquette de veau* and *hors d'œuvres*; *Jorrocks's
Jaunts and Jollities* 12). Eliot's Miss Pratt feels that 'it is easy to see that
Mr Tryan is quite *comme il faw*, to use a French expression' (*Janet's*

Repentance 3). The auctioneer Trumbull offers 'a very recherchy lot' and Raffles claims that he has 'seen the world – used to parley-vous a little' (*Middlemarch* 59, 60). Such linguistic accomplishment, however, may be regarded with suspicion. In Mrs Braddon's *Lady Audley's Secret* (1862), the lady's maid Phoebe has been abroad with her mistress and has learned 'a little French'. Her cousin and sweetheart Luke is not impressed. 'French too! Dang me, Phoebe, I suppose when we've saved enough money between us to buy a bit of a farm, you'll be parleyvooing to the cows?' (3).

When the scene or the character has a closer French connection, the use of spoken French is less artificial. The English girl Ginevra Fanshawe, at school in a French-speaking country, could well speak of a 'tailleuse' and exclaim 'Dieu merci!' (*Villette* 21). Lady Elizabeth Guion converses in a sort of Franglais:

> How delightfully *reclus* and peaceful you are here, Duke . . . I could fancy myself once more in Paris, in the old days, among *les grandes dames* of the Fauxbourg. There was a pretty phrase, I remember, often in their mouths, *L'impiété perd les jeunes esprits*. Ah, in those days it was the best fashion, for women at any rate, to be *dévotes!*' (*Sir Percival* 8)

Latin was more acceptable in the circles where it was understood, and was freely quoted in law courts and Parliament as well as in conversation. Johnson's reply to Wilkes's objection that quotation was pedantry, recorded by Boswell on 8 May 1781, would still have been generally approved. 'No, Sir, it is a good thing; there is community of mind in it. Classical quotation is the *parole* of literary men all over the world.' Guy de Morville asks Philip whether he generally travels without luggage, *impedimentis relictis* and Philip replies, with a nonchalant change of grammatical case, about where he has left 'the *impedimenta*' (*The Heir of Redclyffe* 30). Newman's Campbell follows the French quoted above with 'Horace speaks of the *peregrina lagois*. What nature yields *sponte sua* around you, however delicious, is no luxury' (18). When the struggling writer Biffen has lost everything, he can still say with grim humour and no apparent affectation, 'Behold me undoubtedly a philosopher; in the literal sense of the words *omnia mea mecum porto*' (*New Grub Street* 31).

Although it was still common educated currency, the use of Latin was gradually becoming more self-conscious and the subject of jokes when it was imperfectly known or misunderstood. Brooke approves of

Ladislaw because he 'remembers what the right quotations are, *omne tulit punctum*, and that sort of thing' (*Middlemarch* 34). He expects less from women, telling Mrs Cadwallader: 'Your sex are not thinkers, you know – *varium et mutabile semper* – that kind of thing. You don't know Virgil' (6). His view is shared by Tom Tulliver, whose dismissive 'girls can't learn Latin' is echoed in a different and later social situation by Yule's words to his daughter: 'Don't I know the type of man? *Noscitur ex sociis* – have you Latin enough for that?' (*New Grub Street* 13). Charlotte Yonge, however, suggests that scholarship was not entirely a male prerogative. When a young man says, 'When I got back to my fainting damsel, *non est inventus*', Phoebe remembers the teaching of her governess and murmurs '*inventa*' (*Hopes and Fears* 7). The reader is left to decide whether the aspiring novelist Charley Tudor is preoccupied or ignorant when he replies to his friend's *omne tulit punctum* with 'Yes, I dare say' and the author comments 'too intent on his new profession to attend much to his friend's quotation' (*The Three Clerks* 19). Mrs Gibson reacts to a common Latin word as vigorously as Captain Crackenthorpe does to French; when Roger Hamley uses *ergo* in a sentence, she exclaims, 'Oh, if you are going to chop logic and use Latin words, I think it is time for us to leave the room' (*Wives and Daughters* 24). Mrs Micawber is happy in her rendering of *experientia docet* 'experientia does it – as papa used to say' (*David Copperfield* 11).

Mrs Micawber's error comes from hearing the old or Anglicised pronunciation, which was current for most of the century.[2] There could still be disputes about how to speak what was more familiar on the printed page. Philip is as priggish about the matter as he is about other things; he corrects his cousin Guy: ' "*Ovium*," exclaimed Philip with a face of horror. "Don't you know that the O in *Ovis* is short? Do anything but take liberties with Horace!" ' Later Charles teases Philip: ' "Yours should have been an ovation," said Charles, cutting the *o* absurdly short, and looking at Philip' (*The Heir of Redclyffe* 4). Tom Tulliver laughs at Maggie's reading of Latin since 'a young gentleman does not require an intimate or extensive acquaintance with Latin before he can feel the pitiful absurdity of a false quantity' (*The Mill on the Floss* Book 2, 1). Such episodes make the Victorian age, in some ways so familiar, suddenly seem strange and remote.

By the last decade of the century, respect for classical quotation had declined. 'Some men have a mania for Greek and Latin quotations: this is peculiarly to be avoided. It is like pulling up the stones from a tomb wherewith to kill the living. Nothing is more wearisome than pedantry' (*Enquire Within About Everything* 1891, 78). Nearly forty years earlier, George Eliot had attacked the use of Latin in fictional dialogue on the grounds that it was not true to life; she refers to the heroine of *Laura Gray*, published anonymously in 1856, who knows her classics well: 'It is such a matter of course with her to quote Latin, that she does it at a pic-nic in a very mixed company of ladies and gentlemen.' She continues in terms which seem to contradict some of her own later practice in fiction, as well as that of many of her contemporaries. If her judgement is correct, it suggests that there is sometimes an element of satire when characters in novels use Latin quotations. Usage in male company was perhaps different from what was approved on other occasions. 'It is as little the custom of well-bred men as of well-bred women to quote Latin in mixed parties; they can contain their familiarity with "the humane Cicero" without allowing it to boil over in ordinary conversation' ('Silly novels by lady novelists', *Westminster Review*, October 1856, 305f).

Notes

1. The preference for Saxon words in writing was kept by prescriptivists into the twentieth century. The Fowler brothers' *The King's English* (Clarendon Press, Oxford; 1906) gave the plain imperative, 'Prefer the Saxon word to the Romance', which remains in subsequent editions.

2. The 'English' pronunciation of Latin supports the point made earlier that the educated pronunciation of *says* was /seiz/, in R.H. Barham's couplet:
    What Horace says is
    Eheu fugaces . . .

CHAPTER 10
Conventions of fiction

Despite the growing demand for realism in fiction, Victorian novelists and their readers accepted certain conventions of presentation. Speech created within the text sometimes stood well apart from what might be heard outside it and formed a link with other literary forms rather than with life.

Theatrical speech

There is a strong theatrical element in the heightened speech which often accompanies emotional scenes. The nineteenth century was not a great era for drama, a genre which slowly came back to some intellectual dignity, aided by the Theatre Regulation Act of 1843 which abolished the restriction on legitimate theatre in London. Drama had been compelled to struggle against this inhibition, and against a wider opposition on grounds of its immorality, sowing of false social ideas and representing untrue events – the puritan objections which had been heard since the sixteenth century and which became particularly strong in the early part of the nineteenth. The fact that the theatres were frequently rowdy and sometimes violent was an added disincentive to the respectable of all classes; the novel, which at first met many of the same objections as the theatre, could be read safely at home.

Nevertheless, the theatre flourished as a popular entertainment. Managers in London outside the big patent houses evaded the law by combining drama with other amusements. The provincial theatres, many of them well equipped and supported, gave scope for the actor who was prepared to travel. The most popular type of play was the melodrama, originally, as its name suggests, a way round the patent laws by interspersing so much song and dance that the result could not be considered a straight play. Melodrama came to be an important sub-genre; it was tragedy adapted and simplified for a simple audience, retaining the tragic sense of judgement and consequence, but visiting it only on the wicked while the good ultimately triumphed. The characters and issues were strongly polarised, leaving no doubt where sympathies should be placed. Moral sentiments were uttered by the good characters, in rhetorical and mannered language, and eventually vindicated by the denouement of the plot.

Even as the drama struggled back to better things, the spirit and idiom of melodrama were not forgotten. Kirwan saw a melodrama in the 1860s at the Royal Victoria Theatre in Lambeth (the precursor of the Old Vic) called 'The Terror of London' in which the heroine defied the villain by declaiming, 'The fust m-a-n who places his polyuted touch on the form of my nobil up-e-e-ren-tis, though he were doubly armed with the king's authority, shall find his fate in the point of this pon-yard' (Kirwan 1870, 161). The diction recalls Dickens's rendering of the amateur actor in *Richard III*: 'So much for Bu-u-u-u-uckigham!' (*Sketches by Boz*: 'Private Theatres'). Three examples from successful plays written in the second half of the century illustrate the style, and reveal that it continued as late as Pinero, in the decade when Shaw began his work for the theatre:

(A mother learns that her son has been arrested) Dark blood-hound, have you found him? May the tongue that tells me so be withered from the roots, and the eye that first detected him be darkened in its socket!
                    (Dion Boucicault, *The Colleen Bawn* 1860)

(A man accuses his attacker) Back, woman, and thank that man that you have not my death upon your soul. You will be scorned, loathed, and despised by all. The blow you stuck me rendered me an invalid for months. I have been silent until today, because I gave my word to that poor, dying wretch. But now I am free – free to tell all. Speak to her, Robert, and say I forgive her.
                    (C.H. Hazlewood, *Lady Audley's Secret* 1863)

(A wife accuses her husband of taking her stepdaughter from her.) Listen to *me*! And how do you take her? You pack her off in the care of a woman who has deliberately held aloof from me, who has thrown mud at me! Yet this Cortelyon creature has only to put foot here once to be entrusted with the charge of the girl you know I dearly want to keep near me!   (A.W. Pinero, *The Second Mrs Tanqueray* 1893)

The experienced reader of Victorian novels will find much that is familiar here, including the proliferation of exclamation marks; the second extract is of course from a play based on a novel by Mary Elizabeth Braddon. It is a style in which, as in so much else, Dickens is prominent, effective and sometimes excessive. His love for the theatre is well known and perhaps owed its origin in childhood to the self-dramatising tendencies of his parents as well as visits to the Theatre Royal in Chatham with his step-cousin James Lamert, who was also an amateur producer. In later life Dickens was a champion of the cheap theatres as an entertainment for the people, and although he made fun of melodrama there he also showed some affection for it. He was an enthusiastic amateur actor, and an exacting producer, sometimes in classical plays but also in such distinctly melodramatic offerings as the stage version of Collins's *The Frozen Deep* (1866).

The novel which most fully both honours and subverts melodrama is *Nicholas Nickleby*. Nicholas and Kate are the stock hero and heroine of melodrama, virtuous and courageous, their innocence threatened by the world's villainy: a theme which was always dear to Dickens. That they are brother and sister not lovers, for whom rather shadowy partners are found late in the story, is also attributable to his complex emotions about family and sibling relationships. In moments of strong action, Nicholas speaks in the diction of melodrama. When he attacks Squeers:

'Wretch,' rejoined Nicholas fiercely, 'touch him at your peril! I will not stand by and see it done; my blood is up, and I have the strength of ten such men as you. Look to yourself, for by Heaven I will not spare you, if you drive me on!' (13)

His first sentence here seems to be a cliché of the melodramatic stance; Disraeli's Egremont uses it in a similarly theatrical challenge to his elder brother:

'Touch me at your peril!' exclaimed Egremont, 'and I will forget that you are my mother's son, and cleave you to the ground. You have been the blight of my life; you stole from me my bride, and now you would rob me of my honour.'   (*Sybil* Book 3, 2)

The structure of these speeches echoes a pattern frequent in melodrama and seen in the theatrical passages quoted above. A sharp imperative is followed by a further address or warning to the other

party in the encounter, and then by a comment which invokes the
past or looks to future action.

Kate does equally well in her denunciation of Mulberry Hawk, the
aristocratic villain of melodrama, as Ralph Nickleby is the wicked
financier who tended to displace the wicked squire in the later
development of the form, and Squeers is the semi-comic low
accomplice:

> 'If no regard for my sex or helpless situation will induce you to desist
> from this coarse and unmanly persecution,' said Kate, scarcely knowing,
> in the tumult of her passion, what she said – 'I have a brother who will
> resent it dearly, one day.' (27)

The authorial comment on Kate's words hints at the subversion of
melodrama that is also present in the novel. The overt artificiality of
Vincent Crummles comments on the situations and language of the
serious plot. 'He'll like your way of talking, I know' says the landlord
who introduces Nicholas to Crummles (22). When Nicholas tells
Newman Noggs about his assault on Squeers, he uses a metaphor of
the stage even as he speaks in stage language:

> If the scene were acted over again, I could take no other part than I
> have taken; and whatever consequences may accrue to myself from it, I
> shall never regret doing as I have – never, if I starve or beg in
> consequence. What is a little poverty or suffering, to the disgrace of the
> basest and most inhuman cowardice! (15)

The ironic distancing which accompanies the melodramatic line in
Nicholas Nickleby may be a realisation by Dickens that he had laid on
the melodrama strongly in the previous novel, *Oliver Twist*. 'Wolves
tear your throats!' muttered Sikes, grinding his teeth. 'I wish I were
among some of you; you'd howl the hoarser for it ... Stop, you
white-livered hound!' (27). Fagin in the condemned cell is the very
epitome of the villain brought to justice – 'Strike them all dead!
What right have they to butcher me?' (52). The death of Nancy,
which was later one of the highspots of Dickens's public readings, is
ready-made for the popular stage:

> Bill, dear Bill, you cannot have the heart to kill me. Oh! think of all I
> have given up, only this one night, for you. You *shall* have time to
> think, and save yourself this crime. I will not loose my hold, you cannot

> throw me off. Bill, Bill, for dear God's sake, for your own, for mine, stop
> before you spill my blood! I have been true to you, upon my guilty soul
> I have! (47)

Dickens never completely gave up melodramatic dialogue, although
he clearly saw the comic side of its exaggerations. That it pleased his
readers is evident from its recurrence. Haredale is the repentant
villain – 'I acknowledge to you both that the time has been when I
connived at treachery and falsehood – which if I did not perpetrate
myself, I still permitted – to rend you two asunder' (*Barnaby Rudge*
78). It appears in comic vein when Micawber denounces Heep, and in
high tragic vein when Rosa Dartle attacks Steerforth's mother after
his death:

> 'I *will* speak!' she said, turning on me with her lightning eyes. 'Be silent,
> you! Look at me, I say, proud mother of a proud false son! Moan for
> your nurture of him, moan for your corruption of him, moan for your
> loss of him, moan for mine!'   (*David Copperfield* 56)

With its Dickensian repetition of a keyword, this rivals and outdoes
such stage denunciations as that of *Lady Audley's Secret* quoted above.
A final example – they appear all through the novels of Dickens – is
the showdown between Carker and Edith Dombey with his response,
'Strumpet, it's false!' to her warning, 'Look to yourself . . . you have
been betrayed, as all betrayers are' (*Dombey and Son* 54). 'Look to
yourself' – the very phrase that Nicholas uses to Squeers.

The extensive use of the same style by other novelists shows it to
be part of the accepted currency of fictional speech. When Egremont,
'covered in dust and gore, sabre in hand' rescues Sybil in the attack
on Mowbray Castle, the chapter ending links the Royal Victoria with
1930s Hollywood. 'We will never part again,' said Egremont. 'Never,'
murmured Sybil (Book 6, 13). Harry Carson is worthy of the stage
when he threatens Jem Wilson, 'I will never forgive or forget your
insult. Trust me, Mary shall fare no better for your insolent
interference' (*Mary Barton* 15). Caleb Garth becomes the wronged
noble father when he responds to Bulstrode, 'I am in no fear of you.
Such tales as that will never tempt my tongue' (*Middlemarch* 69).

Some novelists use melodramatic style but then subvert it by
comment, often less concealed than in the sub-text of *Nicholas
Nickleby*. Thackeray can give his speaker a touch of the stage, as when
Blanche says:

I do not disown, I do not disguise – my life is above disguise – to him on whom it is bestowed, my heart must be for ever bare – that I once thought I loved you, yes, thought I was beloved by you! . . . You trifled with the heart of the poor maiden! You flung me back with scorn the troth which I had plighted!   (*Pendennis* 73)

The discerning reader may apply what is already known of Blanche to the obvious falsity of her avowal, and may recall her earlier words, 'I never saw an actress in my life. I would give anything to know one; for I adore talent' (40). If the others choose to take it as it stands, Thackeray implies, let them have their pleasure. Yet Thackeray could rival Dickens in the melodramatic tone when he chose, giving his readers the seasoning of rodomontade that they enjoyed. Major Pendennis defying his blackmailing servant Morgan is fit company for Nicholas Nickleby with Squeers:

One more word, you scoundrel, and I'll shoot you, like a mad dog. Stop – by Jove, I'll do it now. You'll assault me, will you? You'll strike at an old man, will you, you lying coward? Kneel down and say your prayers, sir, for by the Lord you shall die.   (*Pendennis* 680)

Trollope, always quick to mediate between speaker and reader, uses the convention to make an unsympathetic character ridiculous. When Bertie Stanhope catches Mrs Proudie's dress under the sofa:

'Unhand it, sir!' said Mrs Proudie. From what scrap of dramatic poetry she had extracted the word cannot be said; but it must have rested on her memory, and now seemed opportunely dignified for the occasion.
          (*Barchester Towers* 11)

Mrs Proudie might instead have been reading *Nicholas Nickleby*: 'Unhand me Sir, this instant,' cried Kate (19).

Manner as well as content can be deliberately presented by the author as histrionic. The old Duchess of Omnium places 'enormous emphasis on every other word'; when she speaks a commonplace the effect is marked:

'I never knew a house so warm as this, – or, I'm sorry to say', – and here the emphasis was very strong on the word sorry, – 'so cold as Longroyston.' And the tone in which Longroyston was uttered would almost have drawn tears from a critical audience in the pit of a playhouse'   (*Can You Forgive Her?* 22)

George Eliot is scornful about novels in which, 'ladies in full skirts and *manches à la Chinoise* conduct themselves not unlike the heroines of sanguinary melodramas' ('Silly Novels by Lady Novelists', 313). Kingsley tells us that Mrs Lavington speaks 'in a tragedy queen tone' (*Yeast* 7). When he gives distinctly melodramatic tones to O'Flynn and Crossthwaite in *Alton Locke* (1850) he may be parodying the extreme rhetoric of some of the Chartists whose methods he distrusted, though as a good Christian Socialist he desires to turn into pacific channels their spirit of revolt. When Crossthwaite comes near to the diction of a stage hero we may remember that melodrama itself often contained a radical expression of politics in defiance of the rich villain:

> Let there be those who will turn beasts of prey, and feed upon their fellows; but let us at least keep ourselves pure. It may be the law of political civilisation, the law of nature, that the rich should eat up the poor, and the poor eat up each other. Then I here rise up and curse that law, that civilisation, that nature. Either I will destroy them, or they shall destroy me. As a slave, as an increased burden on my fellows, I will not live. So help me God! (10)

Hardy wittily contrasts affected and genuine speech when Festus Derriman pleads with Mrs Loveday:

> 'Ask her to alter her cruel, cruel resolves towards me, on the score of my consuming passion for her. In short,' continued Festus, dropping his parlour language in his warmth, 'I'll tell you what, Dame Loveday, I want the maid, and must have her.'   (*The Trumpet Major* 36)

Eustacia, like Blanche Amory, is the type of character who would readily turn to theatrical language:

> O, the cruelty of putting me into this ill-conceived world! I was capable of much; but I have been injured and blighted and crushed by things beyond my control. O how hard it is of Heaven to devise such tortures for me, who have done no harm to Heaven at all!
> (*The Return of the Native* Book 5, 7)

Madalina Desmolines becomes theatrical in her last bid to secure John Eames: 'You will perhaps have discovered that a woman may be as changeable as the moon, and yet as true as the sun; – that she may flit from flower to flower, quite unheeding when no passion exists, but that a passion fixes her at once.' The humour of the whole episode derives largely from the dialogue, as John's commonsense replies contrast with Madalina's melodramatic passion, and as she at last reverts to colloquial speech when her hope is lost: 'If he thinks I'm going to put up with his nonsense he's mistaken. I've been straightforward and above board with you, Mr Eames, and I expect to be treated in the same way in return' (*The Last Chronicle of Barset* 80).

Characters may themselves comment on the theatrical speech of other characters. Markham tells Guy about Dixon, 'when he heard you had got into disgrace on his account, he raved like a tragedy hero' (*The Heir of Redclyffe* 25). Adrian mocks Richard Feverel's romantic notions about women – 'another groan; an evident internal, "It cannot be – and yet! . . ." that we hear on the stage' (37). Mr Pooter is brusquely put down by his wife when he exclaims 'Caroline!' with, 'Don't be theatrical, it has no effect on me' (*Diary of a Nobody* 5). Jasper Milvain says in self-parody, 'At last we meet, as they say in the melodramas' (*New Grub Street* 8).

The deliberately theatrical passages of speech are easy to identify, and are often identified by the novelists themselves, but an unresolved question remains. How far did the Victorians use exaggerated language under stress of emotion? Did melodrama really influence their speech, as stage and film have done at other times? Or was the idiom of melodrama only a heightening and concentration of the way in which people sometimes talked? Hardy, in one of his rather heavy authorial comments, suggests that the line between theatre and life was not always precise:

> At moments there was something theatrical in the delivery of Fitzpiers's effusion; yet it would have been inexact to say that it was intrinsically theatrical. It often happens that in situations of unrestraint, where there is no thought of the eye of criticism, real feeling glides into a mode of manifestation not easily distinguishable from rodomontade.
>
> (*The Woodlanders* 18)

It seems that the Victorians sometimes tended to use what we should regard as theatrical language. Highly emotional speeches are common in the novels; it may be that they depart from realism in their organisation and articulation of feelings rather than in their tone. The fact that it seems to have been acceptable to readers suggests that it was a convention which was related to experience. When feeling is vivid and uncontrolled, it is difficult to draw a line between it and the sense of melodrama. Sometimes the rhetorical language is appropriate to the context; in *Wuthering Heights*, where everyone is angry or distressed much of the time, we learn to take dialogue as a manifestation of the character rather than as a transcript of something heard. Thus Catherine Linton:

> Hush, this moment! You mention that name and I end the matter instantly by a spring from the window! What you touch at present you may have; but my soul will be on that hill- top before you lay hands on me again. I don't want you, Edgar: I am past wanting you. Return to your books. I'm glad you possess a consolation, for all you had in me is gone. (12)

Brontë characters in general are rich in emotion; and Lucy Snowe has a dramatic turn of phrase when she is upset:

> Your own: yours – the letter you wrote to me. I had come here to read it quietly. I could not find another spot where it was possible to have it to myself. I had saved it all day – never opened it till this evening: it was scarcely glanced over: *I cannot bear* to lose it. Oh, my letter!
>
> (*Villette* 22)

The literary convention, not too far from life, maintained its hold. Later in the century a minor novelist like Shorthouse can use it:

> I beg of you to stop! I have a sense given me that the errand on which you are determined is needless – worse than needless. Were it otherwise I would not stop you, but I am confident that it is not the will of God that we should go on. The air is full of evil omens: let us turn back.
>
> (*Sir Percival* 7)

However, a more sophisticated novelist in the second half of the century, and one capable of quietly subverting the extreme of melodrama, can make a speaker equally passionate:

> 'I tell you it is an infamy, Clare! It's a miserable sin! I tell you, if I had done such a thing I would not live for an hour after it. And coldly to prepare for it! to be busy about your dresses! They told me when I came in that you were with the milliner. To be smiling over the horrible outrage! decorating yourself!' . . . he burst unto tears.
>
> (*The Ordeal of Richard Feverel* 36)

So too speaks Gissing's Amy Reardon: 'Oh, try, try, if you can't save us even yet! You know without my saying it that I do love you; it's dreadful to me to think all our happy life should be at an end, when we thought of such a future together' (*New Grub Street* 15).

The Victorians were apparently accustomed to passionate outbursts, with the intonational equivalent of exclamation marks. Or perhaps the diction of the novels represented feelings that they understood and would have liked to express so articulately. In terms of realism, the statement of controlled emotion is more convincing, and is often effective because the same novel may contain instances of stronger passion. It is psychologically sound when Mary Barton, after a highly emotional speech, 'burst into a passion of tears' and then 'checking herself with a strong effort' adds:

> I must not cry; I must not give way; there will be time enough for that hereafter, if – I only wanted you to speak kindly to me, Margaret, for I am very, very wretched; more wretched than anyone can know; more wretched, I sometimes fancy, than I have deserved. (23)

Trollope's characters in general stay calmer and preserve their dignity even in anger. Eleanor Bold defends Slope:

> If he be ever so improper, how can I help his having written to me? But you are all prejudiced against him to such an extent that that which could be kind and generous in another man is odious and impudent in him. I hate a religion that teaches one to be so one-sided in one's charity. (*Barchester Towers* 28)

Perhaps truest to life are the speeches where emotion breaks the even flow and the character is less articulate. This, rather than the theatrical or the studiedly controlled, seems to bring us to the reality of relationships. Guy Morville shows the temper for which his family is notorious:

> My guardian is a mere weak fool. I don't blame him, – he can't help it; but to see him made a tool of! He twists him round his finger, abuses his weakness to insult – to accuse. But he shall give me an account! (*The Heir of Redclyffe* 16)

Major Pendennis, 'trembling in his wrath', loses his urbanity with Arthur:

> If you choose, sir, after all we've done for you, after all I've done for you
> myself, to insult your mother and disgrace your name, by allying
> yourself with a low-born kitchen-girl, go and do it, by Gad, – but let us,
> ma'am, have no more to do with him. I wash my hands of you, sir, – I
> wash my hands of you.   (*Pendennis* 58)

This has the ring of truth from an outraged elder. There is conviction too when Sue Bridehead, usually provokingly rational in her arguments, breaks into confused speech when she tries to speak of her sexual repulsion;

> I *do* like you! But I didn't reflect it would be – that it would be so much
> more than that . . . For a man and woman to live on intimate terms
> when one feels as I do is adultery, in any circumstances, however legal.
> There – I've said it! . . . Will you let me, Richard?
>   (*Jude the Obscure* Part 4, 3)

Squire Hamley's broken speech is convincing when he learns that his dead son had a French wife: 'It's true . . . she's his wife, and he's her husband – was her husband – that's the word for it – was! Poor lad! poor lad! It's cost him a deal. Pray God, it wasn't my fault' (*Wives and Daughters* 53).

Courtship and proposals

Proposals of marriage are frequent in the Victorian novel, where marriage itself is often the proper ending for the virtuous young. Here we may assume that neither the novelists nor their readers had a great deal of evidence from real life; it was not a situation which they would have experienced very often, and it was one which by its very nature would have no witnesses. A convention of suitably romantic language grows up, assigned almost entirely to male characters, since masculine initiative was to be assumed in these matters. The tone of the Victorian proposal is something of a cliché, easily parodied by later writers who want to give a quick impression of the period.[1] The idiom of proposals remains fairly constant through the century and may be seen as self-perpetuating, derived from even earlier efforts in fiction and drama. There are passages in Victorian novels in lineal descent from the speech of Worthy in Vanbrugh's *The Relapse* (1697):

> Behold a burning lover at your feet, his fever raging in his veins. See
> how he glows, how he consumes! Extend the arms of mercy to his aid –

his zeal may give him title to your pity, although his merit cannot claim your love. (Act 5)

The accents of melodrama are an acceptable part of the code in these intimate scenes; the reader is eavesdropping on a situation where imagination must take the place of reporting. Thus Egremont to Sybil: 'Do not reject my love; it is deep as your nature, and fervent as my own. Banish those prejudices that have embittered your existence, and, if persisted in, may wither mine. Deign to retain this hand!' (*Sybil* Book 5, 1). Philip Wakem is similarly flowery in speaking to Maggie, though she has rather more to say for herself subsequently in rejecting him; she has said that she has no pity for conceited people:

> But suppose, Maggie – suppose it was a man who was not conceited – who felt he had nothing to be conceited about – who had been marked from childhood to a peculiar kind of suffering – and to whom you were the day-star of his life – who loved you, worshipped you, so entirely that he felt it happiness enough for him if you would let him see you at rare moments. . . .   (*The Mill on the Floss* Book 5, 4)

Stephen Guest is even more theatrical when his turn comes: 'If you love me, you are mine. Who can have so great a claim on you as I have? My life is bound up in your love. There is nothing in the past that can annul our right to each other: it is the first time we have either of us loved with our whole heart and soul' (ibid. Book 6, 14). Pleading and a degree of self-depreciation, combined with a modest presentation of credentials, is considered proper for the lover, as Pendennis says to Laura:

> I have lost many an illusion and ambition, but I am not without hope still. Talents I know I have, wretchedly as I have misapplied them: they may serve me yet: they would, had I a motive for action. Let me go away and think that I am pledged to return to you. Let me go and work, and hope that you will share my success if I gain it. You have given me so much, dear Laura, will you take from me nothing? (27)

Even while the convention is honoured, the novelists try to introduce some realism by adapting it to the characters they have created. Gaskell, with her sympathetic ear for the poor and inarticulate, modifies inflated language to the formal but convincing declaration which Jem Wilson makes:

> And now, Mary, I've a home to offer you, and a heart as true as ever man had to love you and cherish you; we shall never be rich folk, I dare say; but if a loving heart and a strong right arm can shield you from sorrow, or from want, mine shall do it. I cannot speak as I would like; my love won't let itself be put in words. But oh! darling, say you believe me, and that you'll be mine.   (*Mary Barton* 11)

Jasper Milvain, in keeping with the concern for a regular income which is his own theme and that of the novel in which he appears, calculates his chances – 'it may be another ten years before I can count on an income of five or six hundred pounds' – before rhetoric takes over:

> I love you, Marian. I want you to be my wife. I have never seen any other girl who impressed me as you did from the first. If I had been weak enough to try to win anyone but you, I should have known that I had turned aside from the path of my true happiness. Let us forget for a moment all our circumstances. I hold your hands, and look into your face, and say that I love you, Whatever answer you give, I love you!

Gissing's naturalism soon reasserts itself and subverts the rhetoric with 'a sense of relief that Jasper had passed from dithyrambs to conversation on practical points' (*New Grub Street* 24). Milvain, it will be remembered, has all the time an eye to Marian's recent legacy. Dickens, never at a loss for direct dialogue in any register, chooses to move into the realm of comedy by giving David's proposal to Dora in *oratio obliqua*: the clichés of fiction are distanced for the reader's amusement, and the dog becomes as articulate as the man:

> I had always loved her every minute, day and night, since I first saw her. I loved her at that minute to distraction. I should always love her, every minute, to distraction. Lovers had loved before, and lovers would love again; but no lover had ever loved, might, could, would, or should ever love, as I loved Dora. The more I raved, the more Jip barked. Each of us, in his own way, got more mad every moment.
>
> (*David Copperfield* 33)

The hero, of course, must keep up the tone even in rejection and prove his manhood by articulate agreement, as when Lancelot is refused by Argemone:

> Yes, I will go. I have had mad dreams, conceited and insolent: and have met with my deserts. Brute and fool as I am, I have aspired even to you! And I have gained in the sunshine of your condescension, strength and purity. – Is not that enough for me? And now, I will show you that I love you – by obeying you. You tell me to depart – I go for ever.
>
> (*Yeast* 10)

Although the prevalence of the style suggests that readers were happy with the conventional declarations of love, reviewers could challenge it. An article on 'The uses of fiction' wonders how the proposals uttered in novels would be received by a girl of nineteen:

> A better judge of the naturalness of the love-scene than the reviewer who has grown grey-haired in dissecting books, and who looks upon such scenes merely as a more or less artistic product. She appeals to her own experiences, and the notions to which they naturally give rise, to say whether at such and such a moment Arthur would be likely to become rhetorical. She says to herself, 'No! If he were so much in love as this, he would sit still and trembling, perhaps seeking to touch her hand, and waiting for the answer of her eyes. He would not begin to rave, any more than to argue her into accepting him by telling her how much he had a-year.'　(*Tinsley's Magazine* 6, March 1870, 183)

Virtue and standard speech

Another convention of the novel is the assignment of standard speech to characters who would realistically speak a non-standard variety. Virtuous characters who play a major part in the story may be treated in this way, the purity of their speech reflecting the purity of their natures and their superiority to their environment. It is a convention which says much about the status accorded to standard speech as a pointer to being a worthy member of society. The improbable diction which Dickens gives to some of his characters has often been noticed. Oliver Twist is brought up in a workhouse and then thrown among London criminals, but his pronunciation continues to be as pure as his sentiments:

'Oh! for God's sake let me go!' cried Oliver; 'let me run away and die in
the fields. I will never come near London; never, never! Oh! pray have
mercy on me, and do not make me steal. For the love of all the bright
angels that rest in Heaven, have mercy upon me!' (22)

Standard speech is given to many more of Dickens's characters
whose natural goodness and salvific effect on others belies their
environment. The 'Little' trio – Nell, Em'ly (despite her moral lapse)
and Dorrit – are honoured in this way; so is Smike. Lizzie Hexam,
daughter of a villainous Thames waterman, speaks as if already
aspiring towards her marriage to Eugene Wrayburn. By this time,
however, the art of Dickens has advanced: her speech is much less
melodramatic than Oliver Twist's and shows some minor
non-standard features. She says to her brother – whose aspirations to
gentility are less creditable – 'as I sit a looking at the fire . . . I look at
it of an evening . . . up comes father' but these are working-class
idioms inserted in articulate language which shows no trace of
non-standard pronunciation. She becomes more articulate and
dramatic as her part in the plot unfolds:

Think of me, as belonging to another station, and quite cut off from
you in honour. Remember that I have no protector near me, unless I
have one in your noble heart. Respect my good name. If you feel
towards me, in one particular, as you might if I was a lady, give me the
full claims of a lady upon your generous behaviour. I am removed from
you and your family by being a working girl. How true a gentleman to
be as considerate of me as if I was removed by being a Queen!
(*Our Mutual Friend* Book 4, 6)

Nevertheless, her way of talking remains simple in lexis and syntax
and her virtuous simplicity is thus suggested without too much
violence to realism; Lizzie Hexam is altogether a more subtle exemplar
of virtuous standard speech than some of Dickens's characters.

The use of the convention by Dickens is striking because his
saintly poor are usually drawn from the most degraded environments
and their speech contrasts with that of those around them. The strain
on credulity is not so great with Tom and Maggie Tulliver, whose
family shows minor rather than heavy dialect. The reader is to accept
Maggie's quality of mind rather than actual purity of diction when she
seems to speak differently from her father. Her description of the devil
in *Pilgrim's Progress* is that of an educated child: 'Here he is . . . and

Tom coloured him for me with his paints when he was at home last holidays – the body's all black, you know, and the eyes red, like fire, because he's all fire inside, and it shines out at his eyes.' Her father's comment is in more demotic speech: 'the child 'ull learn more mischief nor good wi' the book' (*The Mill on the Floss* Book 1, 3). Henry James wrote about another of Eliot's characters, 'Felix Holt converses in the tone of a gentleman and philosopher with cultivated associates, and although he earns a bare livelihood as a journeyman watchmaker, his time seems to be always at his own disposal' (*Nation* iii, 16 August 1866).

Jude Fawley is an important example; he is articulate as becomes his frustrated superior intelligence, and the question of his pronunciation is left unresolved. He is seldom given the dialect pointers which Hardy can use to good effect. There is, however, the revealing comment that Father Time, living with Jude and Sue, 'had learned to use the Wessex tongue quite naturally' (*Jude the Obscure* Part 5, 7). The boy Jude is almost as improbable as Oliver Twist:

'You', he said, addressing the breeze caressingly, 'were in Christminster city between one and two hours ago, floating along the streets, pulling round the weather-cocks, touching Mr Phillotson's face, being breathed by him; and now you are here, breathed by me – you, the very same.'
(Part 1, 3)

When the adult Jude speaks of Christminster like an educated and well-read man, and his speech is sharply contrasted with that of a fellow-countryman, the effect is not to be taken as a graphological realisation of words heard but rather as a symbol of Jude's tragedy where potential is frustrated by opportunity. Indeed, Hardy seems to subvert the portentous words of his hero through the dismissive words of the respondent:

'It is a unique centre of thought and religion – the intellectual and spiritual granary of this country. All that silence and absence of goings-on is the stillness of infinite motion – the sleep of the spinning-top, to borrow the simile of a well-known writer.'
'O, well, it med be all that, or it med not. As I say, I didn't see nothing of it the hour or two I was there; so I went in and had a pot o' beer and a penny loaf, and a ha'porth o' cheese, and waited till it was time to come along home.'
(Part 2, 6)

Kingsley's Tregarva, a gamekeeper who is the son of a Cornish miner, is respectful to the gentry and ever conscious of his lack of education and breeding; but when he has a point to make, he speaks fluently and without trace of dialect:

> We break the dogs, and we load the guns, and we find the game, and mark the game, – and then they call themselves sportsmen; we choose the flies, and we bait the hooks, and we show them where the fish lie, and then when they've hooked them, they can't get them out without us and the spoon-net; and then they go home to the ladies and boast of the lot of fish they killed – and who thinks of the keeper?   (*Yeast* 3)

Expository speech

Sometimes the dialogue in Victorian novels is clearly expository, to inform the reader rather than to develop character and situation. Passages of exposition are, by their nature, usually lengthy and lacking in idiolect, so that reference must suffice instead of quotation. Background information necessary to the plot may be given through a character's autobiographical recollections. This is done in *Villette* when Miss Marchmont tells her story to Lucy, and later when Paulina describes her letter from Bretton (4, 32). Similarly, Molly hears all about Cynthia's background (*Wives and Daughters* 43). Much of the narrative in *Wuthering Heights* is a prolonged discourse from Nellie Dean, which soon ceases to impress the reader as speech.

Another type of exposition gives the opinion of the author through the words attributed to a character. The Victorian novelists, from the greatest to the least, were frequently fired with enthusiasm for a contemporary cause or an enduring moral sentiment. From the 1840s when the 'Condition of England Question' was being widely asked and variously answered, novels often contain a 'message' which authorial skill may subordinate to the imaginative scheme or which may prove obtrusive. Even the best novelists let themselves go on occasion, and transmit through dialogue their views on the issues of the day. Again, the passages are usually too long for quotation and their effect depends on an extended reading of the argument. The more polemical novels naturally have the highest proportion of such speeches. Newman's *Loss and Gain* is full of theological discussion, with a fair statement of different views for most of the book. It is hard to believe that even in that age of theological controversy a young man should actually say to his friends that the Evangelicals 'showed quite plainly, if they were to be trusted, that Luther and Melancthon did not agree together on the prime point of justification by faith, a circumstance which had not come into the Article-lecture' (Part 2, 8). Butler is always ready to expound scepticism in his authorial person, but he sometimes gives the argument to a character like Shaw, the well-read tinker in *The Way of All Flesh* who confuses Ernest Pontifex as a young curate.

Other novelists give vent to political and social questions about which they were concerned. Arthur Pendennis speaks for Thackeray when he makes a prolonged plea for tolerance and abstention from judgement on insufficient evidence – 'our measure of reward and punishments is most partial and incomplete, absurdly inadequate, utterly worldly, and we wish to continue it into the next world . . .' (61). Trollope, the unsuccessful Liberal candidate, gives Palliser an eloquent discourse on Liberalism and its distrust of egalitarian ideas in an imperfect world (*The Prime Minister* 68). Kingsley lets Barnakill expound on the pollution of the Thames and public hygiene in general (*Yeast* 15). Hardy's views often come through the words of his characters, for example in the lengthy discussions about marriage and parenthood in *Jude the Obscure*. Gissing's *New Grub Street* is on one level a prolonged debate on the economics and ethics of contemporary journalism and publishing. There is evidence that Disraeli, Dickens and Kingsley drew verbally on contemporary Government reports for dialogue as well as for direct authorial exposition (Smith 1970).

Characters who speak for their authors often lose some of their distinctive idiolect, as well as becoming unwontedly eloquent and articulate. Sometimes the speaker stays in character, though uttering ideas that he or she would be unlikely to formulate so clearly. Esther Waters speaks movingly in her own idiolect when she resists the suggestion that she could let her child die as she would never bring him up:

> It's none of the child's fault if he hasn't got a father, nor is it right that he should be deserted for that, and it is not for you to tell me to do such a thing. If you had made sacrifice of yourself in the beginning and nursed your own child such thoughts wouldn't have come to you. But when you hire a poor girl such as me to give the milk that belongs to

another to your child, you think nothing of the poor deserted one. He is only a love-child, you say, and had better be dead and done with.

(18)

Direct and indirect speech

Dialogue in the novel is most effective when rendered in direct speech which purports to reproduce in writing the exact words used by the character. Indirect speech emphasises the presence of the author as reporter; it loses the distinctive idiolect of the speaker and merges into the narrative. It is often used simply to convey information which is supposed to come through speech but which is given for its own sake rather than for any development of character and relationship. Sometimes, however, indirect speech can add to characterisation as well as to plot. Political and other public speaking, often reported in newspapers, lends itself to this treatment. The inclusion of the clichés and technicalities of the occasion give their own quiet comment without further authorial intervention. Dickens, master of reiteration in his own narrative voice, used the repeated phrase 'what must be' to show up the hypnotic effect of empty political oratory:

> Sir Matthew Pupker went on to say what must be his feelings on that great occasion, and what must be that occasion in the eyes of the world, and what must be the intelligence of his fellow-countrymen before him, and what must be the wealth and respectability of his honourable friends behind him; and lastly, what must be the importance to the wealth, the happiness, the comfort, the liberty, the very existence of a great and free people, of such an institution as the United Metropolitan Improved Hot Muffin and Crumpet Baking and Punctual Delivery Company.   (*Nicholas Nickleby* 2)

Trollope captures in a reporter's tone the convoluted style of a Parliamentary answer:

> He need hardly remind gentlemen in that House that the Prime Minister was not in a position to devote his undivided time to the management of his own property, or even to the interests of the Borough of Silverbridge. That his Grace had been earnest in his instructions to his agents, the sequel fully proved; but that earnestness his agents had misinterpreted.   (*The Prime Minister* 57)

Another use of indirect speech is to suggest distance or hostility between the parties to a dialogue. Thus the Archdeacon and Mrs Proudie, disliking each other at first sight, move from direct to indirect speech:

> Dr Grantly explained that he lived in his own parish of Plumstead Episcopi, a few miles out of the city. Whereupon the lady hoped that the distance was not too great for country visiting, as she would be so glad to make the acquaintance of Mrs Grantly. She would take the earliest opportunity, after the arrival of her horses at Barchester; their horses were at present in London.   (*Barchester Towers* 5)

The reported speech of William trying to persuade Esther Waters to return to him after his long absence, has a nagging, repetitive tone which suggests her own weary hearing of what no longer moves her: 'If she'd only listen. She was prettier than ever. He had never cared for anyone else. He would marry her when he got his divorce, and then the child would be theirs' (25).

This kind of presentation stands between the formal objectivity of a printed report and the 'free indirect style' which keeps the idiolect and any non-standard variants of the speaker. Even the deviant spelling used to present a dialect may be included in what purports to be the author's statement of what was said. Thackeray thus presents the Irish of Costigan, before moving into direct speech. 'Pen was his dearest boy, his gallant young friend, his noble collagian, whom he had held in his heart ever since they had parted – how was his fawther, no, his mother, and his guardian, the General, the Major' (*Pendennis* 30). Plornish continues to show sub-standard qualities even when he is ostensibly being reported, in speaking of the sufferings of the poor:

> As to who was to blame for it, Mr Plornish didn't know who was to blame for it. He could tell you who suffered, but he couldn't tell you whose fault it was. It wasn't *his* place to find out, and who'd mind what he said, if he did find out? He only know'd that it wasn't put right by them what undertook that line of business, and that it didn't come right of itself.   (*Little Dorrit* Book 1, 12)

This is well realised; Plornish remains an individual, but his voice becomes also the voice of the multitude who feel bewildered pity but not responsibility.[2]

Dialect features may be discarded in the free indirect style, while the distinctive idiolect is kept; this is Meredith's treatment of Farmer Blaize, whose direct speech is marked with dialect forms and deviant spelling. The capitalisation of *Law* conveys both spoken and pragmatic emphasis:

> He had no wish to bring any disgrace anywhere; he respected the inhabitants of Raynham Abbey, as in duty bound; he should be sorry to see them in trouble. Only no tampering with his witnesses. He was a man for Law. Rank was much: money was much: but Law was more. In this country Law was above the sovereign. To tamper with the Law was treason to the realm.   (*The Ordeal of Richard Feverel* 8)

The fussy, rambling idiolect of Mrs Nickleby is kept even when her words are accommodated in the changed tenses and objectifying style of reporting:

> To this Mrs Nickleby only replied that she durst say she was very stupid, indeed she had no doubt she was, for her own children almost as much as told her so, every day of her life; to be sure she was a little older than they, and perhaps some foolish people might think she ought reasonably to know best. However, no doubt, she was wrong, of course she was – she always was – she couldn't be right – couldn't be expected to be – so she had better not expose herself any more. (55)

Free indirect speech retains a girl's nervousness and excitement: 'Oh! it was so long since she had seen a wild flower! Would he be so kind as to stop for one moment to let her gather one. She did so much wish to pick a flower for herself once more!' (*Heartsease* 4).

Direct, indirect and free indirect speech may be combined in a single encounter. Gaskell has a fine passage in *Mary Barton* which uses the different forms to convey the difficulty of communication between the anxiety of the questioner and the complacent calm of the respondent, who keeps her own idiolect but is distanced as her speech moves from direct to free indirect style. Job Legh is trying to get news of Mary and Will Wilson:

> He asked if a young woman had been there that morning, and if she had seen Will Wilson. 'No!'
>   'Why not?'

'Why, bless you, 'cause he had sailed some hours before she came asking for him.'

There was a dead silence, broken only by the even, heavy sound of Mrs Jones's ironing.

'Where is the young woman now?' asked Job.

'Somewhere down at the docks', she thought. 'Charley would know, if he was in, but he wasn't. He was in mischief, somewhere or other, she had no doubt. Boys always were. He would break his neck some day, she knew;' so saying, she quietly spat upon her fresh iron, and then went on with her business. (29)

Notes

1. A nice example is the Victorian episode of the pageant in Virginia Woolf's *Between the Acts* (1941).

2. The original title for *Little Dorrit* was *Nobody's Fault*.

CHAPTER 11
Opinions of authors and critics

A number of contemporary opinions about dialogue in the novel have already been quoted in relation to specific topics. A little further exploration may give more evidence of what the novelists were trying to do and how their efforts were received. The extent of nineteenth-century periodical criticism, like that of the fiction which it reviewed, is so great that any use of it must be highly selective.

Dialogue and actual speech

As the demand for realism in fiction grew after the middle of the century, so critics became more censorious about dialogue which did not read as 'true to life'. The novelists in turn naturally defended their representations of speech. Dickens maintained that he drew upon things that he heard in the streets and public places, and there is support for his claim. For example, there are close parallels between the examination of Jo at the inquest in *Bleak House* and the evidence of a boy called George Ruby in a trial at the Guildhall in 1850 (House 1941, 32). He would take notes of things heard; his youthful work as a reporter had sharpened his naturally acute ear, and had given him the technical skill to record what he heard. His love of the theatre gave him another source; the speech of Jingle follows the staccato style of 'Commodore Cosmogony' created by the comic actor Charles Mathews. He lived with his characters as he created them, and even spoke their words aloud while he wrote.

His early biographer John Forster offers several instances of characters drawn from real people: 'Mrs Gamp's original was in reality a person hired by a most distinguished friend of his own.' The Marchioness in *The Old Curiosity Shop* was based on 'the orphan girl from the Chatham workhouse' who worked for his family when he was a boy. When writing his last, unfinished, novel he went to an opium den with an American friend who recalled 'we found a haggard old woman . . . and the words that Dickens puts into the mouth of this wretched creature in *Edwin Drood* we heard her croon' (Forster II, 30; I, 39; III, 488). Other originals are well known: the caricatures of his mother as Mrs Nickleby and his father as Micawber; the woman of his acquaintance who was so distressed to find herself transformed into Miss Mowcher in *David Copperfield*; the parodies in *Bleak House* of Landor as Boythorn and Leigh Hunt as Skimpole. Recent research has revealed further likely character-sources (Alexander 1991).

Nevertheless, the critics were divided about the credibility of his dialogue. Some were enthusiastic, like the one who wrote of Mrs Gamp, 'To make a monthly nurse talk on for half a page without a break, to make her say something that is peculiarly her own, to make each separate portion of her speech amusing, and yet to make the whole connected and harmonious, is a great feat of art' (*National Review* July 1861). After Dickens was dead, one who knew both his novels and his public readings praised, in an otherwise rather patronising survey, his knowledge of the speech used by the 'masses': 'He knew their way of life, their way of thought, their way of speech; for they have a dialect of their own – more penetrating, more picturesque, more pathetic than the language of the more refined and cultivated' (Lilly 1895, 28)

There were, however, contrary views from contemporary readers who brought the charge of caricature which was to cling to Dickens for many years. Trollope's commentary on how 'Mr Popular Sentiment' might have depicted the old almsmen is famous and has a cutting edge:

> It was shocking to find how the conversation of these eight starved old men in their dormitory shamed that of the clergyman's family in his rich drawing-room. The absolute words they uttered were not perhaps spoken in the purest English, and it might be difficult to distinguish from their dialect to what part of the country they belonged; the beauty of the sentiment, however, amply atoned for the imperfection of the language.   (*The Warden* 15)

G.H. Lewes was even more scathing and challenged Dickens's own claim to regard his characters as real people:

> There are dialogues having the traces of straining effort at effect, which in their incongruity painfully resemble the absurd and eager expositions

which insane patients pour into the listener's ear when detailing the wrongs of their schemes. Dickens once disclosed to me that every word said by his characters was distinctly *heard* by him: I was at first not a little puzzled to account for the fact that he could hear language so utterly unlike the language of real feeling, and not be aware of its preposterousness; but the surprise vanished when I thought of the phenomenon of hallucination.   (*Fortnightly Review* February 1872)

This was a posthumous assessment of the whole art of Dickens; the charge of unnatural dialogue had been levelled at him from the beginning. A severe review of *The Pickwick Papers* compared the dialogue unfavourably with that in *Sketches by Boz*, where Dickens had been 'the first to turn to account the rich and varied stores of wit and humour discernible among the lower classes of the Metropolis'. Now, however, 'the Wellers, both father and son, talk a language and employ allusions utterly irreconcilable with their habits and station, and we constantly detect both in the nice and even critical use of words and images borrowed from sources wholly inaccessible to them' (*Quarterly Review* October 1837).

Is it possible to find the truth beneath these conflicting accounts? It may be said that Dickens had closer experience of London street life than Lewes, or probably the *Quarterly* reviewer. Passages have already been quoted which suggest that Dickens was exaggerating rather than travestying conversations which could really be heard. That his exuberance often carried him away from reality into fantasy, both in episodes and dialogue, cannot be questioned, but he may often have been as near to the facts of contemporary speech as other novelists. We probably cannot do better than accept both the caution and the judgement of a close critic of Dickens's language: 'A novelist is not a philologist, and we are not entitled to assume either his ability or his intention to record the speech of his contemporaries. There is evidence, however, that Dickens, especially in his early novels and sketches, aimed at a high degree of realism' (Brook 1970, 99). It may be added that the evidence of his pursuit of local colour for *Edwin Drood*, cited above, suggests that his aim was not lowered throughout his career. The minor novelist Mrs Oliphant found in Dickens's dialogue the fault not of exaggeration but of flatness. She observes that his heroines making speeches of explanation at the climax of the plot have a remarkable sameness of expression. Louisa Gradgrind follows the line of Kate Nickleby, Mercy Pecksniff,

Florence Dombey and Annie Strong when 'she delivers herself of a number of balanced and measured sentences no doubt quite to the purpose in every instance, but so singularly like each other in form and cadence, that each recalls its predecessor too distinctly to be agreeable' (*Blackwood's Magazine* April 1855).

Where Dickens sometimes destroys the sense of realism is in his authorial comments on what his characters are saying. Authorial interference is of course a characteristic of the Victorian novel which, though it may trouble readers accustomed to the withdrawal of the author characteristic of Modernism, must be accepted as part of the convention. It is a fact that Dickens does not confine his interventions to narrative but too often makes sure that readers are not missing the point of a character's idiolect. The matter was noted by the critic Mowbray Morris in a posthumous assessment of Dickens in the *Fortnightly Review* (December 1882). He cites the way in which Dickens interferes with Mrs Gamp's delightful structures on the 'Ankworks Package' and wishes it was 'in Jonadge's belly', where Dickens cannot resist telling us that she was 'appearing to confound the prophet with the whale in this miraculous aspiration' (*Martin Chuzzlewit* 40)

Morris goes on to make a comparison with Thackeray, to the latter's advantage, which is often found in contemporary criticism. 'Thackeray, let me say, is singularly free from this fault . . . Thackeray never explains. He will talk often enough in his own person, too often, perhaps, we may think; but while his characters are talking he stands aside and lets them speak for themselves.' Over thirty years earlier, another reviewer had compared the dialogue in *David Copperfield* unfavourably with that in *Pendennis*: 'not that the dialect of Mr Peggotty is less racy than the brogue of Captain Costigan, but that in any passage of sentiment Mr Dickens lets the sentiment run away with him.' He continues, quoting David to Steerforth, 'Who ever heard of one young man saying gravely to another, "You are always equally loved, and cherished in my heart"?' (*The Times* 11 June 1851). It is notable that the excessive sentiment which some later readers have disliked in Dickens was more than once attacked by contemporaries. It will not do to say simply that the Victorian reader could take any amount of it, though the great popularity of Dickens in his lifetime suggests that he was satisfying a general desire. The passage quoted by the reviewer is of course part of a highly-charged scene, which builds to the end of the chapter when David soliloquises

retrospectively on what was to come – 'Never more, O God forgive
you, Steerforth! to touch that passive hand in love and friendship.
Never, never more!' (29). That Dickens sometimes heightened the
register of speech to conform to the theme rather than to realism is
part of his total art.

Dickens's ascription of standard speech to lowly but virtuous
characters, noted in a previous chapter, was criticised by Gissing in
his mainly laudatory study:

> At times Dickens's idealism goes further, leading him into
> misrepresentation of social facts. Refining and humouring, even from
> his point of view, must have their limits; and here he altogether
> exceeded in a character such as Lizzie Hexam in *Our Mutual Friend*.
> The child of a Thames-side loafer, uneducated, and brought up amid
> the roughest surroundings, Lizzie uses language and expresses sentiments
> which would do credit to a lady in whatsoever position.
>
> (Gissing 1898, 76f)

Thackeray was generally praised for his dialogue. Some of the
reviews give opinions that would not be invariably echoed today, such
as that of Nassau Senior in the *Edinburgh Review*, who adversely
criticises much of Thackeray's work and then declares, 'Every person
admires the ease and vigour of his dialogue, its sparkling wit and its
humour, sometimes broad, sometimes delicate, but always effective'
(January 1854). Mrs Oliphant qualified her praise by objecting to the
raffish language of some of Thackeray's characters:

> We are not sure how far the English language will be benefited by the
> dialogues of Mr Thackeray; they are very clever, very entertaining, and
> their slang is admirable; but it is very doubtful if it will be an advantage
> to make these Islands no better than a broad margin for the witticisms
> and the dialect of Cockaigne.   (*Blackwood's Magazine* January 1855)

George Eliot also had her champions, although some critics
thought that she obtruded her own ideas into dialogue as well as into
authorial commentary on events in the story. The review of *The Mill
on the Floss* in *The Times* on 18 May 1860 approved that 'she prefers
to make her characters speak for themselves, and the dialogue is
sustained with marvellous ability – the slightest shade of difference
between the personages being rendered with great subtlety'. Another
reviewer noted 'the idiomatic vigour which she throws into her

dialogue' (*Home and Foreign Review* October 1863). There was praise for the talk at the 'Rainbow' in *Silas Marner*, always a favourite with her readers: 'The people in the public-house in *Silas Marner* proclaim in a few words each a distinct and probable character, and sustain it. The things they say are perfectly natural, and yet show at once what the sayers are like' (*Saturday Review* 13 April 1861).

However, this same passage was torn to pieces in the *Dublin University Magazine*. The objection was not to the credibility of the dialogue but to its content: it is the question of the moral and educative value of fiction which runs as a thread through nineteenth-century criticism long after the novel was established as a reputable literary genre:

> What good can anyone gain by reading page after page of the boorish twaddle kept up by the folk who spend their evenings, with the help of pipes and beer, in the 'Rainbow' parlour? It may be very like the talk of such people, but life in a novel is short, and a little of that rubbish goes a long way with all who have any hankering after something better than pothouse gossip, very slightly flavoured with pothouse jokes.
>
> (April 1862)

The reviewer who praised Eliot's 'idiomatic vigour' went on to indict her for authorial intrusion in the presentation of character:

> In dialogue by which character is developed George Eliot is no great artist. If it were not for her own copious comments, the text would often be obscure. She lacks invention, and she lacks subtlety. She can explain how speakers only half reveal their real thoughts, but she cannot exhibit the process; she is soon obliged to pass from dialogue to commentary.

The same view was put succinctly in the *Atlantic Monthly*, claiming that sometimes the characters in *Middlemarch* 'are, after all, only masks through which George Eliot is ventriloquizing' (W.J. Harvey in Hardy 1967, 140).

Trollope is the novelist who receives most approval from reviewers for the natural quality of his dialogue. He would seem to provide the best evidence in fiction of how people really spoke. In his posthumously published *Autobiography* he made the claim that Dickens had made about hearing his characters speak and knowing them intimately:

I have lived with my characters, and thence has come whatever success
I have obtained. There is a gallery of them, and of all in that gallery I
may say that I know the tone of the voice, and the colour of the hair,
every flame of the eye, and the very clothes they wear. Of each man I
could assert whether he would have said these or the other words; of
every woman, whether she would have smiled or frowned. (12)

He continues in the same chapter to give his views on how fictional
dialogue should be written. It must be relevant to the plot, not
extraneously used to express the novelist's own views and concerns.
'The dialogue is generally the most agreeable part of the novel; but it
is only so as long as it tends in some way to the telling of the main
story.' Bulwer-Lytton is a frequent offender with 'devious
conversations'. Speech must be natural, avoiding long 'turns' which
would not be accepted in life. The young novelist may wonder how
such skill is to be acquired: the only in way is through long practice,
as in printing or any other craft:

> Unless it be given to him to listen and to observe, – so to carry away, as
> it were, the manner of people in his memory, as to be able to say to
> himself with assurance that these words might have been said in a
> given position, and that those other words could not have been said, –
> I do not think that in these days he can succeed as a novelist.

How far Trollope succeeded in his high aims can be judged by each
reader of his novels; most would probably agree with the opinion that
his speeches are 'beautifully shaped . . . speeches that do not waste a
word, which know exactly where they are going, and stride ahead
with the utmost confidence' (Tillotson and Tillotson 1965, 59). For
their truth to life we must turn to the reviewers of his own time,
whose verdict is generally favourable: 'Nobody is more literal than Mr
Anthony Trollope in his reproduction of manners and conversation of
the day for which he writes' (*Examiner* 20 July 1867). A slightly
qualified comment observed that 'Mr Trollope's girls, even in their
love-affairs, talk with a commonplace matter-of-fact dulness, which
leaves no doubt about their portraits having been drawn from life'
(*Tinsley's Magazine* March 1870).

One of the most judicious comments on Trollope's dialogue was
written some years after his death, but within the period when
naturalness could still be assessed. Frederic Harrison wrote in *Forum* in
May 1895:

In absolute realism of spoken words, Trollope has barely any equal. His characters utter quite literally the same words, and no more, that such persons utter in actual life. The characters, it is true, are the average men and women we meet in the educated world, and the situations, motives and feelings described are seldom above or below the ordinary incidents of modern life. But within this very limited range of incident, and for this very common average of person and character, the conversations are photographic or stenographic reproductions of actual speech.

Many, perhaps, would give more credit to Trollope for the imaginative presentation of his characters and his ability, at his best moments, to rise about the commonplace; but the testimony to his realism is important. A modern critic who has closely studied Trollope's language considers his dialogue to be overestimated at the expense of his portraits, and much more at that of his passages of psychological analysis: 'Most of the dialogues are short and do little but advance the story; most of the long ones do illustrate character, but these are commonly interrupted by the author's accounts of the state of mind of the speakers' (Clark 1975, 20).

While Trollope was generally praised for the realism of his dialogue, Charlotte Brontë was often attacked for unconvincing speech. The charge of using it in an expository or polemical manner was levelled at *Jane Eyre*; 'Dialogues are carried on to tell the reader something he must know, or to infuse in him some explanation of the writer' (*Spectator* 6 November 1847). George Eliot, who on the whole liked this novel, wrote to Charles Bray, 'I wish the characters would talk a little less like the heroes and heroines of press reports' (*Letters* I, 268). Her comment supports the point made earlier in this book that official reports of speech were often at least as far removed from reality as the more stilted dialogue in fiction. Of *Shirley* she wrote to Catherine Winkworth, 'The conversations seem to me astonishingly poor' (ibid. 147). The *Eclectic Review* was critical of the speech in *Villette*: 'The work mainly consists of dialogue, and although this is sustained with all the vivacity of an unquestionably powerful pen, yet it tires by its sameness' (March 1853). Emily Brontë received similar criticism, though with more admiration, from the *American Review*: 'The dialogue is also singularly effective and dramatic. The principal characters all talk alike; yet they stand before us as definite as so many individuals' (June 1848). Later readers would question the charge of sameness in either writer, even without the varied and extensive use

of dialect. The marked idiolects of Dickens's characters may have set
up expectations which new novelists found hard to meet.

Such criticisms, however, are mild compared with what Leslie
Stephen meted out to Bulwer-Lytton in a posthumous assessment of
his work. He condemned Eugene Aram as a character who deals too
much in opinions and 'pours out his pinchbeck philosophy'. In the
novel of which he is the eponymous hero, 'the central figure – the
character whose passions and sufferings should be the moving power
of the story – is a mere windbag, and a windbag of the most
pretentious kind' (*Cornhill* 27 March 1873).

Much of the criticism of Hardy's dialogue focused on his use of
dialect. The realism of his unmarked dialogue was attacked by
Edmund Gosse, in the famous review of *Jude the Obscure* in which he
asked, 'What has Providence done to Mr Hardy?' (*Cosmopolis* January
1896). 'As for the conversation of his semi-educated characters, they
are really terrible. Sue and Jude talk a sort of University Extension
jargon that breaks the heart. "The mediaevalism of Christminster
must go, be sloughed off, or Christminster will have to go", says Sue . . .
She *could* not have talked like that.' It is certainly true that Hardy's
dialogue, throughout his career, can slip into a stilted tone, but realist
objections to what a character could not have done or said are
unwise. Critics should remember the comment of Brack in *Hedda
Gabler* when Hedda has shot herself, 'One doesn't do that kind of
thing'.

Meredith, often considered in his time superior to Hardy, was
praised for his use of 'the little inflections of voice, the little
finenesses of manner, the choice of ordinary words put in such a way
that they are commonplace no longer; and the voice is heard, the
manner felt' (*Illustrated London News* 28 March 1885). On the other
hand, R.H. Hutton found his dialogue unnatural: 'Of dialogue he is
prodigal; but it is not characteristic dialogue, or rather it is
characteristic of nobody but Mr Meredith. The speeches chime with
context, but not with the people who are made to utter them'
(*Spectator* 1 November 1879). The poet James Thomson, a great
admirer of Meredith, defended his dialogue in poetic terms that
denied the persistent canon of realism in fiction:

> The speeches do not follow one another mechanically adjusted like a
> smooth pavement for easy walking: they leap and break, resilient and
> resurgent, like running foam-crested sea-waves, impelled and repelled

and crossed by under-currents and great tides and broad breezes; in their restless agitation you must divine the immense life abounding beneath and around and above them; and the Mudie novice accustomed to saunter the level pavements, finds that the heaving and falling are sea-sickness to a queasy stomach.   (*Secularist* 3 June 1876)

The judgement would not have been made, even in less extravagant language, thirty years earlier. The possibilities of dialogue, which the early-Victorian novelists had developed, brought sharper critical judgements and greater awareness of what could be achieved.

The movement towards the end of the century brought further expectation of dialogue that would be close to life. Gissing won approval for his attempts: 'the dialogue [in *The Odd Woman*] is of the right sort – natural and to the purpose' (*Athenaeum* 27 May 1893). The critic of the same novel in the *Pall Mall Gazette* praised Gissing for his avoidance of long expositions of character: 'many pages of wiredrawn analysis are replaced by one of living conversation' and declared, 'that parts off good from bad realism' (29 May 1893). An American reviewer of *The Emancipated* wrote, 'the conversations are capital as a rule – simple, natural, often clever without apparent effort, and sometimes impassioned, with a thoroughly modern reserve' (*Critic* 22 February 1896). The taste for melodramatic dialogue had diminished: 'reserve' was the proper accompaniment of emotional speech.

Henry James, however, was more sceptical about the achievements of naturalism: 'It is impossible to read work even as interesting as Mr Gissing's without recognising the impossibility of making people both talk "all the time" and talk with the needful differences. There is always at the best the author's voice to be kept out. It can be kept out for occasions, it cannot be kept out always' (*Harper's Weekly* 31 July 1897). James of course took a sceptical view of the demand for dialogue at the expense of other qualities which he regarded as more important in fiction. In the Preface to *The Awkward Age*[1] he attacked editors and publishers for constantly demanding dialogue:

'We can't have too much of it, we can't have enough of it, and no excess of it, in the form of no matter what savourless dilution, or what boneless dispersion, ever began to injure a book so much as even the very scantest claim put in for form and substance.' This wisdom had always been in one's ears; but it had at the same time been equally in one's eyes that really constructive dialogue, dialogue organic and dramatic, speaking for itself, representing and embodying substance and form, is among us an uncanny and abhorrent thing, not to be dealt with on any terms.

Dialect

The demand for realism inevitably fastened on dialect speech when this appeared in fiction. The gradual acceptance of regional speech as more than incidental or comic was achieved by the latter part of the period. The main critical questions were whether it was accessible or opaque, and whether it seemed appropriate to the imagined characters. As the representation of dialect became more frequent, reviewers were more ready to question its accuracy of reproduction. The reviewer in *Fraser's Magazine* was able to detect the genuine note in *Shirley*: 'Most writers seem to think that they can produce a genuine Yorkshireman by cutting off the final consonant of every word he utters. Currer Bell's Yorkshiremen are not such Cockneyfied automata' (December 1849).

Anne Mozley in *Bentley's* was almost ecstatic about George Eliot's accuracy and discrimination in the dialect used in *Adam Bede*:

> Not only is the dialect of the locality accurately given but the distinct influence of each order. The field labourer's rude utterance, 'as incapable of an undertone as a cow or a stag', receives a touch of cultivation when it is used by the mechanic; and these two, again, are varied in the farmhouse; while each individual has appropriate peculiarities which give a distinct truth of portraiture.   (1 July 1859)

Bulwer-Lytton preferred the portrayal of rural life without overt dialect and found that in *The Mill on the Floss* 'All the Dodson sisters are wonderful. I find it a great relief to get rid of the Provincial dialect and the language of Dialogue in the rural characters is extremely natural without vulgarity and full of point and playfulness' (Letter to John Blackwood 14 April 1860 in Carroll 1971, 120).

Hardy, who made the greatest overall contribution to the use of dialect in fiction, was constantly chided for causing his rustics to speak like educated and informed people. The objections were not so much to inconsistency in the representation of dialect as to its content. The *Athenaeum* reviewer of *Under the Greenwood Tree* referred to 'the tendency of the author to forget his part, as one may call it, and to make his characters now and then drop their personality, and speak too much like educated people' (15 June 1872). Horace Moule, Hardy's friend and mentor, noticed in the same novel 'an occasional tendency of the country folk . . . to express themselves in the language of the author's manner of thought, rather than in their own' (*Saturday Review* 28 September 1872).

R.H. Hutton took the matter more seriously when reviewing *Far From the Madding Crowd*, comparing Hardy unfavourably with Dickens, though depreciating the realism of both authors:

> Mrs Gamp is an impossible though most amusing impersonation of the monthly nurse. But Mrs Gamp makes no claim to any shrewdness beyond the shrewdness of the most profound selfishness; for the rest, she is only a delightful and impossible concentration of the essence of all conceivable monthly-nurse experiences. But these poor men are quizzical critics, inaccurate divines, keen-eyed men of the world, who talk a semi-profane, semi-Biblical dialect full of veins of humour which have passed into it from a different sphere.
>
> (*Spectator* 19 December 1874)

The argument becomes part of the debate about verisimilitude in fictional speech. Was Hardy hopelessly unrealistic in the gnomic and poetic words of his rustics, or did reviewers undervalue the rural culture which was vanishing as he recorded it? As his reputation grew, reviewers were more inclined to defend his practice. The reviewer in the *British Quarterly Review* in 1881, who seems to be one with some knowledge of the 'Wessex' region, defends Hardy for his accurate portrayals of village life and makes a point which Hardy himself frequently urged in defence of Dorset speech:

> The dweller in towns thinks the country labourer a lout because his speech differs greatly from his own, the real fact being that the dialect is far less debased than the clipt and smooth language of educated people, which tends more and more to reduce all the vowels to one sound . . . One who knows the country of which he speaks catches the keynote and has the tune always in his ear: but the outsider is not puzzled by too much dialect and many strange words.

The modern reader is likely to salute the perception of these comments. Dialectology and folk-studies have given us a different perspective on the apparently 'simple' community, while we are less inclined than the Victorians to demand an exact rendering of what people would 'really' say. The powerful choric effect of Hardy's peasants, sometimes tragic and sometimes comic, is a constant reminder that his fiction is the fiction of a poet with epic aspirations. However, some of his contemporaries kept sniping; a review of *The Mayor of Casterbridge* – the most notable of the novels in its subtle pragmatic use of dialect (Chapman 1989) – objected that 'the language of the peasants again is a point on which we have an old quarrel with Mr Hardy. It is neither one thing nor the other – neither dialect exactly reproduced nor a thorough rendering into educated English' (*Athenaeum* 29 May 1886). The assumption that either end of this polarisation is correct for the novel sums up a good deal of Victorian criticism.

Note

1. This novel was published in 1899 and is often considered one of James's least successful in its heavy and sometimes obscure analysis of character. The Preface quoted was written in 1908 for the 'New York' edition of his novels.

CHAPTER 12
Victorian fiction and Victorian reality

The possibility of knowing exactly how the Victorians spoke seems tantalisingly near but is probably unattainable. We cannot hear the sounds of their voices, the pace of utterance, the nuances of stress, pause and intonation which are the making of conversational exchange. Yet written sources bring the spoken word close to our apprehension. The dominance of the novel as a literary genre provides a richer corpus of evidence than is extant for any earlier period. The records of other writers, diarists, reporters, social observers and orthoepists, supplement and frequently confirm what the novelists present.

There is no doubt that Victorian speech was realised in more elaborate codes than are now available. This is not to say that we have lost the power of subtlety in speech, but that the devices are different and not always verbal. We can use body language and unspoken shared assumption to extend the things that are openly said. The erosion of class barriers has been accompanied by a more significant generation gap, with a youth culture that crosses national as well as local frontiers wherever English is spoken. The Victorians had their own way of establishing and changing relationships. Plentiful evidence from fiction has shown that Christian names were used much more sparingly and sometimes not even uttered within families. The use of the Christian name could be an impertinence or a sign of growing favour, especially between the sexes. Titles, from the official ranks of aristocracy to the simple 'Mr', could be similarly used; the word 'sir' had a range of possible connotations, from the servile to the confrontational.

The nineteenth-century novelists wrote in and for an increasingly mobile society which engendered both ambition and anxiety in its members. Speech became a pointer to social status and consequently to the degree of personal success. The spread of education, especially after the Education Act of 1870, brought with it a dissemination of what had been considered upper-class speech. The public schools fostered a particular way of speaking, the new and minor ones earnestly trying to reproduce the usage of the older and more prestigious. The public schools supplied the universities, which in turn produced more public school teachers and the trainers of teachers for state and denominational schools. There were of course other factors, notably the desire of individuals to imitate the speech of their 'betters' whose station they hoped to reach, but the educational system was a major factor in producing the sense that some kinds of speech were 'common' rather than merely regional or comic. To speak in a manner different from those around one had always been a matter for remark, as Chaucer and the Elizabethan dramatists witness, but had never before been a major issue. The time was not far ahead when Bernard Shaw would write, 'it is impossible for an Englishman to open his mouth without making some other Englishman despise him' (Preface to *Pygmalion* 1912).

Regional dialect was receiving attention from two contrary directions. Philological interest in dialect, as preserving older forms of the language and providing evidence of features like sound changes, grew steadily through the period. From the major works of men like Skeat and Wright to the many local dialect societies, there were attempts to record forms of speech that were disappearing. At the same time, pressure for conformity to a national educated standard tended to make the more ambitious youngsters ashamed of their home speech. Examples have been given of the fictional use of diglossia which dialecticians were observing in reality, and of reversion to broader speech under the pressure of emotion. The novelists, as we have seen, could use dialect to indicate close or more distant relationships and to place characters within the rural hierarchy which would scarcely have been noticed by an outsider. Hardy was supreme in this area, but he was not alone.

The use of dialect speech in novels reflects some of the ambiguities of the age. There is not only the uncertainty of social status reflected in speech, but also mingled compassion, condescension and unease with which the class from which readers were principally drawn regarded the poor. Rural pointers can emphasise the honesty and decency of a simple man contrasted with a bad character who is well-spoken. Gabriel Oak is set against Troy, Peggotty against Steerforth, by words as well as deeds. Equally, dialect can reveal comic inferiority in the speaker and confirm complacency in the reader. The cockney landlady Mrs Jupp in *The Way of All Flesh* is light relief to the educated but ingenuous Pontifex; William Worm, in *A Pair of Blue Eyes*, comes from a world outside the cultivated speech of his master Swancourt and his master's daughter Elfride, and is also an uneasy reminder of the society from which Stephen has risen. The Wellers are a continual comic counterpoint to the members of the Pickwick Club, though they have the power to take off into a text of their own.

Hostility and tension could be felt between regions as well as classes. The irruption of Ethelberta's sister and brothers from her Dorset childhood into the fashionable society of London is more than a personal embarrassment. The confusion over 'chippols' quoted in Chapter 3 marks a historical as well as a semantic division, and one which was becoming more acute as travel and communication brought urban influence into the countryside. The contempt of northerners like Yorke and John Barton for London speech, quoted in the same chapter, is also significant; it can still be met today.

The differences of representation between these and other dialect speakers are considerable. Gaskell, the Brontës, Eliot and Hardy use more detailed pointers and attempt more accuracy than Butler, or than Dickens when he moves from cockney to regional speech. The variety of visual devices is interesting for what it reveals about the background of the novelist, but it is secondary to the reader's response to dialogue in its context. No writer of fiction goes so far as Barnes does in poetry to try to represent consistently the precise sounds of dialect. Emily Brontë's first depiction of Joseph showed that the novelist could soon go too far for the reader's comprehension and patience. The written code was equated with 'educated' speech – or perhaps rather the speech with which the reader was best acquainted – and deviant spellings could easily communicate what needed to be said about the status and relationships of characters.

Given the convention that standard spelling is to be equated with standard speech, deliberate misspelling indicates a spoken class or regional variant. This has been a literary convention since the beginnings of the novel; it continues to this day, not only in fiction but in the captions of cartoons and in popular songs, where forms like *wot, sez, gonna*, give a signal independent of the fact that they approximate to relaxed speech in Received Pronunciation (Chapman 1988).

Yet this convenient device could give way to a literary acknowledgement of a social attitude. Victorian ambivalence towards the poor is seen in the giving of standard speech to virtuous but uneducated characters. It was accepted that virtue could reside with poverty and vice with riches, but it seemed to bring a kind of honorary elevation to its possessors. As we have seen, major characters may escape the orthographic signs of their class if they are on the right side. The practice was not universal and tended to be followed mainly for cockney and vaguely lower-class speakers rather than in regional dialect. Gaskell was the boldest in giving strong dialect to those with whom the reader should sympathise; Eliot and Hardy were more cautious. Dickens's treatment of characters like Oliver Twist, Little Nell and Lizzie Hexam is the most striking use of this linguistic bond of fellowship between the middle-class reader and the virtuous poor.

Any attempt to find how closely the speech of fiction approximates to the speech of life must take account of the literary conventions prevailing at the time. In addition to the pretence that good people always speak well, there were a number of other concessions which reflected reality even if they did not perfectly reproduce it. The ban on oaths and obscene words in fictional dialogue was the product of an age more reticent than our own. There is evidence, even in the euphemisms of the novelists and reporters, that language in some social circles could be lurid, and that men of all classes could be profane and bawdy among themselves. The handling of this whole area of speech goes to extreme lengths in avoiding offence, but only because offence could be caused in real situations. What Thackeray wrote about the criminal characters in *Oliver Twist* was true for novels generally: 'no writer can or dare tell the *whole* truth concerning them, and faithfully explain their vices' (*Fraser's Magazine* February 1840).

Similar collusion appears in other conventions. The melodramatic tone of emotional speeches, the lush clichés of romantic proposals, were accepted readily because they were expected when fictional characters were speaking. No doubt some readers were more aware than others of the collusion, and more amused by their part in it. But neither sophisticated nor simple readers would have been happy with inflated speech if it had borne no relationship to its living equivalent. The Victorians, deprived for much of the century of a strong living drama, could easily take a theatrical tone in speech. Such literary conventions – and they have their equivalents in every literate society – must be added to the inevitable constraints on written representation of speech discussed in the first chapter.

We must also remember that the scientific study of speech was not far advanced until the end of the century, when the work of Henry Sweet and others made it possible to record and analyse both phonemic and intonational features. Even then, the lack of sensitive recording equipment was a handicap. The novelists were not skilled in even such pioneer linguistic studies as existed, but they were acute observers of life and some of them at least have a sensitive ear for the sounds as well as the content of speech. For example, George Eliot had an unusual ability to recall the distinctive sounds of voices, the aspect of speech which is known as *phonation*. She wrote to the French translator of *The Mill on the Floss*, whom she had met with his mother, that as she read his letter she was 'hearing the tone of the two voices. I have the happiness of being able to recall beloved faces and accents with great clearness' (*Letters* IV, 82). In her own words, she had the 'nice ear' which 'might have detected a tremor in some of the words' when Mrs Garth speaks 'gravely and decisively' about finding money to pay the debt which Fred Vincy has brought upon the family (*Middlemarch* 24). She would not have been able to make a technical analysis in the terms of pitch height, loudness level, tempo and timbre which a modern linguist would use, though even now this area is often described rather impressionistically with words like 'haughty', 'husky', 'aggressive' and so on.

Hardy was not a student of academic dialectology but he gave thought to the linguistic problems of rendering for a wide readership the dialect which he knew from boyhood. Replying to a reviewer who had accused him of creating 'a series of linguistic puzzles' in his dialect speakers, he wrote:

> The rule of scrupulously preserving the local idiom, together with the words which have no synonym among those in general use, while printing in the ordinary way most of those local expressions which are but a modified articulation of words in use elsewhere, is the rule I usually follow; and it is, I believe, generally recognised as the best, where every such rule must of necessity be a compromise, more or less unsatisfactory to lovers of form.
>
> (*Spectator* 15 October 1881; Orel 1967, 92)

How far then does the dialogue of Victorian novels reflect the living speech of the day? Here we have the help of the reviewers, in an age when the demand for realism in fiction was increasing. Extracts quoted in the previous chapter show that readers expected some verisimilitude in fictional speech. Novelists, major as well as minor, are criticised when they depart from what is considered a reasonable presentation of what people would actually say in such a situation. Yet in the great bulk of reviewing, complaints about unconvincing dialogue are comparatively few. It can be said with some confidence that the dialogue of Victorian fiction brings us close to the realities of contemporary speech. After allowance has been made for the constraints of rendering aural experience in a visual code, it seems clear that speech was more formal and precise, less elliptic and more consciously adapted to the immediate circumstances of conversation. Those of us who in early life had contact with people who were young in the late Victorian period may well feel that memory bears out this reading. We shall never know with phonological and prosodic accuracy exactly how the Victorians spoke, but their fiction brings us closer to the reality. Fictional dialogue and other written reports of speech complement each other, and suggest that even the apparent exaggerations of the novelists were not always far from reality; Dickens always claimed that his characters spoke like people who could be heard in the streets.

At the same time, the art of fiction itself affected everyday speech. Allusions by fictional characters to other works of fiction have been quoted; if realism is granted as the general aim of the novelists, it may be assumed that these too reflect reality. The denunciations of novel-reading made by Utilitarians and Evangelicals are strong enough, especially in the early part of the period, to suggest that people did tend to take fiction into their lives. When Dickens was at the height of his fame, a critic wrote, 'Let anyone observe our table-talk or our current literature and . . . let him note how gladly Dickens is used, and how frequently his phrases, his fancies, and the names of his characters come in, as illustration, embellishment, proverb, and seasoning' (Masson 1859, 252).

The novelists generally honoured the demand for convincing speech. Yet as imaginative writers they knew that the simple reproduction in writing of what could be heard every day was not always appropriate to the created world of the novel. They honoured the demand for realism but they used their art to economise, make more coherent, and sometimes exaggerate the facts of speech. A degree of tension between faithful recording and artistic contrivance was generally valuable in the writing of fiction. Knowledge of the conventions which governed speech in reality aids both comprehension and appreciation of the novelists' art. R.L. Stevenson wrote to Henry James, a short time after the controversy expressed in *The Art of Fiction* and *A Humble Remonstrance*, that people seemed to suppose that 'striking situations, or good dialogue, are got by studying life; they will not rise to understand that they are prepared by deliberate artifice and set off by powerful suppressions'.[1] The confession which Henry Kingsley interpolates suddenly in a passage of emotional dialogue, may speak for the many novelists of the nineteenth century, various in approach and achievement as they are:

> Of course he did not use exactly those words, but words to that effect, only more passionate and even less grammatical. I am not a shorthand writer. I only give you the substance of conversations in the best prose I can command.   (*Ravenshoe* 64)

Note

1. *Letters*, ed. Colvin 1901, Methuen, London; Vol. 1, p. 341 (8 December 1884).

Glossary of linguistic terms

affricate Consonantal sound in which a **plosive** merges into a **fricative**, for example the sound represented by *ch* in 'chip', which is phonetically /t/, /ʃ/ representing the initial sound of 'ship'.

anacoluthon Change in the grammatical structure of a sentence, so that the expected opening sequence is not completed: 'I was going towards the bus stop – you remember the old house on the corner?'

bi-labial Sound made by the two lips coming together; for example, the sounds normally represented in English by *b* and *p*.

connotation The concealed associations of an utterance, as distinct from the overt **denotation**; the name '*Wembley*' denotes a district north-west of London but is likely to connote important football matches with emotive associations for some people.

diglossia Co-existence of two varieties of a language, each with a distinct social status and used by speakers in what is considered the appropriate situation.

elision The omission of sounds in connected speech; for example, the contraction of 'would not' to *wouldn't* or the pronunciation of 'bread and butter' as *bread 'n' butter*.

fricative Consonantal sound produced by the passage of breath through a very narrow space between two speech organs; in English they include the sounds normally represented by *s*, *z*, and the two pronunciations of *th*.

graphological The written realisation of language, as distinct from the spoken.

heteroglossia Use of a number of language varieties within a single speech community or written text.

hypercorrection Language feature not normally found in the variety of language being used, produced by over-anxiety to be 'correct'; a speaker may say 'Thank you for asking my wife and I' through fear of the non-standard 'My wife and me are coming'. The false insertion of an aspirate before a word beginning with a vowel can result from excessive avoidance of 'dropping the h'.

idiolect The language system of an individual, including pronunciation, syntax and specially favoured lexical items.

intonation The pattern of speech created by varying the pitch of the voice. A type of intonation may be general throughout a dialect (for example, Welsh English has a distinctive intonation) or may be used to give implication to an utterance. 'He isn't coming' can be a statement or a question according to intonation; 'yes' can be made affirmative, doubtful or challenging.

labio-dental Consonantal sound made by pressure of one lip against the teeth; the sounds represented by *f* and *v* are labio-dentals in English.

lexis The set of words available in a language, or in the knowledge of an individual user. The vocabulary content of a text or spoken utterance.

marked form Language item with a particular implication beyond its underlying simple form. A plural like *tables* has the plural marker -s to distinguish it from the basic form *table*; *actress* has the feminine marker -ess.

orthoepy Definition and cultivation of the form of speech considered to be 'correct' in a given society. Orthoepists giving instruction for this purpose flourished in the eighteenth and early nineteenth centuries.

phonational Relating to the distinctive quality of a voice, either congenital or at a particular time; it refers to such effects as may be popularly called 'husky', 'breathy', etc.

phoneme The minimal unit of sound in a language. Change of phoneme can cause a change of meaning; thus the vowel sounds in *bit* and *beat* are counted as different phonemes. The *l* sounds in *like* and *well*, although differently articulated, are part of the same phoneme in English but different phonemes in Russian.

phonetics The study of speech-sounds which deals with their description, classification and written transcription.

phonology The study of speech-sounds as they occur in particular languages. English phonology applies the principles of phonetics to the sound-system of English.

plosive Consonantal sound made by a sudden release of breath after closure; The English consonants commonly represented by *p*, *b*, *t*, *d*, *k*, *g* are plosives.

pragmatics The branch of linguistics concerned with the intention of the speaker and its effect on the listener; it takes account of such influences as the situational context and the relationship of the participants.

prosodic Relating to features like pitch, stress, loudness, pace and rhythm in speech, which are not described by analysis of the phonemes uttered.

Received Pronunciation The type of spoken English generally regarded as 'educated'. It is regionally neutral in having no distinctive dialect features. It is the pronunciation commonly heard from media newsreaders and actors playing non-dialect parts but it no longer holds its former social prestige.

register Variety of language chosen by a speaker according to the circumstances of its use. The difference between formal and informal speech, the use of distinctive religious utterance and the deliberate preference for dialect instead of standard usage are examples of register.

schwa Neutral vowel commonly heard in unstressed syllables in English; for example, the first sound in *about* and the last in *paper*. It is shown phonetically by the symbol /ə /.

semantics The branch of linguistics concerned with meaning.

syntax Study and description of the rules by which words combine to form sentences. It has largely replaced the older concept of 'grammar', which dealt more prescriptively with usage and also included the study of changes in word structure now known as *morphology*.

voicing The vibration of the vocal cords which occurs in all vowel sounds and some consonantal. It distinguishes voiced consonants like /d/ and /z/ from their voiceless equivalents /t/ and /s/.

Bibliography

Abercrombie, D. (1965) *Studies in Phonetics and Linguistics*. OUP.

Alexander, D. (1991) *Creating Characters with Charles Dickens*. Pennsylvania State University Press, University Park, Pennsylvania.

Alford, H. (1864) *The Queen's English*. Strahan.

Allott, M. (ed.) (1974) *The Brontës: The Critical Heritage*. RKP.

Axon, W.E.A. (1876–87) 'George Eliot's use of dialect', *English Dialect Society Miscellanies* 19, 37-44.

Bahktin, M.M. (1981) 'Discourse in the novel' in M. Holquist (ed.) *The Dialogic Imagination*. University of Texas Press, Austin.

Bareham, T. (1983) *Trollope, the Barsetshire Novels: A Casebook*. Macmillan.

Barreca, R. (ed.) (1990) *Sex and Death in Victorian Literature*. Macmillan.

Bennett, J. (1948) *George Eliot: Her Mind and Her Art*. CUP.

Blake, N.F. (1981) *Non-standard Language in English Literature*. André Deutsch.

Bolton, W.F. and Crystal, D. (eds) (1987) *The English Language*. Sphere.

Booth, W. (1890) *In Darkest England and the Way Out*. Salvation Army Press.

Bradley, I. (1976) *The Call to Seriousness*. Jonathan Cape.

Brook, G.L. (1970) *The Language of Dickens*. André Deutsch.

Bryant, A. (1940) *English Saga 1840-1940*. Collins.

Bulwer-Lytton, E. (1833) *England and the English* (2 vols). Bentley.

Campbell, Lady C. (1877) *Etiquette of Good Society*. Cassell.

Carroll, D. (ed.) (1971) *George Eliot: The Critical Heritage*. RKP.

'Censor' (1880) *Don't: A Manual of Mistakes and Improprieties more or less Prevalent in Conduct and Speech*. Field and Tuer

Chadwick, O. (1966) *The Victorian Church* Part 1. A. & C. Black

Chambers, J.K. and Trudgill, P. (1980) *Dialectology*. CUP.

Chapman, R. (1984) *The Treatment of Sounds in Language and Literature*. Blackwell.

Chapman, R. (1986) *The Sense of the Past in Victorian Literature*. Croom Helm.

Chapman, R. (1988) 'We gonna rite wot we wanna: the appeal of misspelling'. *English Today* 14, 39-42.

Chapman, R. (1989) 'The reader as listener: dialect and relationships in *The Mayor of Casterbridge* in L. Hickey (ed.) *The Pragmatics of Style*. Routledge.

Chapman, R. (1990) *The Language of Thomas Hardy*. Macmillan.

Chesney, K. (1970) *The Victorian Underworld*. Temple Smith.

Clark, J.W. (1975) *The Language and Style of Anthony Trollope*. André Deutsch.

Cockshut, A.O.J. (1961) *The Imagination of Charles Dickens*. Collins.

Collins, P. (1971) *Dickens: The Critical Heritage*. RKP.

Coussillas, P. and Partridge, C. (eds) (1972) *Gissing: The Critical Heritage*. RKP.

Cox, R.G. (ed.) (1970) *Hardy: The Critical Heritage*. RKP.

Craigie, W.A. (1938) 'Dialect in literature', *Essays by Divers Hands* **17**, 69-91.

Craik, W.A. (1975) *Elizabeth Gaskell and the English Provincial Novel*. Methuen.

Crowley, T. (1989) *The Politics of Discourse: the Standard Language Question in British Cultural Debates*. Macmillan.

Darbyshire, A.E. (1967) *A Description of English*. Edward Arnold.

Davies, C. (1934) *English Pronunciation From the Fifteenth to the Eighteenth Century*. Dent.

Dean, C. (1960) 'Joseph's speech in *Wuthering Heights*', *Notes and Queries* **7**, 73-6.

Doherty, H. (1841) *An Introduction to English Grammar on Historical Principles*. Simpkin Marshall.

Earle, J. (1873) *The Philology of the English Tongue* 2nd edn. Clarendon Press.

Ellis, A.J. (1869) *Early English Pronunciation*. Early English Text Society.

Elliott, R.W.V. (1984) *Thomas Hardy's English*. Blackwell.

Enquire Within About Everything (1891). Houlston. (Author unknown).

Faber, R. (1971) *Proper Studies: Class in Victorian Fiction*. Faber and Faber.

Federico, A. (1991) *Masculine Identity in Hardy and Gissing*. Associated University Presses.

Ferguson, C. (1959) 'Diglossia', *Word* **15**, 325-40.

Forster, J. (1874) *The Life of Charles Dickens* 12th edn. Chapman and Hall.

Foster, J. (1843) *Essays in a Series of Letters* 17th edn. Bohn.

Fowler, R. (ed.) (1970) *Essays on Style and Language*. RKP.

Fowler, R. (1977) *Linguistics and the Novel*. Methuen.

Franklyn, J. (1953) *The Cockney: A Survey of London Life and Language*. André Deutsch.

Garis, R. (1965) *The Dickens Theatre*. Clarendon Press.

Garnett, R. (1859) *Philological Essays*. Williams and Norgate.

Gay, P. (1984-6) *The Bourgeois Experience: Victoria to Freud* (2 vols). OUP, New York.

Gerson, G. (1967) *Sound and Symbol in the Dialogue of the Works of Charles Dickens*. Almquist and Wicksell, Stockholm.

Gilmour, R. (1981) *The Idea of the Gentleman in the Victorian Novel*. George Allen and Unwin.

Gissing, G. (1898) *Charles Dickens*. Blackie & Son Ltd.

Glendinning, V. (1992) *Trollope*. Hutchinson.

Golding, R. (1985) *Idiolects in Dickens*. Macmillan.

Graham, K. (1965) *English Criticism of the Novel 1865-1900*. OUP.

Greenwood, J. (1869) *The Seven Curses of London*. Rivers.

Greenwood, J. (1881) *The Wilds of London*. Chatto and Windus.

Haight, G.S. (ed.) (1954-6) *The George Eliot Letters*. Yale University Press, New Haven.

Hall, F. (1873) *Modern English*. Williams and Norgate.

Hardy, B. (ed.) (1967) *Middlemarch: Critical Approaches to the Novel*. Athlone.

Harrison, M. (1848) *The Rise, Progress and Present Structure of the English Language*. Longman.

Harvey, W.J. (1961) *The Art of George Eliot*. Chatto and Windus.

Harvey, W.J. (1965) *Character and the Novel*. Chatto and Windus.

Hole, S.R. (1901) *Then and Now*. Hutchinson.

Holmberg, B. (1965) *On the Concept of Standard English and the History of Modern English Pronunciation*. Lunds Universitets Arsskrift, Lund.

Honey, J.R. de S. (1977) *Tom Brown's Universe*. Millington.

House, H. (1941) *The Dickens World*. OUP.

Hudson, D. (1972) *Man of Two Worlds: The Life and Diaries of Arthur J. Munby 1828-1910*. John Murray.

Hughes, G. (1991) *Swearing*. Blackwell.

Humphrey, C.E. (1897) *Manners for Men*. Bowden.

Hyde, H.M. (1948) *The Trials of Oscar Wilde*. William Hodge.

Ingham, P. (1986) 'Dialect as realism: *Hard Times* and the industrial novel', *Review of English Studies* NS **37**, 518-27.

Jay, E. (1986) *Faith and Doubt in Victorian Britain*. Macmillan.

Jespersen, O. (1909) *A Modern English Grammar on Historical Principles*. Carl Winter, Heidelberg.

Jones, D. (1987) *An English Pronouncing Dictionary* 17th edn. J.M. Dent & Sons.

Keating, P.J. (1971) *The Working Class in Victorian Fiction*. RKP.

Kingston-Oliphant, H. (1873) *The Sources of Standard English*. Macmillan.

Kirwan, D.J. (1870) *Palace and Hovel: or, Phases of London Life* (A. Allan (ed.) 1963). Abelard-Schuman.

Latham, R.G. (1862) *The English Language* 5th edn. Walton and Maberly.

Lilly, W.S. (1895) *Four English Humourists of the Nineteenth Century*. John Murray.

Lodge, D. (1966) *Language of Fiction*. RKP.

Lucas, J. (1977) *The Literature of Change – Studies in the Nineteenth-Century Provincial Novel*. Harvester Wheatsheaf.

Lysons, S. (1868) *Our Vulgar Tongue*. London.

Marcus, S. (1969) *The Other Victorians*. Corgi.

Marsh, G.P. (1862) *Lectures on the English Language*. John Murray.

Masson, D. (1859) *British Novelists and their Styles*. Macmillan.

Matthews, W. (1938) *Cockney Past and Present*. Routledge.

Mayhew, H. (1862) *Those that Will Not Work* (ed. P. Quennell 1950), *London's Underworld*. Kimber.

McCrum, R. *et al* (1987) *The Story of English*. Faber and Faber.

Moon, G.W. (1865) *The Dean's English* 4th edn. Hatchard.

Munster, Countess of (1904) *My Memories and Miscellanies*. Eveleigh Nash.

Olmsted, J.C. (1979) *A Victorian Art of Fiction: Essays on the Novel in British Periodicals 1870-1900*. Garland, New York.

Orel, H. (1967) *Thomas Hardy's Personal Writings*. Macmillan.

O'Rell, M. (pseudonym of Blouet, P.) (n.d.) *John Bull and his Island*. Field and Tuer.

Owens, R.J. (1958) 'The effect of George Eliot's linguistic interests on her work', *Notes and Queries* 203, 311-13.

Page, N. (1969a) 'A language fit for heroes: speech in *Oliver Twist* and *Our Mutual Friend*', *Dickensian* 65, 100-7.

Page, N. (1969b) 'Eccentric speech in Dickens', *Critical Survey* 4, 96-100.

Page, N. (1970) 'Convention and consistency in Dickens's cockney dialects', *English Studies* 51, 339-44.

Page, N. (1973) *Speech in the English Novel*. Longman.

Partridge, E. (1974) *A Dictionary of Slang and Unconventional English* 2 vols. RKP.

Pearsall, R. (1969) *The Worm in the Bud*. Weidenfeld and Nicolson.

Phillipps, K.C. (1978) *The Language of Thackeray*. André Deutsch.

Phillipps, K.C. (1984) *Language and Class in Victorian England*. Blackwell.

Pollard, A. (1982) 'Trollope and the Evangelicals' *Nineteenth-Century Fiction* 37, 329-39.

Quinlan, M.J. (1941) *Victorian Prelude*. Columbia University Press, New York.

Ritchie, J.E. (1869) *The Night Side of London*. Tinsley.

Russell, G.W.E. (1898) *Collections and Recollections*. Smith Elder.

Russell, G.W.E. (1902) *The Household of Faith*. Hodder and Stoughton.

Russell, G.W.E. (1912) *One Look Back*. Wells, Gardner, Darton.

Sanders, A.L. (1978) *The Victorian Historical Novel 1840-1880*. Macmillan.

Scherer, K.R. and Giles, H. (eds) (1980) *Social Markers in Speech*. CUP.

Sheets, R. (1982) '*Felix Holt*: language, the Bible and the problematic of meaning', *Nineteenth-Century Fiction* 37, 146-69.

Sheridan, T. (1762) *A Course of Lectures on Elocution*. Facsimile reprint, 1968. Scolar Press, Menton.

Slater, M. (1983) *Dickens and women*. J.M. Dent & Sons.

Smart, B.H. (1836) *Walker Remodelled: A New Critical Pronouncing Dictionary*. London.

Smith, S.M. (1970) 'Blue books and Victorian novelists', *Review of English Studies* NS 21, 23-40.

Society Small Talk or What to Say and When to Say It, by a Member of the Aristocracy (1879).

Sutherland, J. (ed.) (1953) *The Oxford Book of English Talk*. Clarendon Press.

Sweet, H. (1890) *A Primer of Spoken English*. Clarendon Press.

Tillotson, G. and Hawes, D. (eds) (1969) *Thackeray: The Critical Heritage*. RKP.

Tillotson, G. and Tillotson, K. (1965) *Mid-Victorian Studies*. Athlone Press.

Tillotson, K. (1954) *Novels of the 1840s*. OUP.

Trease, G. (1959) 'Language in the historical novel', *English* **12**.

Trench, R.C. (1873) *English Past and Present* 8th edn. Macmillan.

Vicunus, M. (1974) *The Industrial Muse*. Croom Helm.

Waddington-Feather, J. (1966) 'Emily Brontë's use of dialect in *Wuthering Heights*', *Brontë Society Transactions* **15**, 12-19.

Walder, D. (1981) *Dickens and Religion*. Allen and Unwin.

Walker, J. (1774) *A Critical Pronouncing Dictionary of the English Language*. London.

Watson, G. (1973) *The English Ideology: Studies in the Language of Victorian Politics*. Allen Lane.

Watson, K. (1971) 'Dinah Morris and Mrs Evans: a comparative study of Methodist diction', *Review of English Studies* NS **22**, 282-94.

Wall, S. (1988) *Trollope and Character*. Faber and Faber.

Watt, G. (1984) *The Fallen Woman in the Nineteenth-Century Novel*. Croom Helm.

Weekley, E. (1930) *Adjectives and Other Words*. John Murray.

Williams, I. (1971) *Meredith: The Critical Heritage*. RKP.

Williams, R. (1961) *The Long Revolution*. Chatto and Windus.

Wyld, H.C. (1936) *A History of Modern Colloquial English*. Blackwell.

Young, G.M. (1936) *Portrait of an Age*. OUP.

Zimmerman, B. (1980) 'Gwendolen Harleth and "The Girl of the Period" ' in A. Smith (ed.) *George Eliot: Centenary Essays and an Unpublished Fragment*. Vision Press.

General index

Index of novelists mentioned or quoted